The Founding Mothers
of Mackinac Island

Earliest photograph of Mackinac Island, 1856. COURTESY OF MACKINAC STATE HISTORIC PARKS.

The Founding Mothers of Mackinac Island

THE AGATHA BIDDLE BAND OF 1870

Theresa L. Weller

MICHIGAN STATE UNIVERSITY PRESS | *East Lansing*

♾ The paper used in this publication meets the minimum requirements
of ANSI/NISO Z39.48-1992 (R 1997) (Permanence of Paper).

Michigan State University Press
East Lansing, Michigan 48823-5245

LIBRARY OF CONGRESS CATALOGING-IN-PUBLICATION DATA
Names: Weller, Theresa Lynn, author.
Title: The founding mothers of Mackinac Island : the Agatha Biddle Band of 1870 / Theresa L. Weller.
Other titles: Agatha Biddle Band of 1870
Description: East Lansing : Michigan State University Press, [2021] |
Includes bibliographical references.
Identifiers: LCCN 2020033982 | ISBN 978-1-61186-395-6 (paperback)
| ISBN 978-1-60917-668-6 (pdf) | ISBN 978-1-62895-428-9 (epub) | ISBN 978-1-62896-429-5 (kindle)
Subjects: LCSH: Biddle, Agatha, 1797-1873. | Indian women—Michigan—Mackinac Island.
| Indians of North America—Michigan—Mackinac Island—Genealogy.
| Indians of North America—Mixed descent—Michigan—Mackinac Island—Genealogy.
| Ojibwa Indians—Michigan—Mackinac Island—History—19th century.
| Ottawa Indians—Michigan—Mackinac Island—History—19th century. | Mackinac Island (Mich.)—Genealogy.
Classification: LCC E78.M6 W45 2021 | DDC 929.37749/23—dc23
LC record available at https://lccn.loc.gov/2020033982

Book design and typesetting by Charlie Sharp, Sharp Designs, East Lansing, Michigan
Cover design by Erin Kirk
Cover art: photo of Angeline Boulanger Therrien, Roma Therrien Brake, Florence Therrien, and children.

Michigan State University Press is a member of the Green Press Initiative and is committed to developing
and encouraging ecologically responsible publishing practices. For more information about the Green
Press Initiative and the use of recycled paper in book publishing, please visit www.greenpressinitiative.org.

Visit Michigan State University Press at *www.msupress.org*

For my parents,
Vern and Maryalice Weller

Indian Lodges on the Beach of the Island of Mackinac, 1837. Anna Jameson Sketchbook.

Contents

Preface xi

A Word about Names in This Book xix

38   Mrs. Louis Beaubien (Christine Otapitakewinam). 1

43   Mrs. Louis Belonzhay (Genevieve Montreuil). 3

26   Mrs. Paul Belonzhay (Angelique Montreuil) 4

6   Mrs. Charles Bennett (Angelique Antoine) 7

56   Miss Mary Bezonette (Miss Mary Dufina, Mrs. Jean Baptiste

Bazinet). 9

1   Mrs. Agatha Biddle (Agatha Sarrasin) 11

36   Mrs. Isaac Blanchard (Mary Babeau, Babbien) 16

20   Mrs. Vital Bourassa (Angelique Fountain) 20

8   Mrs. Louis Cadotte (Marie Louise Laverdure). 21

5   Mrs. Joseph Caron (Louise Vasseur). 22

17   Mrs. Betsey Champagne (Unknown) 24

34   Mrs. Moses Champagne (Sarah Martin) 24

30   Mrs. Bela Chapman (Marie Charette). 26

39   Mrs. Joseph Cheverow (Marie Charlotte Dejadon). 28

64   Mrs. Peter Closs (Julia Pond) 30

9	Mrs. Alice Cushway (Alice Graveraet Couchoise)	30
31	Mrs. Ambrose Davenport (Susan Descarreaux)	32
42	Mrs. William Davenport (Marie Dufault)	37
60	Alexsie Dophena	39
23	Mrs. Hyacinthe (François) Dophena (Josette Dejadon)	39
14	Mrs. Joseph Fountain (Angelique Fagnant)	41
16	Mrs. Henry Hudson's Children (Angeline Caron)	43
22	Mrs. Peter Jacobear (Poline Martin)	44
15	Mrs. Francis Johnston (Margaret Bennett-Beaubin)	46
57	Edward Karrow	46
10	Mrs. Henry Karrow (Judithe Diotte)	48
29	Mary A. Karrow (Marianne Kedegekwanabe)	49
7	Mrs. William Karrow (Isabelle Morin)	50
19	Mrs. David Kniffen (Marie Bennet-Beaubin)	51
25	Mrs. Michael Kuthron (Sophie Pogay)	53
58	Mrs. Mary LaDuke (Mary Bruneau, Mrs. Jeremie LeDuc)	57
32	Mrs. Joseph Lalotte (Lozon) (Marie Boyd)	59
12 a, b, c	Sarah, Louisa, and Charles Lalotte (Lozon)	60
12 a	Sarah Lalotte (Mrs. Paul Lancour)	61
12 b	Marie Louise Lozon (Mrs. John Poupard)	62
12 c	Charles Lozon	63
51	Mrs. Jane Lancour (Genevieve Pond)	64
62	Josephine LaPierre (Unknown)	68
4	Mrs. Edward Lasley (Therese Bennett)	68
40	Mrs. Joseph Laslin (Julia Lesieur Aslin)	70
45	Mrs. Samuel LeBlanc (Elizabeth Belonga)	73
35	Mrs. Alixse Lelone (Marie Louise Cadotte)	74
54	Mrs. Angeline Louisignon (Angelique Aslin)	74
47	Miss Rosalie Louisignan (Lusignan)	76
53	Mrs. Moses Maillet (Angelique McClure)	77
2	Mrs. Louis Maishtaw (Marie Bennett-Beaubin)	79
21	Mrs. Francis Martin (Agatha Fountain)	80
55	Miss Lizzette Martin (later Mrs. Antoine Truckey)	81
49	Mrs. Benjamin McGulpin (Elizabeth Boyd)	82
52	Miss Mary McGulphin (later Mrs. Mary Garrison)	85
41	Miss Nancy McGulpin	86
44	Mrs. Joseph Menasaw (Mary Belanger)	87

18   Mrs. Daniel Moore (Louise Charbonneau) 89
3   Mrs. Andrew Moran (Mary Kekematiwain) 91
11   Mrs. Ignace Pelotte (Rosalie Boucher) 92
65   Victoire Peltier (Mrs. David Bellaire) 95
13   Mrs. Francis Rastoul (Christine Bennet-Beaubin) 97
48   Mrs. Benjamin A. Rice (Ursula Lusignan) 98
59   Angel Robinson (Mrs. George Lamyott) 99
33   David Robinson 101
27   Mrs. Charles Roussain (Rousseau) (Charlotte Martin) 102
46   Mrs. Louis St. Onge (Catharine Peltier) 104
37   Miss Martha Tanner 106
24 a, b, c   Hester Terrien, sister, and Peter 110
24 a Hester Terrien 110
24 b Genevieve Terrien 111
24 c Peter Isaac Terrien 111
61   Mrs. Margueritta Thompson (Margaret Pouillat) 114
66   William Valier 115
50   Mrs. Henry Vaillancourt (Catherine LaCroix) 116
28   Mrs. Thomas Valliere (Josette Thibault) 118
60   Mama Walsh 122

      APPENDIX: Durant Correspondence to the Commissioner
          of Indian Affairs 123
      Notes 127
      Bibliography 221

Front Street, Mackinac Island circa 1870. One half of stereoscopic card.

Preface

This project began with an interest in *Anishinaabe* names on annuity payments from Mackinac Island, Michigan.[1] Using the annuity payments in my possession for the years 1839, 1842, 1857, and 1870 for the Mackinac Island band, I tried to match the names from one year to another with little success. My goal was to find the Anishinaabe name of my ancestor—Angelique Belonzhay. When I posted a query about annuities on a Michigan Anishinaabe site, Larry Wyckoff offered his copies of the 1858 and 1859 annuity payment rosters. I gratefully accepted. These rosters contained crucial information because it was during the 1859 payment year that the payees were listed for the first time by their married names in English. The 1858 payment was the last year the payees were enumerated in their Anishinaabe names.

The Mackinac Island band was unique from other bands because it consisted of unrelated women. Not all the people in the band were Ojibwe or Odawa, there were at least two Cree (Pond and Fountain), one Sioux (Lapines), and one Osage (Vaillancourts). Many of the women came from Wisconsin—from the Lapointe and the St. Croix River areas and Green Bay—while others came from L'Arbre Croche, Cross Village, or Canada. Usual rules of behavior, such as the choice of marriage partners, was not applicable in this case. Members of an Odawa or Ojibwe band were exogamous, that is, they could marry only those individuals from outside

Augustin Hamlin. McKenney & Hall prints. IMAGE COURTESY OF THE US LIBRARY OF CONGRESS.

their birth clan. Since the members of Agatha Biddle's band were not based on a single patrilineal ancestor, exogamy did not exist. The exogamous taboo was not enforced in the Mackinac Island band as there was much intermarriage among the members' children.

Throughout much of the Great Lakes, children belonged to the father's clan or *ododem* as Charles Cleland describes in *Rites of Conquest*:

> Among both the northern and southern Anishnabeg, [a] family consisted of a group of people related through the father to a distant, and perhaps, mythical progenitor. ... The Anishnabeg system of descent recognition was lineal; a person belonged to the lineage and clan of the father. It was through this line alone that descent was traced. And from which rights and obligations of the children were derived. This did not mean that the Anishnabe lacked identity with their mother's family. In fact, that connection was important, but those people were not part of one's family. The brothers and sisters of a family shared with the father the rituals and duties of clan hood. ... The mother's interests were in the clan of her birth, her family of blood.[2]

As such, the Mackinac Island band was unique, not conforming to the traditional description of a band, but it, nevertheless, was formed as a band and recognized by the US government as an entity unto itself over the course of many years.

The chief of the Mackinac Island band, listed on the 1839 annuity roster, was Augustin Hamlin. He was an Odawa from L'Arbre Croche who was an educated man, having trained for the priesthood in Rome. It is likely that he advised and guided the women throughout his life. While Agatha Biddle was a member of this band from the first enumeration to the last, she did not become chief until sometime during the early 1860s. What were the duties and responsibilities of being the chief of this band? What were the membership requirements? While some women's children were members of the band during their lifetimes, other children were not added until their mothers died. Was need or relation a determining factor? After having worked with the rosters for more than twelve years, developing the families and their genealogies, I have more questions than answers.

Developing genealogies for all sixty-six individuals and their families appeared at first to be a daunting task. For help in beginning and organizing this task, I turned to my good friend, Jim LaLone, who shared information from his database of more than 32,000 Anishinaabeg accumulated over the years. Armed with his data, I began to gather information and research the families. I am very grateful to him for his friendship, generosity, and assistance.

My project to research the descendants of those original women was based on material that already existed—the Durant Roll and all its genealogical material from the 1870 annuity payment. The Anishinaabeg on the 1870 annuity payment were recognized as mixed-blood individuals who qualified for annuity payments from the Treaty of Washington, DC, of 1836, and the Treaty of Detroit of 1855.

The 1836 Treaty of Washington, DC, ceded more than 13 million acres of land in parts of the Lower Peninsula and the eastern part of the Upper Peninsula of Michigan. It was orchestrated by Henry Schoolcraft who was the Indian agent at Mackinac and later, the superintendent of Indian Affairs for Michigan. In exchange, the Anishinaabeg (Odawa and Ojibwe) were to receive land, blacksmith shops, implements and animals for farming, education, and repayment of debts to traders. Ever mindful of mixed-blood relations, the chiefs requested and were granted annuity payments for the mixed-bloods for the next twenty years. Unfortunately, after the treaty was negotiated and agreed upon by all parties, it was sent to the US Senate for ratification. The Senate added a clause that the lands were to be used for a limit of five years. After the expiration of five years, the decision for the Anishinaabeg to be removed or remain was to be determined by the president.

Because of the added clause, the Indians affected by the treaty were confused and unsure about clearing land or developing permanent dwellings. By 1855, with new agents and different views, a new treaty was requested to resolve the residency issue, outstanding payments, and other matters. The chiefs and US officials met in Detroit and created a supplement to the 1836 Treaty of Washington, known as the Treaty of Detroit, 1855. In this treaty, the US government agreed to provide the Odawa and Ojibwe individual land awards, payment for outstanding debts to traders, and another ten years of annuity payments for the mixed-blood relations with an additional four years' payment on any balance remaining. As referenced in the Treaty of Detroit (31 July 1855), fourth part of Article 2, below:

> Fourth; The sum of three hundred and six thousand dollars in coin, as follows: ten thousand dollars of the principle, and the interest on the whole of said last-mentioned sum remaining unpaid at the rate of five per cent [*sic*] annually for ten years, to be distributed per capita in the usual manner for paying annuities. And the sum of two hundred and six thousand dollars remaining unpaid at the expiration of ten years, shall be then due and payable, and if the Indians then require the payment of said sum in coin the same shall be distributed per capita in the same manner as annuities are paid, and not in less than four equal annual installments.[3]

Annuities were paid to the Mackinac Island band until 1872. In 1905, the Odawa and Ojibwe filed a lawsuit against the US government to request an accounting of treaty monies that were held in trust for them by the US government. The US Court of Claims determined that more than one hundred and thirty thousand dollars were due to the Odawa and Ojibwe. In order to pay out the monies, Charles McNichols, special agent, was ordered to prepare rolls of qualified individuals. Unable to complete the task in the allotted time, McNichols was replaced by special agent Horace Durant in 1907.

Horace Durant took over the task and was charged with determining the final number of claimants in Michigan for the award made by the US Court of Claims. Using the annuity payments from 1870, Durant spoke to the chiefs, headmen, or elders of each band in all the communities involved. He created a preprinted sheet called a Field Note. Each Field Note is grouped by band with the chief's name. Each band has a number derived from the original 1870 roll known as the page number. Each family in the band then has its own number. When referring to a certain page of the Field Notes, the individual's number comes first followed by the page number. For example, in 1870, Agatha Biddle's band was written on pages 13 and 14. Agatha Biddle was listed first as chieftainess, so her Field Note is 1/13. One was her number on the list, and 13 was the page from the 1870 annuity she was originally listed on.

Durant made several errors on the Field Notes he created. The 1870 annuity list named each payee followed by a set of numbers. The numbers followed this order: the number of males, females, then children. The last number represented children—no names or sex of the children were provided. So, Durant was faced with the formidable task of deciding which of the children were counted.

To determine who should be on the 1908 payment lists, Durant interviewed thousands of individuals when gathering his information. The informants' names are listed on the top of each page of the Field Notes. They provided Durant with the information on each individual and children to the best of their recollections. The informants were usually elderly *Anishinaabeg*, family members, or descendants.

The errors Durant made on the Mackinac Island band are most notable on pages 10/13 and 16/13. Page 10/13 is Mrs. Henry Carrow, née Judithe Diotte. Listed on this page were the children of Mrs. Henry Hudson, née Angeline Caron (Carrow), who should appear on page 16/13. Listed on page 16/13 are the children of Mrs. David Hudson, not Mrs. Henry Hudson. Mrs. David Hudson was not enumerated on the original 1870 Agatha Biddle annuity list and should not have appeared on this page of the Durant Roll. Angeline Caron Hudson died on 4 September 1869. The children who should be on this page are listed on page 10/13. This means Judithe Diotte Carrow's children were not enumerated or paid. They were Charles, Clement, Joseph, Edward, Mary Louise, Julie, and Elisabeth Karrow (see individual pages for citation information).

In the correspondence pertaining to the Durant Roll, there is a letter from the 1909 Mackinac-area chiefs who wanted no one added who was not part of the 1870 annuity payment. This letter was witnessed and signed by Durant on 9 August 1909 at St. Ignace, Michigan. The living descendants agreed that only the individuals named on the 1870 annuity payment would be allowed in the payment of 1910. No additions were to be made for siblings not enrolled in 1870. Therefore, it was important that Durant determine who the children—represented by the numbers following each payee—were. In the end, known children were listed according to the informants.[4]

Durant wrote it was particularly true of the Mackinac band that "intermarriage with the white race has eradicated all trace of Indian blood" and that the chiefs allowed the band "out of custom" for the last payment. This claim on both counts is false. Since annuity payment rosters exist, we can see that the band was first enumerated and compensated in the late 1830s. All the women's names were written in *Anishinaabe*, and some have an English first name, possibly due to baptism or assimilation. Some of those first ladies from the 1839 annuity list can be identified;

others are probably lost to history. Occasionally the ladies' *Anishinaabe* names were written by priests when recording the baptisms of their children. Rarely, some of the mothers themselves were baptized, and in addition to their *Anishinaabe* names, their place of birth was recorded. This usually preceded their marriage. Other priests recorded the mother's names simply as *Sauvagess, Sauteuse, Matris Indiani,* or just the letter "N."

My purpose in writing this book was to give the *Sauvagess* a name. Who were these women? Where did they come from? What were their lives like? Agatha Biddle's band contains sixty-six family sheets for a total of seventy-four individuals. Out of these seventy-four, eight were men and sixty-six were women. Most of the women married men who were in the fur trade and retired to Mackinac Island. Many of these men became fishermen after the fur trade died out in the area. Most were poor and illiterate. Three women never married and at least one was college educated. At least two husbands fought in the War of 1812, and several husbands and sons fought in the Civil War. Most of the women in Agatha's band were at least half-blood and the daughters of fur traders.

The data in this work has been derived from as many primary source documents as possible. In large part, the information is from the registers of Ste. Anne's Catholic Church of Mackinac Island. Additional sources are Ste. Anne's of Detroit exterior parishes; St. Ignatius Loyola of St. Ignace Michigan; St. Mary's of Cheboygan, Michigan; Ste. Mary's of Sault Ste. Marie, Michigan; St. Joseph Mission of LaPointe, Wisconsin; Ste. Croix records from Cross Village, Michigan; Ste. Croix register of Wikwemikong, Ontario; St. Ann's of Penetanguishene, Ontario; the Denissen, the Tanguay, and St. Boniface of Manitoba Voyageur Database; and other Catholic records from Quebec and Ontario. Other works include the 1836 Treaty of Washington's Half-Breed Census, the 1837 Treaty with the Ojibwe (including the Half-Breed Census), *All Our Relations* by Dr. Theresa Schenck, diaries, newspapers, US war and veteran records, and US lighthouse and county records.

I have many people to thank for this work. Librarians from the Burton Collection in Detroit to the Bayliss Library in Sault Ste. Marie, including the main library at my alma mater, Michigan State University; the Clark Library at Central Michigan University; the Clements and Bentley Libraries at the University of Michigan; and Brian Jaeschke, archivist at the Petersen Center Library, Mackinac State Historic Parks. I especially want to thank the members of the Mackinac Area Genealogy and Family History page, especially Jami Innerebner Moran, Richard Renaud, Dr. Art Dembinski, Corey Lasley, Rane Walker, Michelle Goudreau Helgesen, Jim LaLone, H. J. Armstrong, and many, many others. I would also like to thank all the kind people from the churches I visited to review registers especially at St. Mary's in Cheboygan, and of course, Leanne Brodeur from Ste. Anne's on Mackinac Island. To all the people who shared their family photo treasures, you have my deepest appreciation. Genealogy friends Sharon Laakko, Carol Brown, Rae Tamlyn, Roger Horn, and Smi Horn for their love and support. Finally, I owe much loving gratitude to the following: my parents, Vern and Maryalice Weller, who are my number one fans; my grandfather, Coy Abraham Weller, from whom I got my genealogy bug; and my nana, Theresa Martell Scholl, who is my constant inspiration.

It is my hope that this work will assist other researchers in working on their Mackinac Island and Mackinac-area families. I look forward to hearing from those researchers who wish to add information or corrections to this book to be incorporated in possible future editions. I also encourage anyone with images to share them giving these founding Mackinac mothers a face to go with their names.

Island of Mackinaw, 1837. Anna Jameson. Note Agency House, compare to figure 36.

A Word about Names in This Book

I n this book you will find a variety of spellings of each family name within the biographies. Most French-Canadian genealogical researchers will be familiar with the variety of spellings, but for those who are reading for pleasure, the various name spellings can be confusing. Many names changed from one generation to the next, and some members of the same family spelled their surnames differently, e.g., Morin, Moran, Moreau, Morrow; Catrin, Cadran, Cadreau; Caron, Karrow, Carrow.

First, the names in the headings of each person are spelled according to the worksheets Durant used when compiling the rolls in the early 1900s. Different spellings within the biographies were used because their names appeared in other documents or censuses with that spelling.

The variation in name spellings was caused by many circumstances including illiteracy, lack of French fluency, and "dit" names, to name a few.

Many of our French-Canadian ancestors were illiterate and did not know how to sign their names. Fortunately, many of the priests were French-speaking and provided us with an approximate spelling of those surnames. The "dit" name is an alternate surname and can reflect a personal characteristic (LeBlond) and occupation (Boulanger [baker] or Lefebvre [blacksmith]), or an origin in France

(Montreuil, LeBreton). These are only a few examples of where a "dit" name may come from. "Dit" names may or may not be combined with the family name.

Keep an open mind while researching. It will help you discover possibilities. Also, a French-Canadian genealogy "how-to," such as *Miller's Manual: A Research Guide to the Major French-Canadian Genealogical Resources, What They Are and How to Use Them*, would be a very helpful resource for a beginning researcher.

The Founding Mothers of Mackinac Island

The Agatha Biddle Band of 1870

38. Mrs. Louis Beaubien (Christine Otapitakewinam)

Christine Otapitakewinam was born around 1800. Little has been recorded about her life before she married Louis Beaubien (Bennett-Beaubin). They were married at Ste. Anne's on Mackinac Island on 28 October 1827.[1] Children from this marriage include the following:

1. Marie was born around 1820. She married Louis Masta. (See no. 2 Mrs. Louis Maishtaw.)
2. Therese was born 1 March 1826.[2] She married Edward Lasley. (See no. 4 Mrs. Edward Lasley.)
3. Marguerite was born 1 February 1828.[3] She first married Toussaint Masta, then she married Francis Johnston. (See no. 15 Mrs. Francis Johnston.)
4. Marie was born 15 November 1829.[4] She married Hollis Kniffen. (See no. 19 Mrs. David Kniffen.)
5. Christina was baptized on 18 July 1831.[5] She died young.
6. Louis was born 13 August 1832.[6] He was enumerated on the 1836 Half-Breed Census, as no. 220, as half-Odawa and Chippewa.[7] He married Rachael St. Andrew (or St. Andre) at St. Ignatius Loyola in St. Ignace on 28 November

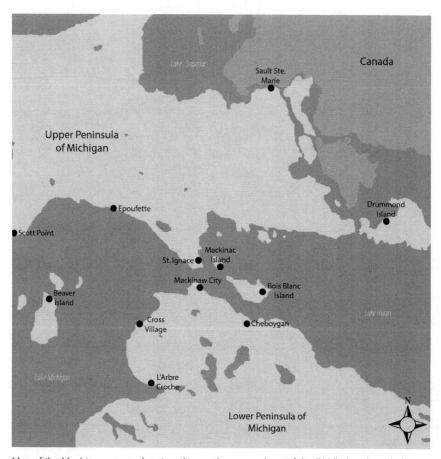

Map of the Mackinac arean, showing places where members of the Biddle band resided.

1859.[8] Louis was a member of the famed Company K, 1st Michigan Sharp Shooters.[9] He survived the war and returned home. Louis and Rachael had one child, Mary Jane, before he died on 19 September 1869.[10]

7. Christine was born in the month of September 1834.[11] She married François Rastoule (See no. 13, Mrs. Francis Rastoul.)

8. Charles was born 27 October 1836.[12] He married Angelique Sagitondaway. (See no. 6 Mrs. Charles Bennet.)

9. Amable was born 13 March 1839 and baptized at Ste. Anne's.[13]

10. Joseph was born 5 March 1842 and baptized at Ste. Anne's.[14]

Tombstone of Louis Bennett in Ste. Anne's Cemetery, Mackinac Island. COURTESY OF THE AUTHOR.

Louis died on 10 October 1846 and was buried on Mackinac Island.[15] By 1860, most of the family moved from the island to Cheboygan County, with Christine comfortably situated with daughters and their families living on either side of her. She lived in Cheboygan County until her death on 9 December 1876.[16]

43. Mrs. Louis Belonzhay (Genevieve Montreuil)

Genevieve is the sister of no. 26 Mrs. Paul Belonzhay, no. 39 Mrs. Joseph Cheverow (Aslin), and no. 23 Mrs. Francis Dophena. Their mother was probably Josephine Louise Mischovassi. Genevieve and Mrs. Paul Belonzhay had the same father, Joseph Montreuil. The elder sisters, Mrs. Cheverow (Aslin) and Mrs. Francis Dufina, had a different father named Dejadon. On 23 December 1832, Father Samuel Mazzuchelli of Ste. Anne's on Mackinac Island baptized Genevieve and recorded that she was born at *Lac Superior* in March of 1818.[1] Louis Belonzhay (Belanger, Belonga) was born in Quebec in the parish of St. Michel d'Yamaska on 21 March 1809. His parents were Chrysostome Belanger and Therese Petrin according to the St. Michel d'Yamaska register.[2]

Genevieve and Louis married at Ste. Anne's on Mackinac Island on 6 January 1834.[3] From this marriage at least six children were born.

1. Marie was born in October 1834.[4] (See no. 44 Mrs. Joseph Menawsaw.)
2. Elizabeth was born 8 February 1836.[5] (See no. 45 Mrs. Samuel LeBlanc.)
3. Joseph was born 10 December 1837.[6] He married Angelique Satigo, daughter of Joseph Satigo.

4. Louis was born 25 April 1839[7] and died 1 August 1923 at Carp River, Mackinac County.[8] He married Rose Martineau, daughter of Oliver Martineau and Marie McGulpin.
5. Antoine was born 12 April 1841.[9]
6. Genevieve was born 30 July 1848.[10]

Genevieve Montreuil Belanger died 27 July 1879,[11] and Louis died 10 March 1895.[12] They were buried in St. Ignace, Michigan.

This family is still visibly prominent in the St. Ignace area. The Belanger name is now spelled Belonga and pronounced "blahn-gee." The family owns the local plumbing company, and their trucks advertising *Belonga Plumbing* are seen daily around the St. Ignace area. The author visited Mrs. Anne (Robert) Belonga for an afternoon and got a good deal of information about the children of Louis Jr. and Rose Martineau. Mr. Robert Belonga is a direct descendent of Louis and Genevieve, the original Louis Belanger being his three-times-great-grandfather.

26. Mrs. Paul Belonzhay (Angelique Montreuil)

Angelique Montreuil was born around 1815, near Red Cedar Lake, Minnesota. Her parents were probably Josephine Louise Mischovassi and Joseph Montreuil. Information about her childhood years is scarce, but vital information in the Lucius Lyons Papers, from the Clements Library at the University of Michigan, indicates Angelique had at least three sisters. They were no. 43 Mrs. Louis Belonzhay, no. 23 Mrs. Hyacinthe (François) Dophena Sr., and no. 39 Mrs. Joseph Chevrow.[1]

There were a couple of brothers. François Dejadon was identified as a brother in *All Our Relations.*[2] His father was recorded in the application for funds as part of the Chippewa mixed-bloods in the Treaty of St. Peters, 1837, as Pierre Dijaddon (Dejadon), and his mother was a "Chippewa woman of La Pointe." Another probable brother was Pierre Dejadon who remained at LaPointe. The two eldest sisters (Mrs. Dophena and Mrs. Chevreau) and Pierre used the surname Dejadon or Henry. Their father was most likely Pierre Henri Dejadon, a trader in the region. There are at least two instances of a Louise Montreuil acting as godmother in the St. Joseph baptisms of LaPointe. This woman was possibly their mother (or sister-in-law). To date, no other records regarding Louise Montreuil have been located.

Angelique and one sister appeared in the Indian Day Book of 1836 from Mackinac Island where Angelique's Indian name was written as a customer. Comparing

Benjamin Boulanger.
COURTESY OF JULI PIONK.

annuity payment records prior to 1859, Angelique was listed as *Key-way-ke-num*.[3] The Indian Day Book listed her as "living with Debadon [*sic*] sister." Another "Debadon" sister's Indian name was recorded as *"Ne-say-wa-quit."*[4] She was either Mrs. Aslin or Mrs. Dufina; however, that name does not correspond to any name on the band listing or annuity recipients on lists prior to 1859. Beginning in 1859, most of the women were recorded under their married English names.

Angelique was married 4 August 1831 at Mackinac by Father Mazzuchelli.[5] Her groom was Paul LeFebvre dit Boulanger, more commonly known in records as Paul Belanger or Belonzhay. Paul was the son of Joseph LeFebvre Boulanger and Josephte Fortier of Yamachiche, Quebec. He was born 12 December 1809 and baptized at Ste. Anne's of Yamachiche.[6] At least two siblings joined Paul at Mackinac: Marie Rose, who married Jacob Wertz (the family appears as *Verse* in the 1850 Michilimackinac County census), and Benjamin, who married at least three times. His wives were Marguerite Therrien, Genevieve Maranda, and Catharine Plante, respectively. Another possible sibling was Marie, who married George Hull at Ste. Anne's on Mackinac Island with Paul and Angelique as witnesses. Both the bride and groom were from Canada.

Paul and Angelique had at least twelve children. Of the children that survived to maturity, four married into the Davenport family. (See no. 31 Mrs. Ambrose Davenport.)

1. The eldest child, Lucy, married William Davenport (son of Ambrose and no. 31 Susan DesCarreux Davenport) on 26 February 1850.[7] Lucy's life was tragically cut short. She gave birth to a son on 12 April 1853, and in July of the

Left to right: Sophie Boulanger Chapman, Clement Boulanger, and his wife, Grace Plant.
COURTESY OF ROGER HORN.

same year, "[she was] shot accidentally by her husband while hunting . . . at Birch Point in that county."[8]

2. Leon married Elizabeth "Betsy" Davenport, William's sister, on 10 December 1855.[9] He died 28 February 1915 and was buried on Mackinac Island.[10]
3. Isabelle "Liset" married John Davenport (a sibling of William and Elizabeth Davenport), on 21 January 1867.[11]
4. Delphine married Robert Davenport on 13 May 1867.[12] According to the marriage certificate, Robert was the son of William Davenport Sr and no. 42 Marie Dufault. William Davenport Sr. was a brother of Ambrose Davenport.
5. Frederick was born 13 January 1837.[13]
6. Marie was born 17 December 1838.[14] She married John Wachter on 5 June 1855.[15]
7. Charles was born 9 July 1844,[16] and he married Elise Mincier (daughter of Charles Mincier and Marie Gendron) on 29 November 1865.[17]
8. Sophia was born 9 March 1852,[18] and married Andrew Jackson Chapman (son of no. 30 Marie Charette Chapman), 2 February 1879.[19]

9. Louis was born 8 March 1854.[20] He married Mollie Mary McGulpin on 22 September 1878.[21] Louis was enumerated on the Durant Roll as no. 29/11.[22]

10. Angelique Felicity was born 15 August 1856,[23] and she was first married to Daniel Donovan, then to William Hull, and lastly, she was married to Peter Isaac Therrien (son of Olivier Therrien and Isabelle Lozon).

11. Joseph was born 13 November 1858,[24] and married Bridget Gallagher on 15 October 1886 in Mackinac County.[25]

12. Clement was born 30 July 1860.[26] He first married Isabelle "Libby" Fountain (daughter of Andre Fountain and Marianne Lozon) on 1 September 1889 at Ste. Anne's on Mackinac Island.[27] After she died, he married Grace Plant.

According to baptism records at Ste. Anne's from the 1880s, some of the Boulanger family left Mackinac Island and went to Scott Point, a fishing and lumbering village near present-day Gould City, Michigan. Marie Boulanger Wachter (wife of John Wachter) was buried in the Newton Township Cemetery there.[28]

From the documents at the Register of Deeds office in the Mackinac County Courthouse, it appears that, sometime between 1892 and late 1893, the senior Boulangers moved from Mackinac Island to Newton Township, near Gould City. To date, no death records or burial information have been located for Paul and Angelique. The last legal information found is an indenture from the Register of Deeds office in Mackinac County from Paul and Angelique to their grandson Walter Donovan, dated 6 December 1893.[29] They were not found on the 1900 census.

6. Mrs. Charles Bennett (Angelique Antoine)

Angelique Antoine was born circa 1840, probably at L'Arbre Croche.[1] Her father was named Antoine Sagitondaway and is listed as a second-class chief from L'Arbre Croche in the 1836 Treaty of Washington.[2] He was enumerated on his own Durant Roll worksheet under page 31, no. 4. Angelique Antoine was also known by her father's surname of Sagitondaway on annuity payment documents.

St. Anne's of Detroit, Exterior Parishes, has recorded several generations of this family. Antoine was born 1 January 1819 at L'Arbre Croche, son of Louis Wabini and Marie Osanwoui.[3] Antoine's siblings include Elizabeth Ozawanaanokoue Sagitandaway, born in 1806;[4] Therese Makokoue Sagitandaway, born March 1820;[5] and Louis Sagitandaway, born June 1826.[6]

Angelique's grandfather, Louis Sagitandaway Wabini was born circa 1786.[7] He was the son of Wabini and Obagiminikoue.[8] Louis married Marie Osanwoui on 12 September 1826 at L'Arbre Croche. She was the daughter of Pinesiouapami and Ozikikoue and was born circa 1786.[9] Both Wabini and Obagiminikoue were present when their son Louis was married in 1826.[10]

On the Field Note for Angelique's page, Durant wrote the name *Captain* in parentheses. He was, perhaps, her first husband, but information on an individual or children with that name was not found.

Angelique married Charles Bennett (date and location unknown). He was the son of Louis Bennett-Beaubin and no. 38 Christine Otapitakiwinam and was born 27 October 1836 and baptized at Ste. Anne's on Mackinac Island.[11]

Angelique and Charles had at least eleven children.

1. Jane was born 29 December 1858.[12] She married William Onenagons (son of Peter Omaynawgoonse and Josephte Ginibissikwe) on 22 February 1876 in Emmet County.[13]
2. Lucy was born May 1861 at Old Mackinaw (current day Mackinaw City).[14] She married Frank Duffina (son of Hyacinthe Daufina and Josette Andress) on 19 November 1883 in Mackinaw City, Michigan.[15]
3. Marie was born 1 January 1863 and died 30 December 1881.[16]
4. Charles François was born 18 December 1864,[17] and died 9 November 1871.[18]
5. Therese was born 1 November 1866.[19] She married Alfred Cadran/Cadreau, son of no. 25 Mrs. Michael Kuthron.
6. Toussaint Ambrose, known as Samuel, was born 16 January 1869 and died 27 September 1870.[20]
7. Margaret was born 11 March 1872 and died 30 March 1872.[21]
8. Elisabeth was born 25 March 1874 and died 7 June 1874.[22]
9. John Charles was born 11 April 1876.[23]
10. Elisabeth was born 15 September 1878.[24]

In 1910, Charles and Angeline lived in Mackinaw Township, next door to Charles's sister, Mary Kniffen (no. 19 Mrs. Hollis Kniffen).[25] Charles died first on 6 August 1916 and was buried in Mackinaw City.[26] Angeline died a couple of years later on 8 March 1919.[27]

56. Miss Mary Bezonette (Miss Mary Dufina, Mrs. Jean Baptiste Bazinet)

Mary Dufina was the daughter of François Dauphinet (Dufina) and no. 23 Josette
Dejadon Dufina Numinville. She was born 26 September 1839 on Mackinac Island
and baptized at Ste. Anne's Catholic Church.[1] The worksheets (56/14 and 4/17)
support Mary Dufina as the correct person here; however, in 1870 she was a married
woman with three children.

Michel Bazinet (Bazinaw, Besinet) was the father of Jean Baptiste Bazinet and
made an application to the 1837 treaty with the Lake Superior Chippewa (Treaty
of St. Peters):

> Michelle (*sic*) Bazinet ½ breed, 39 years of age, was born at La Pointe. Has generally
> lived in the Lac Court [*sic*] Oreille and Lac du Flambeau country with the exception
> of 5 years at Mackinac. He also claims for 4 children, ¾ bloods. The names are
> Augustine 14 years of age and Alexis 12 both born at Lac du Flambeau. Jean Baptiste
> 10 years, Joseph 8, born at Lac Court [*sic*] Oreille. The children have always resided
> with their parents. The father has generally been in the employ of Indian traders.
> Their mother was a full Chippewa of Lac du Flambeau.
>
> History confirmed. The mother of Michell Bazinette was a full Chippewa
> woman from La Pointe. He is somewhat inclined to drink and is extravagant, not
> well calculated to take care of money.[2]

Earlier, the three oldest sons, Augustin, Alexis and John, applied for funds from
the 1836 Treaty of Washington, DC. Their names appear on the Half-Breed list that
was made in September of 1836. They were denied funds because their mother
was Menominee.[3]

The identity of Jean Baptiste's mother is not clear. His two older brothers were
baptized at Ste. Anne's on Mackinac Island in 1830, and their mother was Naukouékijiokoué.[4] Theresa Scheck wrote in *All Our Relations* that Michel Bazinet, "married
the sister of the Lac du Flambeau chief known as La Loche,"[5] but it is not known
if Naukouékijiokoué and La Loche's sister are the same person. Jean Baptiste's
marriage record lists his parents as Michel and Angelique Basinet.[6] Later, Michel
married Marie Anna Bagotigokwe on 28 July 1839 at LaPointe,[7] then he married
Margaretha Ochikigikwe, 22 September 1850.[8] It is not known which woman was
Osquequa Bazina (from the census). Most likely she was Margaretha Ochikigikwe.
Among the people in the household was nineteen-year-old Jean Baptiste, earning
a living as a voyageur.[9]

Partial image, 1850 census. LaPoint, Wisconsin, page 2 (Bezina).

Mary and Jean Baptiste Bazinet were married 24 September 1861 at Ste. Anne's.[10] From this union, there were at least eight children.

1. Augustin was born around 1859. He married Emma Massaway (daughter of Peter Meswewinini and Marie Louise St. Andre)[11] on 25 July 1885.[12] Augustin suffered a tragic end, dying in a house fire on Mackinac Island on 29 December 1915.[13]
2. Jean Baptiste was born 18 August 1861 at Grand Island (*Ile Haut*) and baptized on Mackinac Island, 18 November 1861.[14]
3. William Alfred was born 18 October 1865 on Bois Blanc Island and baptized 26 November 1865 at Ste. Anne's on Mackinac Island.[15] He married Mary Andress (daughter of David and Mary Andress) on 3 June 1899 on Bois Blanc Island.[16] He died 18 January 1913 and was buried on Mackinac Island.[17]
4. François Olivier was born on Bois Blanc Island in April 1868 and baptized at Ste. Anne's on 26 May 1868.[18]
5. Joseph Thomas was born in March 1870 and baptized at Ste. Anne's on Mackinac Island on 2 April 1870.[19]
6. Jeanne Josephine was born 7 May 1874 and baptized at Ste. Anne's on Mackinac Island.[20]
7. Julien Olivier was born 27 April 1875.[21] Julius, as he was known, suffered a similar fate to that of his brother Augustin. He died in a barn fire on Mackinac Island on 19 October 1920.[22]
8. Marie Elizabeth was born 27 February 1878.[23]

Jean Baptiste Bazinet died 26 August 1885 and was buried at Ste. Anne's on Mackinac Island. Mary died 28 May 1909 and was buried next to her husband.[24]

1. Mrs. Agatha Biddle (Agatha Sarrasin)

Agatha Biddle was most likely the daughter of Jawoue Kougacomma Sarasin or de la Vigne (Odawa) and Marie LeFebvre (Potawatomi). After Jaowoue's death around 1804, Marie married Joseph Bailly, a prosperous and prominent fur trader at Mackinac Island and Montreal. By 1820, Bailly left Mackinac and relocated his family and business on the Calumet River in Indiana.

Edward Biddle was born about 1790 to John Biddle and Sophia Boone and arrived at Mackinac Island around 1808. Emerson Smith writes, "Edward Biddle could read and write, which gave him an advantage. If so, he was one of the small percentage who was not illiterate. Agatha Biddle could not read or [write], and it is a question whether there were many women residents who possessed these talents. . . . She was of humble origin, and, [there was] not much difference, of course, between her and other residents in this respect."[1]

Various sources differ about the degree of Indian blood that Agatha possessed. Therese Baird wrote in her *Reminiscences* that, "She was fair complexioned for an Indian, although her eyes were very black, and her hair equally so."[2] Emerson Smith writes, "the marriage of Edward Biddle was not to an Indian woman . . . but to Joseph Bailly's stepdaughter who was at the most quarter-blood."[3] Sarah Biddle, Agatha's daughter, was enumerated on the 1836 Treaty of Washington Half Breed Census (no. 538) with blood quantum of half-Odawa.[4] If their daughter was half-blood and Edward Biddle was of European descent, Agatha would have to be full-blood according to the treaty census.

Agatha married Edward Biddle in 1819. The service performed by Samuel Abbott, a justice of the peace.[5] Throughout their lives together, Agatha remained Catholic, while Edward preferred Protestantism. Of their children, the girls were baptized at Ste. Anne's, the Catholic Church, while the boys were not. This difference in religion was maintained even in death. Edward, who died first was buried in the Post Cemetery, while Agatha was buried in Ste. Anne's cemetery.

From this marriage at least four children were born.

1. Agatha Sophia was born around 1822 and baptized at Ste. Anne's in 1834.[6] She never married. There is a local legend about her beauty and refinement. In her early years, she was formally educated and spent time away from the island. When she returned to her parents, she participated in local society, which included officers from Fort Mackinac and friends and associates of her parents. She developed an attachment to a Lieutenant John C.

Tombstone of Sophia
Biddle taken at Ste. Anne's
Cemetery, Mackinac Island.
Courtesy of the author.

Pemberton who was stationed at Fort Mackinac. He had also formed a
strong attachment to her and asked Sophia for her hand in marriage. Sophia
agreed to marry him, but she told him he must first meet her mother. When
he met Agatha and saw she was an Indian, he left Sophia and severed their
relationship. After an illness, Sophia reportedly wasted away and died. She
was buried in Ste. Anne's Cemetery.[7]

2. John was born 23 November 1823 and married Lucy Chapman.[8] Lucy was the
   daughter of Bela Chapman and no. 30 Marie Charette. John died 4 January
   1879 and was buried in the Protestant Cemetery on Mackinac Island.[9]
3. Marie was born 10 November 1825 and baptized at Ste. Anne's.[10] She died on
   19 December 1833 according to her tombstone in Ste. Anne's Cemetery.
4. Sarah was born 12 October 1833, and also was baptized at Ste. Anne's.[11] She
   married Charles Durfee at Ste. Anne's on 27 June 1854.[12] Sarah appeared
   on the 1836 Treaty of Washington's Half-Breed Census (no. 538); her other
   siblings were not listed.[13] She was rejected from that treaty because Agatha
   and her children were previously awarded payment from the 1833 Treaty
   of Chicago. Sarah died on 27 January 1923 and was buried in Ste. Anne's
   Cemetery on Mackinac Island.[14]

The 1836 Treaty of Washington, Article 5, provided for the repayment of
debts owed by the Indians to local traders. From written affidavits in support of
Mrs. Biddle's claim (no. 156) comes a picture of generosity and compassion. John
Beaubien stated he has,

probably never known Mrs. Biddle being without some Indians, to a greater or less amount in her kitchen and about her private house; that such inmates were supplied with food, lodging and fuel, when sick they were nursed, furnished with medicines and with a Doctor, if necessary, all of which was done by Mrs. Biddle. . . . [Also] that funeral services have been rendered to many individuals, coffins made for them, shrouds and funeral garments provided, graves dug and the corpses carried there and interred by said Mrs. Biddle's husband and at their expense. . . . The persons entertained in and about Mrs. Biddle's house were so numerous that [Beaubien] could not fix the precise number thereof, but he is of the opinion that two hundred persons annually would be a small estimate; that Mrs. Biddle's kindness encouraged many to come, that [Beaubien] has sometimes known twenty or thirty at a time who have remained more or less according to circumstances . . . the services were purely personal and rendered in and about Mrs. Biddle's own house; that all of them were gratuitous and charitable, never paid for or otherwise compensated and many of the objects on whom they were expended were destitute and forlorn.[15]

David McGulpin's affidavit states,

The Establishment of Mr. Biddle was as a kind of Foreman to attend on the Indians and furnish them with provisions, which consisted of pork, fish, flour, potatoes, corn and such like which [was] got out of Mrs. Biddle's house from her own stock; sometimes the outhouse attached to Mrs. Biddle's dwelling for the use of the men was filled with Indians; this house is not the same as that used by the Firm of Biddle and Drew for like purpose that [McGulpin] has known to have Indians to remain two weeks.[16]

Samuel Abbott's affidavit states,

That she as well as her husband are of very humane and benevolent dispositions, given to hospitalities and the friends of the poor and needy; that Mrs. Biddle is an Indian and therefore, the more sure to visits from Indians; that [Abbott] has known repeated instances of benevolence and hospitality on the part of Mr. and Mrs. Biddle since their marriage nearly twenty years ago, that the objects thereof was the Indians generally visiting at Mackinaw among them the aged, infirm, sick or crippled of both sexes.[17]

Emerson Smith, writing in 1961, said Edward Biddle,

was not affluent—none of the regular Mackinac Island residents of his day were well off. He took the position of sheriff when he could not make a living bartering with the Indians. Mackinac Island was a poor community, with poor people in it, and did not have much of an economy to support it after the offices [of John Jacob Astor] . . . left there. . . . The whole Island situation bears the same mediocrity which was prevalent in remote pioneer communities.[18]

From the Mackinac Island newspaper, Frank Straus wrote that Edward Biddle was a cousin to Nicholas Biddle, who controlled the largest bank in the United States at the time; they were an extremely affluent family.

Mackinac Island residents, such as the Biddles . . . did not want to live down on the shoreline close to the summer fur traders and their wigwams or tents. Contemporary records indicate that Mackinac Island's summer rendezvous was a fun-loving, raucous place to be, an atmosphere especially disturbing to early Victorian Americans who were working hard to construct a cultural space of gentility around themselves. As an economically successful couple, Agatha and Edward Biddle were eligible to occupy this kind of space. Today's Biddle House . . . has been restored to pay tribute to this life of gentility. . . . The Biddles were highly respected by their neighbors and fellow taxpayers. Records indicate that Edward Biddle was elected annual Warden of the Borough of Mackinac, a position parallel to that of Mayor, in 1831 and again in 1844.[19]

Finally, another contemporary account from 1841 mentions Agatha's Indian heritage and her kindness and concern for island residents and visitors alike. James Silk Buckingham provides this first-hand observation:

An Indian lady, who is called "a great squaw" here, the wife of an opulent white trader, Mr. Biddle, is a person of considerable influence, and greatly respected. She is thought to understand English, but will not speak it, she wears the Indian costume of her tribe, using, however, only the finest materials; she does not eat with her husband, but after him; and sits on the floor in her own apartment, though her house is well furnished with tables and chairs. Her daughters, who are reputed to be handsome, though dark, have been educated at first-rate and fashionable boarding-schools, and are considered highly accomplished; yet even they are proud of their Indian origin, and consider themselves of richer and purer blood than their "pale-faced" sisters.[20]

Agatha Biddle.
COURTESY OF MACKINAC ISLAND STATE
HISTORICAL PARKS/THOMAS PFEIFFELMANN.

This description is contrary to the Smith opinion. Surely the term *opulent* denotes a high level of success and comfortable living as applied to the Biddles' home and lifestyle of the early 1840s. Smith's determination of Agatha's degree of Odawa blood quantum also appears to be at odds with Buckingham's description. The description of Agatha and her children being "dark" is also the opposite of Mrs. Baird's description of Mrs. Biddle as "very fair." Mrs. Baird was born and lived on the island until her marriage and would have been personally acquainted with the Biddle family, but her *Recollections* were written well after the fact and have been labeled "fiction" and "misinformation" by Smith.[21]

There is no disagreement about the great level of respect Agatha earned from island citizens. Dr. John R. Bailey described her: "Mrs. Edward Biddle was Indian of queenly appearance; she dressed in Indian costume, the finest black or blue broadcloth, beautifully ornamented with silk and moose-hair work."[22]

Contemporary accounts describe the Biddles as having the means and willingness to help those who came to their door. These extraordinary accounts of the Biddles give us a rare firsthand glimpse of Mackinac Island and its people in the 1830s and 1840s. That the Biddles were generous individuals to the poor of the region speaks of another time when survival meant living off the land and depending on your neighbors. The Biddles raised a family of more than just their own children—those in need were given hospitality and compassion in a harsh world. With a lifelong example of kindness and generosity, there is little question of how Agatha Biddle became chieftainess of the Mackinac Island band.

36. Mrs. Isaac Blanchard (Mary Babeau, Babbien)

Mary Babeau was the daughter of Louis Babeau and Josephte Otchipewa and was born circa 1805 in Wisconsin. Mary's mother, Josephte, was most likely the daughter of Chief Kabemappa (He who sits to the side) of the St. Croix River region in Wisconsin; Mary's brother Nodin (Wind) was a principal chief in the Snake River region and was painted by James Otto Lewis in 1827.[1]

Chief Kabemappa appears in *Schoolcraft's Expedition to Lake Itasca*, where he is described as friendly to Americans and gave Schoolcraft and his party a "feeling of welcome" when encountered at nightfall on the St. Croix River. While directing them to a suitable location to set up camp, Schoolcraft provides this ethereal description of the chief, "As the tall and gaunt form of the chief glided by, with his spear-pole elevated in the direction we were to go, it might have needed but little power of the imagination, to transform him into a spirit of supernatural power."[2]

Kabemappa was baptized into the Catholic faith at the age of seventy on 2 March 1847 and took the name Joseph.[3] The same day he married Marie Pinessi, age sixty.[4] It is not clear if this woman was the mother of Nodin and Josephte, as it was not uncommon for a chief to have more than one wife.

According to information in *All Our Relations*, there was a close kinship connection between Kabemappa's family and the Cadotte family. "Michel Cadotte was, on his mother's side, first cousin to Nodin one of the principal chiefs of Snake River. . . . He was also first cousin to Buffalo, chief at La Pointe."[5] According to this information, Michel Cadotte's mother and Kabemappa's wife were sisters to Buffalo, all members of the powerful Crane clan. Kabemappa and his son Nodin were members of the *A-Waus-e*, or Great Fish Clan.

Nodin married Angelique Ogagwedakwadokwe (Lace sewing woman) on 28 August 1836.[6] On the same date, Nodin was baptized and also took the name of Joseph.[7] He was forty years old and died on 4 November 1842, leaving no known male heir.[8] The St. Joseph Mission (LaPointe, Wisconsin) baptisms record that Nodin and Angelique had six daughters. Only one child appears to have survived to adulthood and was married. Therese, born 1822, married George Millette 6 January 1839.[9]

Josephte appears to have had a country marriage with Louis Babeau. From this relationship, Marie and a brother named Joseph were born. Little is known about Joseph Babeu; however, his name is listed as an heir of Louis Babeu.[10]

Marie was baptized 10 August 1823 at Ste. Anne's, the same day as half-sister, Suzanne.[11] Suzanne's birth date was recorded as 12 June 1809 in her baptismal record, and her parents, Pierre Assalier dit LaJeunesse and Josephte Otchipewa,

Chief Notin (McKenney Hall), brother
of Mary Babeu. COURTESY OF DR. WILLIAM CROSS.

were mariés [*sic*] in a civil ceremony.[12] A marriage between Pierre Sillier and an
Indian woman named Josette dated 10 June 1829 was performed by Reverend J. J.
Mullen in Mackinac County,[13] but a marriage record prior to the 1823 baptism has
yet to be found.

An *engagé* named "Babeux" was mentioned several times in *A Wisconsin Fur
Trader's Journal, 1803–1804* by Michel Curot. This man was most likely Mary's father.
Curot was sent to the Folle Avoine (northwestern Wisconsin) area to operate a
trading post and recorded the hardships and activities during his time there. The
journal mentions "the wife of Babeux" but does not name her. At some point in
time Assalier married Josephte. Louis ended his work in the fur trade and relocated
his children to the Mackinac area as early as 1811.

Louis Babeu was awarded Private Claim No. 6 at the Pointe de St. Ignace (now
known as St. Ignace, Michigan).[14] According to the *American State Papers*, Louis
Babeu (Babbien) arrived at Pointe de St. Ignace around 1811 and began cultivating
land. Here he built a homestead and lived with his children. The same papers
indicate Louis died during the autumn of 1821.[15] It is not known who cared for
Babeu's children between the time of his death and Mary's marriage in 1824, but
it is probable that Josephte and Pierre followed Babeu to St. Ignace. The 1820
Michilimackinac census recorded Pierre Asseliea in a household with two girls
between ten and sixteen. Both Mary and Suzanne would fall into this age bracket.
No boys were recorded.

The 1830 Michilimackinac census for the Blanchard household lists several
children, one male between twenty and thirty years old, who may have been Joseph
Babeu, and one male between forty and fifty, who was likely Isaac Blanchard. There

William Henry Blanchard.
COURTESY OF JIM CYR.

were two males between ages fifty and sixty. Perhaps one of these men was Pierre Assalier. Perhaps Pierre and Josette/Josephte lived in the Blanchard household.[16]

Mary married Isaac Blanchard in a civil ceremony performed by J. N. Bailey, Esq., on 9 December 1824.[17] Isaac Blanchard was from New Hampshire, born 19 May 1787 and came to Michigan just before the War of 1812.[18] He enlisted in Captain Benjamin K. Pierce's artillery corps at Fort Mackinac on 13 February 1813 for a period of five years.[19] He reenlisted in 1817 and was promoted to sergeant in Company I of the Second Artillery at Fort Mackinac. He served until November 1822.[20] After the war, Blanchard became engaged in commerce and held a trader's license issued by Henry Schoolcraft in 1839.[21] He was also a justice of the peace, performing many marriages in the area.

The Blanchard's family included the following children:

1. Mary Belle was born 19 September 1826,[22] and she married John Shurtleff on 13 October 1843.[23] She died 11 February 1896 in Moran, Mackinac County.[24]
2. Susanne was born 20 November 1827 and baptized at Ste. Anne's.[25]
3. Joseph was born 25 June 1828,[26] and he married Elizabeth Vallier on 6 August 1851 at Ste. Anne's on Mackinac Island.[27] He died 29 April 1880 and was buried in Gros Cap Cemetery.[28]

4. François was baptized 1 February 1831 at Ste. Anne's.[29]
5. Isaac was born 20 March 1837.[30] He was killed in a now-famous dispute on 18 June 1859 at Seul Choix Point,[31] a fishing village in Schoolcraft County, Michigan. He was buried in Gros Cap Cemetery in Mackinac County. Isaac Jr. was killed by Augustus Pond. (This case has been extensively written about. It began the precedent that an individual can defend his home with deadly force.)
6. John was born 28 November 1839,[32] and married Elizabeth Leveille on 12 February 1872 at Ste. Anne's on Mackinac Island.[33] He died 1 October 1903 in St. Ignace, Michigan.[34]
7. Phebe was born 10 November 1843,[35] and married Louis Recollet on 10 July 1865 at Ste. Anne's on Mackinac Island.[36] She died 22 February 1923 and was buried at Mullett Lake, Cheboygan County, Michigan.[37]
8. William Henry was born 12 December 1846,[38] and became a veteran of the Civil War, serving in the 7th Michigan Cavalry, Company K.[39] This company fought at Gettysburg in July 1863 and was present at Appomattox when Lee surrendered. The company mustered out in December 1865. William survived the war but lost a hand at Leavenworth, Kansas. After his discharge, he was given an Invalid war pension.[40] Later, in 1867, he was admitted to the Soldier's Home in Dayton, Ohio. He died on 21 March 1879 at thirty-two years of age and was buried there with a military stone.[41]
9. Agnes Elvira was born 25 June 1850 and baptized at St. Ignatius church in St. Ignace.[42] She married Ambrose Corp at St. Ignatius on 17 September 1865.[43] She died 8 January 1924 in Moran Township, Mackinac County.[44]

Isaac Blanchard was a respected member of the community and served as the Moran Township justice of the peace from 1859 to his death in 1866. He was a religious person and, as such, became one of eight charter members of William Ferry's Presbyterian Church on Mackinac Island in 1823.[45]

An interesting source of personal information about the relationship between Mary and her mother, Josette, comes from David Corp:

Mrs. Blanchard (Me-san-jean-o-qua) was a very hard-working woman, full of energy, who was very temperamental; hated very much when she hated, but kind and considerate at other times. Her mother, No Ko, was of a different nature, being kind and good natured, and making many friends. Being an Indian woman, she would go on a spree occasionally. Mrs. Isaac Blanchard did not drink nor smoke.

While living at Gros Cap, there would be periods as much as three years, when she did not speak to her Mother.[46]

Isaac Blanchard died 10 June 1866 and was buried in the Gros Cap Cemetery.[47] Mary died 12 November 1876,[48] and Josette died 5 September 1871.[49] Both women were buried in the Blanchard plot.

20. Mrs. Vital Bourassa (Angelique Fountain)

Angelique Fountain was probably born in the Red River region of Manitoba circa 1831. Her parents were Joseph Fountain and no. 14 Angelique Fagnant. Angelique's mother was Knisteneaux or Cree and most likely the reason the family did not appear on the Treaty of Washington, DC, Half Breed Census. Her father was active in the fur trade, and like many, he retired from that business to become a fisherman at Mackinac. At Mackinac, Angelique met and married Vital Bourassa (Bourisaw).

Vital Bourassa was the son of Louis Bourassa and Marie Naganaché. The Bourassa family had been in the Mackinac area for several generations by the time Vital was born on 19 September 1825.[1] He was enumerated on the 1836 Half Breed Census along with the rest of his family and listed as Odawa.[2]

He married Angelique Fountain 3 January 1843 at Ste. Anne's on Mackinac Island.[3] From this marriage at least eight children were born.

1. Joseph Vital was born 5 February 1849 and baptized at Ste. Anne's.[4]
2. François/Frank was born 16 September 1851 and baptized at Ste. Anne's.[5] Frank served in the Lighthouse Service under his father at Skillagalee Island Light (Ile aux Galets). First as a second assistant keeper from 1875 to 1879, and later he was promoted to first assistant keeper from 1879 to 1882.[6] He married Harriet Lasley (daughter of James Lasley and Elizabeth Cown) on 13 July 1883.[7] He died 29 June 1930 and was buried on Mackinac Island.[8]
3. Gabriel was born 4 February 1854 and baptized at Ste. Anne's.[9] He first married Anna Mirandette at Ste. Anne's.[10] Gabriel served in the Lighthouse Service as first assistant keeper under his father at Skillagalee Island Light from 1875 to 1879.[11] He died 11 April 1885 and was buried on Mackinac Island.[12]
4. Vital Benjamin was born 1 January 1857 and baptized at Ste. Anne's.[13]
5. Marie June was born and baptized in April 1858 at Ste. Anne's.[14]

Above: Vital Bourassa in his
lighthouse keeper's uniform.
COURTESY OF MARY SCHADEL.

Right: Frank Bourassa.
COURTESY OF MARY SCHADEL.

6. Vital was born 19 June 1859 at Birch Point and baptized at Ste. Anne's 29 August 1859.[15] He died 11 May 1875 and was buried on Mackinac Island.[16]

7. Felix was born 12 December 1861 and baptized at Ste. Anne's.[17]

8. Andre was born 17 November 1866 and baptized at Ste. Anne's.[18]

Angelique Bourassa died 2 June 1879 and was buried at Ste. Anne's Cemetery on Mackinac Island.[19] After her death, Vital married Sarah Anne Chapman on 12 July 1886 at Ste. Anne's.[20] He died 3 March 1904 and was buried in Ste. Anne's Cemetery.[21]

8. Mrs. Louis Cadotte (Marie Louise Laverdure)

Louise Laverdure was born circa 1812 to unknown parents. According to the baptism of her first child, Marie, her full name was Louise Piquette dit Laverdure.[1] It appears Louise had a hard life. Her first relationship with Jean Isaac Levake gave her two known children. Marie was born when Louise was around fourteen years old; Louise's second child was named Xavier. Xavier was enumerated on the Durant Roll on his mother's page, with a notation that Durant could not find this man.[2]

Louise then met George Lasley and had one child named John, who was born

19 May 1836 and baptized at Ste. Anne's on Mackinac Island.[3] John does not appear with Louise and husband Louis Cadotte on the 1850 Mackinac County census; he may have died young. Next, Louise met Pierre Louisignan, with whom she had two children. Rosalie was born in 1837 and married Alex Lozon at Ste. Anne's on 29 December 1863.[4] Rosalie died 3 July 1878 and was buried on Mackinac Island. Peter was born 2 March 1838 and baptized at Ste. Anne's.[5] He married Marie Louise (Lucy) St. Andre at Ste. Anne's on 11 February 1872.[6]

She then married Louis Cadotte on 23 May 1842 in a civil ceremony in St. Ignace.[7] Louis Cadotte was the son of Augustin Cadotte and Madeleine, an Ojibwe woman.[8] He was the nephew of Michel Cadotte, known as Le Grand, the head of a powerful and successful fur-trade business.

This couple had at least seven children:

1. Marie-Louise was born 27 October 1842 and baptized at Ste. Anne's.[9] She married first Alexander LaLonde 5 March 1862 in a civil ceremony.[10] After his death, she married James Delaurier on 31 March 1872 at Ste. Anne's.[11]
2. Augustin was born 9 June 1845,[12] died 12 August 1846, and was buried at Ste. Anne's.[13]
3. Louis was born 2 December 1847.[14] He first married Elizabeth McCollick on 21 April 1871 at Ste. Anne's.[15] After her death, he married Lucy St. Andre, 9 February 1874.[16]
4. Madeleine was born October 1849 and baptized at Ste. Anne's.[17]
5. Michel was born 5 May 1851.[18]
6. Edward was born 22 September 1853 and baptized at Ste. Anne's.[19] He married Jane Garouet on 24 January 1878 at Ste. Anne's.[20]
7. Francis was born 27 July 1856 and baptized at Ste. Anne's.[21]

Louise died 2 September 1873,[22] and Louis died 1 August.[23] They were buried in Ste. Anne's Cemetery on Mackinac Island.

5. Mrs. Joseph Caron (Louise Vasseur)

Louise Vasseur was baptized 25 August 1787 at St. Ignace de Michilimackinac.[1] Her parents were Joseph Vasseur and Madeleine Ouiskoin (Wisconsin?) who was from Lac Courte Oreille (now in present-day Wisconsin). Louise married Joseph Gauthier dit Caron on 1 July 1804.[2] The couple had at least two children before their union was blessed by the priest. This was not an uncommon practice at the time since several years might pass before a priest or missionary visited the region. Couples were viewed as married by the community and were not disparaged in any way.[3] When a priest visited a village and married a couple, any children were noted at the end of the sacrament and were listed as the couple's legitimate children.

Six children are recorded from this marriage.

1. The first child, Joseph, was born 20 March 1802.[4] He married twice, first to Catherine Anthenemie (daughter of Joseph Anthenemie and Enebitas Aiabe), on 8 February 1835, at Ste. Anne's.[5] They had one child, Joseph, born 3 July 1836.[6] Catherine died after the baby's birth, and Joseph then married Mary Anne Kedegekwanebe (no. 29 Mrs. Mary A. Karrow) on 2 July 1840.[7]

2. Marie was born 18 April 1803 and baptized 17 June 1804.[8]

3. Louis was born circa 1816 and married Lucie Beaubin (daughter of Charles Beaubin and Therese Makakons) on 3 January 1837 on Mackinac Island.[9] Louis died on 30 May 1845.[10]

4. Angelique was born circa 1822. She married twice. Her first husband was Jean Baptiste Therrien (son of Peter Isaac Therrien and Angelique Majibinokwe), whom she married 15 November 1841 at Ste. Anne's.[11] He died on 10 November 1846.[12] She then married Henry Hudson on 4 February 1849.[13] Angelique and Jean Baptiste had four children, and she had at least six children with Henry. She died 15 August 1863.[14] (See no. 16 Mrs. Henry Hudson's children.)

5. William was born 15 September 1825 on Drummond Island, Michigan,[15] and married Isabelle Morin (see no. 7 Mrs. William Karrow) on 7 November 1844. She was the daughter of Andre Morin and Marianne Naanwaandago.[16]

6. Henry was born 9 May 1828 at Drummond Island.[17] He married Judithe Diotte (See no. 10 Mrs. Henry Karrow) on 31 May 1847 at Ste. Anne's.[18] Judithe was the daughter of Jean Baptiste Diotte and Marguerite Kabina of Folle Avoine, Wisconsin.[19] Her parents died, and she was adopted into the household of Paul and Angelique Boulanger (See no. 26 Mrs. Paul Belonzhay).[20]

Louise and some of her children applied for funds under the sixth article of the 1836 Treaty of Washington, DC (nos. 193–199). They were enumerated in the "Half-Breed Census" where they were admitted in council and received monies.[21]

Louise was still living in 1870 and was eighty-three years old. Her death record has not been found.

17. Mrs. Betsey Champagne (Unknown)

The worksheet for Betsey Champagne contains no clues to establish her identity. It lists that her children were dead (the children's names were not listed), and there were no heirs. Research was conducted for Elizabeth or Isabelle Champagne with no result. Other Champagne families were researched for a spouse with that name with the same result.

34. Mrs. Moses Champagne (Sarah Martin)

Sarah Martin was born circa 1818 according to her baptism of 30 July 1835.[1] This birth year is consistent with the information on the 1836 Half Breed Census, where she appears as Sarah Plante.[2] Her parents were Antoine Martin Jr. and most likely Helen Midwewinni. According to the 1836 Half Breed Census, Sarah was the granddaughter of the Bear Skin.[3]

Sarah was first married to Michel Plante at Ste. Anne's on Mackinac Island on 14 January 1836.[4] Michel was the son of Peter Plante and Josette Bouillette.[5] One child named Letitia was born on 20 December 1838.[6] No additional information has been found on this child. The marriage appears to have been annulled, because both Sarah and Michel later married different spouses in the Catholic Church. Michel married Marie LeDuc at Ste. Anne's on 3 April 1842,[7] and Sarah married Moses Champagne (Shampine, Shompine) at St. Ignatius Loyola on 13 October 1855.[8]

Moses and Sarah made their home in Moran where they had at least eight children:

1. Sarah was born November 1856 in St. Ignace.[9] She married Patrick Holland in St. Ignace on 31 January 1876.[10]
2. Flavie Delima was born 8 June 1858,[11] and died 30 August 1859 in St. Ignace.[12]
3. Marie Elisabeth was born 26 March 1861 in St Ignace.[13]
4. Jean Baptiste was born 14 July 1862 in St. Ignace (see note concerning his birth date). He died 30 November 1938 and was buried in Naubinway.[14]
5. Charles Augustin was born 16 October 1862 and baptized at St. Ignatius.[15] He married Rosie Levake on 3 Jan 1876 at Ste. Anne's.[16] He died 27 May 1928 in Charlevoix, Michigan.[17]
6. Mary was born circa 1865.
7. Joseph Napolean was born 24 November 1867.[18] He married Mary Lavake

(daughter of Jean Baptiste Lavake and Catherine Plante) on 28 January 1890 in Hendricks Township by a justice of the peace.[19]

8. William was born around 1872 and married Pearl Boutin in St. Ignace, 29 November 1896.[20] Sarah was fifty-four years old when her last child, William, was born.

Aunt Jane Goudreau, a popular, long-lived figure in St. Ignace, was acquainted with Mrs. Champagne and had this story about her, as written by Richard M. Dorson:

> It was my good fortune to meet two more old residents, who came to visit her the last evening of my April stay: her brother, Frank Derusha, ten years her junior, and Jenny Belanger. The three became utterly absorbed in the old tales, quite forgetful of my presence, corroborated details, chimed in with expression of horror at such antics, and recalled further mysteries and haunts; Aunt Jane's voice rose almost to frenzy as she told again about Mrs. Lozon and the *ghibou*.
>
> Old Sarah Champain [Mrs. Moses Champaign] was very sick all the time, she was choking, because Mrs. Lozon didn't like her. Sarah came from Pointe La Barbe to St. Ignace. Every night she took ill and had to go to bed, when a great big ghibou (a corruption of the French hibou—owl) came and perched on her clothesline. It came the same hour every night. It is unusual to see an owl right in the city. The clothesline ran right out under the window (she was in an upstairs apartment), right next to my aunt's house. Mrs. Champain got the doctor and the priest, but they couldn't help her; they couldn't tell her what was wrong.
>
> The door of my aunt's room was open in the summer, and she would see the owl when she went to take her clothes in. She told her nephew to kill the ghibou because he would get the chickens. So, he takes a shotgun and shoots the ghibou. He sees it flop over, puts the gun away, and goes out to pick up the ghibou, to cut it up for a feather duster. But he can't find it. He goes around the house to the highway, down to the trail—the building was set up on the hill—and sees old Mrs. Lozon, lame, trying to crawl up the hill. A rig picked her up and took her over to one of her sisters. She never got over it; she stayed there till she died. . . . And do you know, when Old Mrs. Lozon died, old Sarah got better right away.[21]

According to the State of Michigan death records, Moses died of influenza at age fifty-eight on 28 March 1895 and was buried in the Gros Cap Cemetery.[22] Sarah died 5 July 1906 of senility, complicated by a severe fall.[23] At the time of her death, she was living with her daughter, Lizzie Cadran, on Mackinac Island, where she was buried.

30. Mrs. Bela Chapman (Marie Charette)

Marie Charette was born about 1806, probably in the Fond du Lac area of Wisconsin. Her parents were Simon Charette and Equameeg, or Marguerite *La Grue* (crane, her clan or *ododem*) Kinikinokwe, the daughter of Chief Keeshkemun.[1] On the American Fur Company roster of employees for 1818–1819, her father, Simon Charette was listed as an interpreter, and her mother, a trader in her own right, was stationed at Lac du Flambeau, Wisconsin.[2]

Mary and her children born before 1836 appear on the Treaty of Washington Half Breed Census (nos. 557–564), where they are listed as Chippewa. Similar perhaps to the situation of no. 36 Mary Blanchard, Mrs. Chapman was born outside the treaty area but was admitted "at the request of the Council of Chiefs." Mary and her eldest daughter were awarded first class payments of $1,812.50, while the remaining six listed children were awarded second class payments of $305.89.[3]

Bela Chapman was born circa 1793 in either New Hampshire or Vermont. He was employed by the American Fur Company and was a trader at Grand Marais in 1823.[4] At some point during this time, Chapman met Mary, and they began their family. The Chapmans were married at Mackinac by the Rev. William Ferry on 15 July 1830.[5]

The following children were born to the Chapmans:

1. Elizabeth or Eliza was born circa 1822. She was married to Horatio Pease on 6 December 1838.[6]
2. Reuben was born 1824 and died 31 July 1860.[7] He married Louise Gravareat on 22 January 1855,[8] daughter of Henry Gravareat and Charlotte Livingston. He built, owned, and operated the Lake View Hotel on Mackinac Island.
3. Amanda was born at Fond du Lac about 1826 and married Edward Ashmun on 30 June 1849.[9] He was the son of Samuel and Nancy Ashmun of Sault Ste. Marie, Chippewa County, Michigan.
4. Bela Jr. was born circa 1828.
5. Lucy Chapman was born 9 July 1830,[10] and she married John Biddle (son of no. 1 Agatha Biddle) in Cheboygan, 7 February 1852.[11] Though Lucy was baptized a Catholic, she was buried with her husband in the Protestant Cemetery on Mackinac Island. She died 4 January 1879,[12] and John died 3 March 1886.[13]
6. James was born circa 1833.
7. John was born around 1835, and he married Sarah Ann Hudson 25 August 1858.[14]

Military marker of John B. Shomin.
COURTESY OF WEENGUSH ODEIMIN.

8. Levi was born in 1839, and he married Harriet Pelotte (daughter of no. 11 Rosalie Pelotte).

9. Mary Mathilda born 9 July 1843,[15] and married Jean Baptiste Shomin on 29 May 1868.[16] Jean Baptiste was also known as John B. Shomin. He was a member of the famed Company K, 1st Michigan Sharpshooters, during the Civil War. He enlisted 17 August 1863 at the age of twenty. During the battle of Petersburg (Virginia), he was captured (17 June 1864) and imprisoned at Andersonville. Nearly one year later, on 6 May 1865, he was released. At the end of the war, he was mustered out in Washington, DC, on 3 July 1865.[17]

10. Andrew Jackson was born on 4 January 1846 and died 27 November 1929.[18] He was a veteran of the Civil War, serving in Company K, 7th Michigan Cavalry. He mustered in 29 February 1864 and was transferred to Company C, 1st Cavalry, where he went to California. He was discharged at Detroit, Michigan, on 11 May 1866.[19] After Mary Mathilda's death, he married Sophia Boulanger (daughter of no. 26 Angelique Boulanger) on 2 February 1879.[20]

Bela Chapman was an influential man in the Mackinac region. He was involved in state politics and helped the Michigan territory become a state. Later, he was elected as a probate judge in Mackinac County. He spent seven years in Cheboygan County where he helped shape the town of Cheboygan. He returned to Mackinac Island where he again served as judge until his death in 1873. No information

Mrs. Mary Charette Chapman.
COURTESY OF ANCESTRY.COM.

Mr. Bela Chapman.
COURTESY OF ANCESTRY.COM.

regarding Marie Charette Chapman's death or burial was located. Her death occurred after 14 June 1880 because she appeared on the 1880 Mackinac County census living in the home of her son John.

39. Mrs. Joseph Cheverow (Marie Charlotte Dejadon)

The Field Note lists the children of Joseph Aslin Jr and is a duplicate of no. 40 Mrs. Joseph Laslin (Aslin). Mrs. Cheverow was Marie Charlotte Dejadon (Mrs. Joseph Aslin Sr.) who was born around 1809 at Red Cedar Lake, Minnesota, according to the Mixed Blood Census of the 1873 Treaty with the Lake Superior Chippewa. Her parents were probably Pierre Henri Dejadon and Josephine Louise Michovassi, and she had at least three sisters. They were no. 43 Mrs. Hyacinthe Dophena Sr., no. 26 Mrs. Paul Belonzhay, and no. 43 Mrs. Louis Belonzhay.

Aslin also went by the name Chevreau. This name was used on the 1836 Half Breed Census.[1] Three of the sisters are listed on the same page, with Angelique Boulanger's (Belonzhay) family and Josette Dophena's (Dauphiny) family. The family applications for all four sisters for the 1836 Treaty of Washington were denied, and no monetary awards were given. Comments in the Remarks Column say Marie Cheverau was "of Mississippi origin, B[azile] Jellee [Jolie] says she is from Fond du Lac."[2]

Marie and Joseph Aslin were married in the Protestant church on 4 April 1828 by the Rev. William Ferry. Later, there was a Catholic ceremony at Ste. Anne's on

Mackinac Island, where, on 9 March 1834, "Joseph Aslin de la Paroisse de St. Vincent de Paul á Montreal married Enerica Henry Ojibowe Sauvagesse."[3]

Joseph and Marie had at least twelve children:

1. Joseph Hillaire was born 12 January 1830 and baptized at Ste. Anne's.[4] He married no. 40 Julia Victoria Lessieur (daughter of Edward Lessieur and Angelique Peltier) on 21 January 1853 at Ste. Anne's.[5]
2. Angelique was born circa 1834 and first married Alexis Therrien (son of Peter Isaac Therrien and Angelique Majibinokwe) on 11 November 1850.[6] After his death, she married Charles Louisignan on 2 March 1862 (son of François Louisignan and Agatha Langlade)[7].
3. Elizabeth was baptized 24 November 1836 at Ste. Anne's.[8] She married Joseph Lapine (son of Joseph Lapine and Marie Louise Charbonneau) on 31 March 1856 at Ste. Anne's.[9]
4. Pierre or Peter was born 25 May 1839 and baptized at Ste. Anne's.[10] He married Elizabeth Jeanne Mettez (Metty) on 14 April 1861 at Ste. Anne's.[11]
5. Paul was born 11 June 1841 and baptized at Ste. Anne's.[12] He first married Angelique Lessieur,[13] then Jane Davenport,[14] and finally married Joanna Matilda Lasley.[15] Paul was enumerated with his own page on the Durant Roll under no. 25/11. He died 1 November 1876.
6. Theophile was born 24 September 1843 and was baptized at Ste. Anne's.[16]
7. Marie Isabelle was born 25 March 1846 and was baptized at Ste. Anne's.[17] She married Jean Baptiste Caron (son of Joseph Caron and no. 29 Marianne Kedegekwanabe) on 25 May 1862 at Ste. Anne's.[18]
8. Magdeleine was born 13 May 1848 and baptized at Ste. Anne's.[19] She married Joseph Besina (son of Michel Besina, Bezonette, or Bazinet).[20]
9. Esther was born 18 April 1851 and baptized at Ste. Anne's.[21]
10. Marguerite was born 15 July 1853 and baptized at Ste. Anne's.[22] She married David Andress (son of William Andress and Josette Bazinaw) on 2 May 1870 at Ste. Anne's.[23]
11. Marie Louise was born January 1856.[24]

Marie Dejadon Aslin died 10 November 1869 and was buried in Ste. Anne's cemetery on Mackinac Island.[25] Joseph died on St. Helena Island on 22 July 1887 and was buried on Mackinac Island.[26]

64. Mrs. Peter Closs (Julia Pond)

Julia Pond was the daughter of Augustin Peter Pond and Louise Boucher. She was born 19 December 1831 and baptized at Ste. Anne's of Mackinac Island on 5 February 1832.[1] See no. 51 Mrs. Jane Lancour (Julia's sister) for the history of her parents.

Peter Closs was born in Canada and immigrated with his parents to the Mackinac area around 1844. Peter first appeared in documents of the Mackinac area on the 1850 Michilimackinac census with his parents, Louis Closs and Catharine Plaunte, at thirteen years of age.[2] Louis Closs died in St. Ignace on 15 March 1857,[3] and Catharine died on 12 May 1873.[4] They were buried in St. Ignatius Cemetery in St. Ignace.

Julia Pond married Peter/Pierre Closs on 4 May 1857 in St. Ignace.[5] From this marriage there were at least ten children:

1. Pierre Julian was born 20 March 1858 and baptized at St. Ignace.[6]
2. Louis was born circa 1861.
3-4. William Isidore and Julie Virginia were born circa 1864. She married John Bouchard (son of Abraham Bouchard and Madeline Matha) on 12 November 1892.[7]
5. Sophie S. was born circa 1866.
6. Annie Elizabeth was born circa 1866. She married Stephen Riell (son of Nicholas Riell and Julia St. Bernard) on 14 November 1888.[8]
7. Elizabeth was born circa 1868.
8. Adeline was born circa 1870 and married Amos R. Olmstead (son of Peter Olmstead and Rhoda Stiles) in Sault Ste. Marie, Michigan, on 26 July 1888.[9]
9. Marie Louise was born 24 July 1872 and baptized at St. Mary's in Cheboygan.
10. Mary A. was born 18 September 1885.[10]
11. Oliver was born 17 July 1876 in St. Ignace.[11]

Peter Closs died 15 November 1890,[12] and Julia died 26 January 1912.[13] They were buried in St. Ignace, Michigan.

9. Mrs. Alice Cushway (Alice Graveraet Couchoise)

Sophia Alice Graveraet was the daughter of Henry Garret Graveraet, Jr. and Sophie Bailly. She was born in 1836. Henry was the son of Henry Graveraet and Charlotte

Left: Henry Graveraet, husband of Sophie Bailly, and father of Garrett.
COURTESY OF THE EMERSON SMITH COLLECTION AT BENTLEY HISTORICAL LIBRARY, UNIVERSITY OF MICHIGAN.

Right: Garrett Graveraet, son of Henry and Sophie Graveraet.
COURTESY OF THE EMERSON SMITH COLLECTION AT THE BENTLEY HISTORICAL LIBRARY, UNIVERSITY OF MICHIGAN.

Livingston. Like other women on this list, Alice became part of this band through heredity. Her grandmother, Charlotte, was one of its original members back in 1839 and was enumerated until her death. Sophie Bailly's parents were Joseph Bailly and Angelique McGulpin.

Sophie Bailly was a schoolteacher, and Henry was a carpenter. They were married 11 January 1836 at Ste. Anne's.[1] From this marriage there were three children.

During the Civil War, their son, Garrett, organized Company K of the First Michigan Sharpshooters and recruited mainly Native Americans from the Northport, Michigan, area. His father, Henry Jr., was his sergeant. He was killed at Spotsylvania, Virginia, and buried in the Fredericksburg National Cemetery.[2] In the Siege of Petersburg, Garrett was wounded in the left arm, which was later amputated. He died from his wounds at a Washington, DC, Army Hospital.[3] There is a marker in Ste. Anne's cemetery for Henry and Garrett but only Garrett's body was returned to Mackinac Island for burial. Sophie received a pension and lived comfortably until her death on 8 January of 1892. She was buried in Cross Village, Emmet County, Michigan.[4]

Alice was married to John Baptiste Couchoise on 5 March 1859 at Ste. Anne's on Mackinac Island.[5] John was the son of John Baptiste Couchoise and Catherine Lyons of Detroit.

Sophia Bailly Graveraet.
COURTESY OF THE EMERSON SMITH COLLECTION
AT THE BENTLEY HISTORICAL LIBRARY,
UNIVERSITY OF MICHIGAN.

From this marriage there were three children:

1. Robert John was born on 25 May 1860 and baptized at Ste. Anne's.[6]
2. Sophie Rosine born 2 October 1863 and baptized at Ste. Anne's. She died 15 February 1944 in Chicago, Illinois.[7]
3. Helen Elisabeth born 23 August 1866 and baptized 26 August 1866.[8]

Alice died 27 February 1873 and was buried in Ste. Anne's Cemetery.[9] John married Alice's sister Marie Rosine (who had been previously married to Robert F. Wright). They were only married a brief period before John died on 11 October 1873.[10] From that marriage one child, John C. Couchoise, was born. He became a writer and recorded stories of his childhood and those of his grandmother, Sophie Bailly.

31. Mrs. Ambrose Davenport (Susan Descarreaux)

Susan Descarreaux was born around 1804 at a trading post on the Crow Wing River in Minnesota. She was the eldest of four children born to François Descarreaux and a native woman, believed to be a daughter of Waubojeeg, a chief at LaPointe, Wisconsin. Susan's brother François, born circa 1808 at Sandy Lake, Minnesota, was later given the Christian name of Henry Blatchford at the Mackinac Missionary School. Her sister, Marguerite, was born circa 1811 at Rabbit Lake, Minnesota, and her other sister, Mary, was born around 1816 at Sandy Lake, Minnesota.

Ambrose and Susan Davenport.

Ambrose Davenport Jr. was the son of Ambrose Davenport Sr., known as the Yankee Rebel. He refused to give his allegiance to the British Crown when Mackinac Island was lost during the War of 1812. Ambrose Jr. followed in his father's footsteps by earning his living in the fur trade. During his service with the American Fur Trade, he met Susan. Later, they were married at LaPointe on 12 August 1835.[1]

This family applied for funds from the 1837 Treaty of St. Peters, and appears in *All Our Relations*. The recorded application follows:

Ambrose Davenport residing at la Pointe and in the service of the American Fur Company, claims for wife Susan ½ breed 32 years of age born at Crow Wing River, was raised in the ceded territory and remained in it until she was married about 14 yrs since. From that time to the present she has been residing with her husband and accompanying him through the Indian Country to the different places that he was sent to by the Company. Her father (Mr. Decharrault) was an Indian trader for a number of years in the country up to the time of his death in 1822. The mother was a full Indian woman from Mille Lac where she always lived until she was married. He also claims for his children ¼ breeds. William, 12 yrs of age born at Rainy Lake, Henry 10 yrs of age born at Fond du Lac Portage, Mary 8 yrs of age born at Vermillion Lake, Joseph 6 yrs of age born at Gull Lake, Betsy 4 yrs of age born at La Pointe and John I, born at L'Ance.[2]

John Davenport with second wife, Julia Dufina, and family. COURTESY OF KAREN FRAZIER.

Between the birth of John at L'Anse and the 1840 census, the Davenports relocated to Mackinac Island. Later, Ambrose was appointed the fish inspector on the island, and in 1853, he became the keeper of the Skillagalee Light on Lake Michigan. Skillagalee is a remote location on Lake Michigan, roughly between Cross Village and Beaver Island. He served several years there with his son, John, who was his first assistant keeper.[3] By 1870, he was back on Mackinac Island living comfortably as a fisherman with Susan and their youngest children. Ambrose died on 4 November 1879 in Moran, Michigan, and was buried in the Protestant Cemetery on Mackinac Island.[4] Susan outlived her husband by nine years. She died in Cross Village on 29 November 1888 and was buried next to her husband in the Protestant Cemetery on Mackinac Island.[5]

During their long life together, witnessing such things as the War of 1812, the fur trade, the fish trade, and lighthouse service, this couple raised a large family:

1. William was born 13 July 1826 at Rainy Lake, Minnesota.[6] He married Lucy Boulanger on 26 February 1850,[7] then married Harriet Flint. He died 11 July 1860 and was buried in the Protestant Cemetery on Mackinac Island.[8]
2. Henry L. Davenport was born 14 June 1828 at Fond du Lac, Minnesota.[9] He

married Julia Perrault on 14 June 1853,[10] and died 30 August 1912 in Detroit, Michigan.[11]

3. Mary was born 3 March 1831 at Vermillion Lake, Minnesota.[12] She married Charles James Lusignan on 9 May 1850,[13] and died July 1855.[14]

4. Joseph was born 24 March 1833 at Gull Island, Minnesota,[15] and he died 16 February 1862 at Mackinac Island.[16]

5. Elizabeth or Betsey was born around 1836 at LaPointe, Wisconsin. She married Leon Boulanger on 8 December 1855 at Ste. Anne's.[17] She died 12 May 1874 and was buried in Ste. Anne's cemetery on Mackinac Island.

6. John was born 14 December 1837.[18] He married Liset Isabelle Boulanger on 21 January 1867 at Ste. Anne's.[19] After she died, he married Julie Dufina on 13 May 1876.[20] He died 30 November 1913 in Naubinway, Michigan.[21]

7. Jane was born 9 June 1842.[22] She married Paul Aslin 7 February 1865 at Ste. Anne's on Mackinac Island.[23] She died 13 October 1872 and was buried in the Protestant Cemetery there.[24]

8. Julia was born 25 April 1845 on Mackinac Island.[25] She married William Henry Duclon on 2 May 1867.[26] William was a Civil War veteran who served in Company K, 14th New York Heavy Artillery. In 1883 William took over the lighthouse keeper's position at Eagle Bluff, Door County, Wisconsin. He served there for the next thirty-five years where they raised seven children. Julia died 20 September 1922,[27] and William died 2 September 1926.[28] The couple were buried in the Blossomberg Cemetery, Fish Creek, Wisconsin.

9. James was born in 1 April 1847 on Mackinac Island.[29] He married Madeleine Lasley on 18 April 1870.[30] He died 18 March 1932 and was buried in Mackinaw City, Michigan.[31]

10. Susan was born 15 April 1849 on Mackinac Island. She died 18 January 1870.[32]

11. Margaret Caroline was born on Mackinac Island on 12 October 1851.[33] She married Samuel Morris 26 May 1874 at Trinity Church on Mackinac Island.[34] She died 5 August 1933 in Petoskey and was buried there with her husband in Greenwood Cemetery.[35]

12. Andrew Jackson was born 6 December 1854 on Mackinac Island.[36] He married Clara Hamann on 6 July 1874 in St. Ignace, Michigan.[37] He died in Chicago, Illinois, on 25 April 1929.

Before Susan's death, an encounter with her was recorded in the *Friends' Intelligencer*, a Quaker publication from Philadelphia:

Left: Julia Davenport and William H. Duclon. COURTESY OF EAGLE BLUFF LIGHTHOUSE MUSEUM, DOOR COUNTY, WISCONSIN.

Right: Susan DesCarreux Davenport. COURTESY OF JEAN LHODE.

One moon-lit evening, as we walked westward along the roadway which skirts the south shore of Mackinaw, passing the lowly, simple homes of half-breed and Indian fisher folk, we were attracted by an open door and a pleasant, comely Indian woman who held a little child on her knee as she sat at her threshold. We paused to say a pleasant word to the little papoose and to the venerable-looking grandmother. To our surprise, in very imperfect English, she announced herself to us as the widow of Ambrose Davenport. She is a Chippeway Indian from the country beyond Lake Superior and was brought by her Anglo-Saxon lover to this island more than fifty years ago. He built this low-browed cottage on the shore of the glittering lake, and here they reared their dusky children, and here their children's children yet abide in unprogressive content, while the great wave of advancing civilization rolls past and onward to the western ocean's marge. The Indian widow yet prefers the Chippewayan speech, and laughingly names for us the resplendent evening star, the full moon, the lake and other objects. She is skilled in cookery and alluded very slightingly to the efforts of the hotel cooks, wondering how the "strangers" could eat such things as they knew how to make. She is also highly valued for her gifts in the art of healing, knowing all the mysteries of Indian "medicine," and having the nerve and the faith to apply them.[38]

Susan died 29 November 1888 and was buried in the Protestant Cemetery on Mackinac Island.

42. Mrs. William Davenport (Marie Dufault)

The children listed on the Durant worksheet of Mrs. William Davenport are the children of Robert Davenport and Dolphine Boulanger and the grandchildren of William Davenport and Marie Dufault.

Mrs. William Davenport (Marie Dufault) was enumerated on the Mackinac Island band annuities as early as 1859. Prior to that year, Anishinaabe names were used.

According to *All Our Relations*, William was the brother of Ambrose Davenport,[1] whose father, Ambrose Davenport Sr., was born in Virginia and came to Mackinac to work in the fur trade. Here, William learned the trade until he got his own license and worked for the American Fur Company at various posts in the Wisconsin area. While in this region, he met Marie, and they began their family. To date, a marriage record for them has not been found. A baptism for a woman named Marie Dufault was found in the St. Joseph Mission of LaPointe dated 28 August 1836.[2] This Marie Dufault was twenty-two years old, and no parents were listed. It is not known if this is the same woman who married William Davenport.

Marie Dufault's father was probably Louis Dufault Sr, who was the son of Louis Dufault and Marie Louise Mentosaky, daughter of Mentosaky and Penymeny.[3]

Trading at Leech Lake, William applied for funds available from the 1837 Treaty with the Lake Superior Chippewa. These applications were transcribed in *All Our Relations*:

William Davenport of La Pointe claims for his wife Mary, ½ breed 26 yrs of age born at Sandy Lake where she resided for several years, accompanying her father (Louis Dufaut Senr an Indian Trader) in his migrations throughout the Indian country until her marriage when she accompanied her husband also a trader wintering in many parts of the Indian Country. (Mr. Davenport now in the employ of the American Fur Company.) He also claims for his 3 children ¼ breeds. William 7 yrs. old, born at Leech Lake, Robert 5 yrs. born at Leech Lake and Martha Jane 1 yr. born at Fond du Lac. They have always resided with their parents.[4]

The application was accepted and approved. Each claimant received $258.40, half paid in gold and coin and the remainder paid in bank notes.[5]

From the marriage of William and Marie, there were at least three children:

1. William was born circa 1834, near Leech Lake, Minnesota. He married

Robert Davenport.
COURTESY OF KAREN FRAZIER.

Therese Dailey on 22 November 1863 in Emmet County.[6] Because of the marriage date, Therese cannot be the Mrs. William Davenport enumerated in the annuities prior to 1860. William died 9 August 1901 in Cross Village and was buried there.[7]

2. Robert was born near Leech Lake, Minnesota, circa 1836. He married Dolphine Boulanger (daughter of Paul Boulanger and no. 26 Angelique Montreuil) on 13 May 1867 at Ste. Anne's.[8] He served in the Civil War, enlisting in Detroit on 20 August 1862, in Company G, 5th Michigan infantry.[9] Robert survived the war and was mustered out 16 May 1865 in Detroit. He died 24 January 1885 in Newton Township,[10] and was buried in the Protestant Cemetery on Mackinac Island.[11] His grave is marked with a soldier's stone in recognition of his service.

3. Martha Jane was born circa 1838, near Fond du Lac, Wisconsin.[12]

William Davenport retired from the fur trade and brought his family to the Mackinac area, first appearing in the 1850 Michilimackinac County census living next door to his brother Ambrose and family.[13]

According to Mackinac County death records, William Davenport died in 1875 on Mackinac Island.[14] No information was found regarding Marie Dufault Davenport's death and burial.

60. Alexsie Dophena

The worksheet Durant made for Alexsie Dophena does not indicate if this person is male or female, nor is there any information regarding a spouse or children to help identify the individual.

The applicant could be Alexander Dophena son of Francis Dophena and Therese Mukademunk. Francis and Therese married at Ste. Anne's on Mackinac Island on 18 March 1851.[1] If this is the correct person, Alexander was the grandson of no. 23 Mrs. Hyacinthe Dophena Sr. (see below).

Francis and Therese had at least three children:

1. Julia was born 8 February 1852 and baptized on Mackinac Island.[2]
2. François was born 15 January 1853 and baptized on Mackinac Island.[3]
3. Alexander was born 15 February 1854 and baptized on Mackinac Island.[4]

After Therese died, Francis married Marie Madeleine Cadotte on 31 January 1861.[5] No additional information was found about Therese Mukademunk.

Alexander married Mary Harriet Donais on 7 April 1874 in Mackinac County.[6] The 1880 Mackinac County census for Holmes Township showed the couple with no children and that they lived near his brothers and widowed grandmother, Josette Dophena, on Mackinac Island.[7]

By the 1900 census, Alex was living with his brother, Samuel, in Cheboygan County where he is a widower, with no children.[8] Alex died 15 January 1907,[9] and he was buried in Mackinaw City, Michigan.[10]

23. Mrs. Hyacinthe (François) Dophena (Josette Dejadon)

Josette Dejadon was probably born near Red Cedar Lake in what is now Minnesota around 1807. Her parents most likely were Pierre Dejadon and Josephine Michovassi. Josette had three sisters who also lived in the Mackinac area. They were no. 43 Mrs. Louis Belonzhay, no. 26 Mrs. Paul Belonzhay, and no. 39 Mrs. Joseph Cheverow. All

Alexander Dufina.
COURTESY OF MARY SCHADEL.

four women married men who were engaged in the fur trade, retired to Mackinac Island, and became fishermen.

Josette and François Dauphinet (presently spelled Dufina) were married on 14 April 1828 by Reverend William Ferry.[1] Even though the Dufinas were married in a Protestant service, their children were baptized by the Catholic priest on the island:

1. François, was born on 27 August 1828, and baptized at Ste. Anne's.[2] He first married Therese Mukademunk on 18 April 1851 at Ste. Anne's.[3] After she died, he married Marie-Madeleine Cadotte on 31 January 1862, also at Ste. Anne's.[4] François died 9 September 1898 in Mackinaw City, Michigan.[5]
2. Hyacinthe was baptized 28 April 1831 at Ste. Anne's.[6] He and Josette Andress were married on 7 March 1859 by Bela Chapman, justice of the peace.[7]
3. Julia was born 6 November 1832 and was baptized at Ste. Anne's.[8]
4. Alexander was born 12 February 1835 and baptized at Ste. Anne's.[9] He married Ursula Lesieur, daughter of Edward Lesieur and Angelique Peltier,[10] on 16 April 1859, at Ste. Anne's.[11] Alexander died 23 October 1926 and was buried in Ste. Anne's cemetery.[12] Ursula died 28 January 1923 and was buried there as well.[13]
5. Guillaume was born 29 October 1838 and baptized at Ste. Anne's.[14]
6. Marie was born 26 September 1839 and baptized at Ste. Anne's.[15] She married Jean Baptiste Bazinet, son of Michel Bazinet and Marie Anne Bagotigokwe on 24 September 1861 at Ste. Anne's.[16] Jean Baptiste died 28 August 1885,[17] and Marie died 28 May 1909.[18] They were both buried in Ste. Anne's cemetery.

7. Madorus was born 12 February 1843 and baptized at Ste. Anne's.[19] He married Christine Leveille 13 September 1868.[20]

An island story says that François Dauphinet Sr. was a carpenter and house-builder there. One day tragedy struck when a wall he was working on collapsed, killing him instantly. Whether this is true or not, François died young, sometime between 1843 and 1846. Josette then married Peter Numanville, son of Jean Baptiste Numanville, on 23 September 1846.[21] The marriage produced one child, Peter, in 1848. The next year, Peter Numanville died on 6 October 1849, victim of a cholera epidemic.[22] Josette was probably the woman named Josephine Duffina who died 14 July 1891 and was buried on the 17 July on Mackinac Island. Her age was listed as ninety-six and her place of birth Bayfield, Michigan (Wisconsin?).[23]

14. Mrs. Joseph Fountain (Angelique Fagnant)

Angelique Fagnant (Faillant, Fayant) was born around 1810, probably somewhere near St. Boniface, Manitoba. Her father was Raphael Fagnant and an unknown Cree woman.[1] Raphael and his wife had several children who lived in the Winnipeg area. Raphael died on 22 November 1836 at eighty-one years of age and was buried at St. Francis Xavier, Manitoba.[2] No additional information about Angelique's mother has been located.

Not much is known of Angelique's life until she began having children with Joseph Fontaine. No marriage record was found, but it is probable that they were married somewhere in the St. Boniface area of Manitoba, as the baptismal record of their second child was found there. From Manitoba, Joseph and Angelique came to Mackinac Island where they made their home. Joseph and his sons, like other men who had worked in the fur trade, became fishermen.

Joseph and Angelique had at least ten children:

1. Angelique was born around 1831. She married Vital Bourassa. (See no. 20 Mrs. Vital Bourassa.)
2. Mary, also known as Nancy, was born 27 October 1832 and baptized at St. Boniface, Manitoba.[3] She married Simon Martin, son of Simon Martin and Marie Lisette Leveille, on 4 May 1858 at Ste. Anne's on Mackinac Island.[4]
3. Andre or Andrew was born circa 1836, possibly near La Cloche, Ontario. He married Marianne Lozon, daughter of Joseph and Elizabeth-Nancy Lozon,

Joseph Fountain Jr., lighthouse keeper, circa 1882. COURTESY OF MARILYN FISCHER.

on 12 July 1863, at Ste. Anne's on Mackinac Island.[5] Andrew died 13 April 1926 at the Newberry State Hospital in Chippewa County and was buried in the Gould City (Newton Township) Cemetery in Mackinac County.[6]

4. Agatha was born 9 September 1840 and baptized at Ste. Anne's.[7] She married Francis Martin. (See no. 21 Mrs. Francis Martin.)

5. Joseph was born 29 August 1843 and baptized at Ste. Anne's.[8] Joseph married Christine Lozon, daughter of Joseph and Elizabeth-Nancy Lozon, on 11 February 1872 at Ste. Anne's.[9] In 1882 he began to work for the Lighthouse Service at Skillagalee (Ile aux Galets) as first assistant keeper. Later, he became the lighthouse keeper at Sand Point in Escanaba, Beaver Island Harbor (St. James) Light, Seul Choix Light, and finally St. Helena, where he served from 1901 to 1918. He retired from the service in 1918 and died in May 1925. He was buried at Gros Cap Cemetery in Mackinac County.

6. Theophilus was born 13 December 1846 and baptized at Ste. Anne's.[10]

7. Marie was born 25 November 1849 and baptized at Ste. Anne's.[11]

8. Theophile was born 29 April 1853 and baptized at Ste. Anne's.[12]

9. Matilda was born 13 September 1854 and baptized at Ste. Anne's.[13]

10. Jane was born in 1855 and died 27 September 1876.[14] She was buried at Ste. Anne's Cemetery.

Joseph died 21 November 1868 and was buried in Ste. Anne's Cemetery on Mackinac Island.[15] Angelique died a couple years later, on 16 January 1875, and was buried next to her husband.[16]

16. Mrs. Henry Hudson's Children (Angeline Caron)

Mrs. Henry Hudson was Angeline Caron, the daughter of no. 5 Louise Vasseur and Joseph Gauthier Caron. The children listed on this page were the children of David Hudson and Catherine Andress and were not enumerated on the annuity lists paid to the Biddle band.

Angeline's children appear under no. 10 Mrs. Henry Caron, who was Judithe Diotte. Mrs. Henry Caron's children were, therefore, left off the Durant Roll.

Angeline Caron was born circa 1822, probably in the Mackinac area. She first married Jean Baptiste Therrien, son of Peter Isaac Therrien and Angelique Majibinokoue.[1] With Jean Baptiste, she had at least three children: Marie Magdeleine was born 26 February 1844 and died at seven months old; Jean Baptiste was born 18 September 1845 and lived for just over a month; and Marguerite was born 25 October 1846. On the same day, 10 November 1846,[2] Marguerite and her father, Jean Baptiste died, according to parish records. Angeline survived to bury her husband and two-week old infant in Ste. Anne's Cemetery with the other babies. There is no indication in the records what caused their deaths.

On 4 February 1849, she married Henry Hudson at Ste. Anne's.[3] From this marriage, several children were born:

1. Emily was born 15 October 1849 and was baptized at Ste. Anne's.[4] She married Benjamin Fisher and died 12 December 1885 in Cheboygan, Michigan.[5]
2. William Hudson was baptized 21 March 1852 at Ste. Anne's.[6]
3. Louis Napoleon was born 6 April 1854 and baptized at Ste. Anne's.[7] He married Mathilda Donner.
4. James Hudson was born 4 May 1855. It appears he did not marry and lived to be 102 years old. There was an application for a service marker that listed his death on 31 May 1957.[8] He served in the Spanish-American War in 1898.
5. Mary Hudson was born circa 1859.
6. Alice Hudson was born circa 1861. She married John Andress in Cheboygan on 16 June 1876.[9]
7. Angeline Hudson was baptized 25 December 1862 at St. Mary's in Cheboygan.[10] She married John McCarty on 27 February 1880 in Cheboygan, Michigan.[11]

Henry Hudson was a paid substitute in the Civil War.[12] He enlisted on 16 June

Henry Hudson. COURTESY OF PATTI LYLES.

1864 and was mustered out 9 July 1865.[13] He survived the war and came back to Michigan. Later, according to Army records, he applied for an invalid pension, citing "nearly total deafness in both ears."[14] Angeline died 4 September 1869 and was buried in the Calvary Cemetery in Cheboygan, Michigan.[15] After Angeline's death, records indicate Henry married Mary LaLonde, but no record was found. Henry died 9 December 1910 and was buried in the Calvary Cemetery in Cheboygan, Michigan.

22. Mrs. Peter Jacobear (Poline Martin)

Mrs. Peter Jacobear (Jockabare, Hebert, Abare) is a mystery. She was born perhaps near Sault Ste. Marie, Michigan, but no record of her birth was found. She appeared in only one census under the name Poline. Her parents are unknown.[1]

Her husband, Pierre, offered more data, but a snag (like so many other members on this list) was the multiple surname spellings used by those who recorded this family. The following information is given with little concrete evidence except where noted. Pierre Hebert was (probably) born 18 January 1844 at *vieux fort* (old fort, Mackinaw City).[2] His parents were listed as François Abey and Marie Jolon. He was baptized at Ste. Anne's on Mackinac Island on 18 September 1844. Subsequent census records list his father as François Hebert (1850) and James Hebert (1860). He was François Jacques Hebert and his mother Marie Chalue (Chalut), probably from Red Cedar Lake.

Partial image, 1870 census, Mackinac County, Holmes Township, page 17 (Jacobear, Hebert).

Poline Martin and Pierre Hebert were married at St. Ignatius in St. Ignace, Michigan, on 18 November 1862.[3] The marriage record listed the bride's birthplace as Sault Ste. Marie but listed no parents. The following children were born to this couple:

1. Peter was born February 1863 and baptized at St. Mary's (Sault Ste. Marie, Michigan) on 24 August 1863.[4]
2. Charles was born circa 1864 and died 18 April 1880 on Bois Blanc Island and was buried at Ste. Anne's on Mackinac Island.[5]
3. William was born circa 1865. He appears on the 1870 census (See above).
4. Joseph was born circa 1867. He appears on the 1880 census (See below. Could he be the same person as William?)
5. Margaret was born July 1869. She appears on the 1870 census (See above).
6. Nancy was born around 1869 and married James Lefevere of Saginaw, Michigan (son of Henry Lefevere and Ann Settles) on 30 September 1896 in St. Ignace, Michigan.[6] Their marriage must have been annulled because James is listed as single on later censuses. Nancy later married Thomas Vallier (son of Thomas Vallier and Marianne Martin). No record of the marriage was located but several children were found in later censuses. The 1910 census indicated they were married circa 1899.[7] Nancy's death record listed Jack Abare as her father and her birth date as 6 March 1869.[8] Perhaps Nancy and Margaret are the same person.
7. Genevieve Paulee was born 26 March 1873 and baptized at St. Mary's in Sault Ste. Marie, Michigan.[9] She died 3 August 1873 and was buried the next day in the Ste. Anne's Cemetery on Mackinac Island.[10]

Both Peter and his mother were listed as widowers on the 1880 census. It is possible that Poline died after giving birth to Genevieve, but no record of her death was found. Peter died, age forty-one, on 6 October 1884, and was buried in Ste. Anne's Cemetery on Mackinac Island.

15. Mrs. Francis Johnston (Margaret Bennett-Beaubin)

Margaret Bennett-Beaubin was the daughter of Louis Bennet-Beaubin and no. 38 Christine Outapitakawinam. She was sister to no. 19 Mrs. David Kniffen, no. 4 Mrs. Edward Lasley, no. 2 Mrs. Louis Maishtaw, and no. 13 Mrs. Francis Rastoul

When the 1836 Half Breed Census was taken, Margaret was six years old. Margaret and her siblings were enumerated, admitted in council, and received third class awards of $95.14 each.[1]

She married Francis Johnston from Sweden, who came to the United States in 1856.[2] They were married on Mackinac Island by the justice of the peace, Bela Chapman, on 28 April 1859.[3]

Margaret Johnston's obituary appeared in the 3 October 1913 *Cheboygan Democrat*:

> Mrs. Johnston, wife of Frank Johnston, died Wednesday Sept 24, at the home of Mr. and Mrs. Theodore Duffiner. Mrs. Johnston was born at Mackinac Island and was married to Frank Johnston at the age of 31 and lived to the good old age of 85, spending the 54 years of her life on a farm near Mackinaw City. Last winter Mrs. Johnston commenced to fail and having no children of their own they moved to Mackinaw City to the home of Mr. and Mrs. Theodore Duffiner, where they were tenderly cared for. Mrs. Johnston died very peaceful with her aged husband at her bed side where he remained until the body was carried to its last resting place. Beautiful flowers from loving friends surrounded the casket and the dear old lady has gone to be at rest in the mansion prepared for her. The funeral was held from St. Anthony's church Friday morning, Father Nye officiating. Interment at Lakeside cemetery.[4]

57. Edward Karrow

Edward Karrow (Carrow, Corrow, Caron) was the son of no. 10 Judithe Diotte and Henry Carrow. He was born on Bois Blanc Island and baptized at Ste. Anne's on 8 April 1861.[1] He later moved to Cheboygan, Michigan, where he married Elizabeth Viedmer on 29 June 1885.[2] Elizabeth, or "Lizzie" as she was known, was from Pennsylvania.[3]

Edward and Lizzie produced four children, and it appears Lizzie had a hard life. Her husband, whom she did not live with, was a shiftless man and non-supportive.

He was listed in the Cheboygan newspaper several times for misdemeanors, including one for stealing chickens,[4] and another where he was ordered to leave town for ninety days.[5] To support her children, Elizabeth did laundry and occasionally received funds from the Cheboygan County Poor Fund.[6] The month after Lizzie's death, Edward received four months of support and funds to pay her funeral expenses.[7]

Lizzie met a horrific end. On 3 April 1899, Lizzie and her son Edward traveled by dogsled into Cheboygan to do laundry. Apparently, the dogsled blades stuck on the track and Lizzie and one of the dogs were killed by a train and Edward Alfred was injured.[8]

Their father, unable to provide for his children, apparently counted on the charity of others to take them in. They were found living with various families in the 1900 census. Edward was listed as a "servant" in the Louis Gerard household.[9] Herbert was found as a "ward" in the William Fullerton household.[10] Rachel was listed as a "cousin" in the Andrew Corrow household in the city of Cheboygan.[11] Joseph, as seen below, was adopted by the Mallette family.

Edward and Lizzie's children were:

1. Edward Alfred Karrow was born 10 March 1886 in Cheboygan, Michigan.[12] He married Ethel Izora McCash (daughter of James McCash) 16 October 1912 in Cheboygan.[13] Ethel was born 15 September 1891,[14] and she died 17 November 1972.[15] Edward died 30 March 1977. He was buried with his wife in Cheboygan.

2. Herbert Ash was born 7 November 1888 in Cedar Township.[16] He first married Delia Mae "Lila" Dettling (daughter of Anthony and Mary Dettling) on 30 December 1911 in Grand Ledge, Michigan.[17] After she died, he married Electa Swarthwood (daughter of John and Florence Swarthwood) on 8 April 1944 in Henry, Ohio.[18]

3. Rachel Eva was born 15 February 1891.[19] She first married Harvey Logan Millett (son of Gilbert and Hattie Millett) on 23 December 1911.[20] He died 5 February 1912 of injuries from a fall.[21] Later, she married Seth Tubbs Kingsley (son of William and Mary Kingsley) on 18 October 1913 in Lansing, Michigan.[22] Rachel died 11 June 1984 and was buried in Grand Ledge, Michigan, with her husband.[23]

4. Joseph Sherman was born 10 May 1895.[24] He was four years old when his mother died. By 1900, he had been adopted by Alexander and Odile (Vieau) Mallett.[25] He enlisted in the army before the end of World War I, on 24 June

Military marker of Joseph Mallette, Pine Hill Cemetery, Cheboygan, Michigan.
COURTESY OF THE AUTHOR.

1918. He served in the 4th Infantry in France, and after the end of the war, the division was relocated to Germany to serve as occupation forces. He landed in Brooklyn, New York, 23 August 1919,[26] and discharged 27 August 1919.[27]

After Joseph returned home, he married Emma Davis Blay (daughter of Robert and Mary Davis) circa 1922.[28] Their marriage record was not found. She died 10 March 1933.[29] He then married Margaret Imason Bellant (daughter of Alexander Imason and Mary Crowe), on 10 June 1935, in Cheboygan.[30]

10. Mrs. Henry Karrow (Judithe Diotte)

Mrs. Henry Karrow/Caron was Judithe Diotte. Durant made an error on this worksheet, listing the children of Angelique Caron Hudson. These children should have been listed on the page of no. 16 Mrs. Henry Hudson's children. According to annuity records, Judithe had been receiving annual payments since at least 1859. Prior to this, the annuities listed the recipients under their Native names.

Judithe Diotte was probably born near Lac du Flambeau around 1830. Her father was Jean Baptiste Diotte and her mother Marguerite Kabina. She was about five years old when she was baptized on 2 August 1835 at the St. Joseph Mission in LaPointe, Wisconsin.[1] In an application for the 1837 mixed-blood Chippewa funds, Paul Belanger (Boulanger) applied for Judithe as her adoptive father. He stated that she was born at the mouth of the Montreal River in the Folle Avoine–St. Croix River region. At the time (1839), he reported she was eleven years of age and that she had been with him for eight years. He adopted her because she was destitute, and both parents were dead.[2]

Judithe married Henry Caron, 31 May 1847 at Ste. Anne's on Mackinac Island. Witnesses were Paul Bellanger and Joseph Carron.[3]

Henry Caron was the son of Joseph Louis Gautier dit Caron and no. 5 Louise Vasseur. He was born 9 May 1828 at Drummond Island, Michigan,[4] and appears on the 1836 Half Breed Census with the other members of his family (nos. 194–199).[5]

Henry and Judithe had at least six children:

1. Louise was born 6 June 1848 and baptized at Ste. Anne's on Mackinac Island.[6]
2. Julie was born 11 October 1850 and baptized at Ste. Anne's.[7]
3. Charles was born 7 February 1852 and baptized at Ste. Anne's.[8]
4. Elisabeth was born 10 April 1854 and baptized at Ste. Anne's.[9]
5. Clement Olivier was born 6 October 1856 and baptized at Ste. Anne's.[10]
6. Joseph Alexander was baptized 22 May 1858 at Ste. Anne's.[11]
7. Edward Alfred was born 8 April 1861 and baptized at two months of age at Ste. Anne's.[12]

Henry Caron died 10 January 1863 at thirty-five years of age.[13] Sometime after Henry's death, Judithe moved her family to Duncan Township in Cheboygan County. She was enumerated there on 1870 census,[14] perhaps to be close to Karrow/Caron relatives. Judithe died 5 April 1885 and was buried in Cheboygan.[15]

29. Mary A. Karrow (Marianne Kedegekwanabe)

To date, limited information has been found about the early life of Marianne Kedegekwanabe. She was born about 1815 and first appears in the records of Ste. Anne's on Mackinac Island when she married Joseph Kekematiwain on 7 September 1833.[1] From this marriage, one daughter, Marianne was born (see no. 3, Mrs. Andrew Morin). Joseph Kekematiwain died young, and Marianne then married Joseph Caron Jr. on 22 July 1839 at St. Ignatius Loyola in St. Ignace.[2]

Joseph Caron was the son of Joseph Louis Gauthier dit Caron, born 17 December 1763, at Bécancour, Quebec,[3] and Louise Vasseur (see no. 5, Mrs. Joseph Karrow) was born circa 1787. Joseph Sr. and Louise were married on 1 July 1804.[4] Joseph Jr. was born 20 March 1802 on Mackinac Island and baptized at the Mission of Ste. Anne de Michilimackinak.[5] Joseph was first married to Catherine Anthenimus on

8 February 1835 at Ste. Anne's.[6] With him, Catherine had Joseph who was born 24 June 1836 on Bois Blanc Island and baptized at Mackinac Island.[7] Catherine died young, and Joseph later married Marianne Kedegekwanabe.

With Joseph, Marianne had the following children:

1. Jean Baptiste was born 6 May 1840 on Mackinac Island and baptized at Ste. Anne's.[8] He married Mary Aslin (daughter of Joseph Aslin and Marie Dejadon), 25 May 1862 on Mackinac Island.[9] He died 15 December 1920 and was buried in Cheboygan, Michigan.[10]
2. Alexis was born 8 January 1842 on Mackinac Island and baptized at Ste. Anne's.[11]
3. Marianne was born circa 1843. She married Antoine Dumas (son of Antoine Dumas and Jeanne Henderside), 2 March 1862 at Ste. Anne's.[12] She died 13 August 1883 in Cheboygan, Michigan.[13]
4. Angelique was born 27 December 1845 and baptized at Ste. Anne's.[14]
5. Joseph was born 15 October 1847 and baptized at Ste. Anne's.[15]
6. Margaret was born 14 March 1850 and baptized at Ste. Anne's.[16]
7. Joseph was born 5 February 1852 in Cheboygan,[17] and he died 2 October 1869 in Duncan, Cheboygan County.[18]
8. William, no data was found.
9. Louis, born circa 1856.
10. Agatha, born circa 1859.

Joseph died 28 July 1863 and was buried in the Ste. Anne's Cemetery.[19] Marianne may have lived for many years at the Cheboygan County Poor Farm. A woman named Agnes Carrow was listed there as a "boarder" on the 1900 and an "inmate" on the 1910 Cheboygan County Census.[20] Both records indicate she was "Indian" and did not speak English, nor could she read or write. A woman named Mary Agnes Karrow, born in France, died 12 September 1910, at one hundred and eleven years of age in Benton, Cheboygan County.[21] It is possible this woman was Marianne Carrow—on the bottom of the certificate it says she had been an invalid for many years.

7. Mrs. William Karrow (Isabelle Morin)

Isabelle Morin was the daughter of Andre Morin and Marianne Naanwandago. Andre was a French-Canadian born 24 February 1797 in Montreal, Canada.[1] He died

22 August 1878 in Benton Township, Cheboygan County.[2] Marianne and Isabelle were baptized together on 31 July 1834 at Ste. Anne's on Mackinac Island.[3] According to the baptismal record, Marianne was born circa 1806, and Isabelle (or Lisabeth as she was christened) was born circa 1822. According to the 1860 Mackinac County census, Isabelle was born in Wisconsin.[4]

William Karrow/Caron was the son of Joseph Gauthier dit Caron and no. 5 Louise Vasseur. He was baptized as Guillaume Caron on 15 September 1825 at Drummond Island, Chippewa County, Michigan.[5]

William and Isabelle were married at Ste. Anne's on Mackinac Island on 2 July 1840.[6] From this marriage at least eight children were born:

1. Isabelle was born 3 March 1846 on Bois Blanc Island, Mackinac County, Michigan.[7] She first married William Benoni McGulpin on 6 July 1862.[8] She then married George Labelle (born 10 November 1844),[9] and died on 30 December 1867 in Duncan, Cheboygan County.[10]
2. Madeleine was born 9 May 1849.[11]
3. Andrew was born 15 December 1850 and baptized at Ste. Anne's on 8 March 1851.[12]
4. Marie Louise was born 27 August 1852 and baptized 27 September 1852.[13]
5. Oliver was born 27 October 1859 on Bois Blanc Island and baptized at Ste. Anne's of Mackinac Island on 18 April 1860.[14]
6-7. Twins, Marie Louise and Elisabeth Jeanne, were born 5 December 1863.[15]
8. Marianne was born 4 August 1868,[16] and died 4 March 1870 in Duncan, Cheboygan County, Michigan.[17]

Isabelle/Elizabeth died 19 August 1910 and was buried in Calvary Cemetery in Cheboygan.[18] William died 25 June 1918 in Beaugrand Township, Cheboygan County, Michigan.[19] He was also buried in Calvary Cemetery.

19. Mrs. David Kniffen (Marie Bennet-Beaubin)

Father Samuel Mazzuchelli baptized Marie Bennet, daughter of Louis and Christine Bennet, on 16 December 1830 at Ste. Anne's on Mackinac Island.[1] There were several Marie Bennets in the area, so to have both the baptism and death record confirms the correct person for the researcher.

Hollis or David Kniffen was born in Ohio or New York. He made his living as a cooper and passed these skills to his son, David. The earliest date he was found in the Mackinac area was on the 1850 Michilimackinac census living in the home of the Henry and Charlotte Furlan (Feurtin, Fertie) family. This is the same home where Simon Martin (see under no. 21 Mrs. Francis Martin) was living in 1850.[2]

Marie Bennet married Hollis "David" Kniffen on 8 May 1854 at Ste. Anne's.[3] From this marriage there were at least nine children:

1. Mary Helen was born 15 March 1855 and baptized at Cross Village.[4] She married Eustache Plant on 7 June 1874 in Mackinaw City, Cheboygan County.[5] She died 30 May 1944 and was buried in Cheboygan, Michigan.[6]
2. Harriet Christina was born 23 October 1856 and was baptized at Cross Village.[7] She died 23 October 1884 in Mackinaw City.[8]
3. Julia was born in 1857. She does not appear on the 1860 census.
4. David Louis was born 23 June 1859 and baptized at Cross Village.[9] He died 23 January 1883 in Mackinaw City, Michigan.[10] He earned his living as a cooper, no doubt taught by his father.
5. John was born in 1859. He does not appear on the 1860 census.
6. Mary was born 23 September 1861,[11] and baptized 9 February 1862 at St. Mary's in Cheboygan.[12]
7. Samuel Walter was born 23 May 1865 and baptized at Cross Village.[13] He married Annie Josephine Dufina (daughter of Alexander Dufina and Ursula Lesieur), born 10 April 1865.[14] He died in Mackinaw City on 10 May 1946.[15]
8. Phillip was born on 6 February 1869.[16]
9. Charles L. was born circa 1870. He first married Margaret Andress (daughter of John Andress and Alice Hudson) on 23 January 1883 in Mackinaw City, Cheboygan County.[17] After her death, he married Lizzie Richards on 18 September 1918 in Petoskey, Michigan.[18]
10. Jacobus/James was born 24 June 1872 and baptized at Cross Village.[19] He married Ella Wing (daughter of George Wing and Carrie Smith) on 26 June 1920 in St. Ignace.[20]

Marie Bennet Kniffen died on 17 November 1911 and was buried in Mackinaw City.[21] A death record or burial information was not located for Hollis Kniffen.

25. Mrs. Michael Kuthron (Sophie Pogay)

According to her death certificate, Sophie Pogay (Paget, Page, Besson) was born 21 December 1821 at Red River, Canada.[1] Another source, written during her lifetime says, "She was born in the Churchill River country, between Hudson's Bay and Great and Little Slave Lakes."[2]

Sophie's husband was Michel Cadran born 11 October 1795 at St. Michel d'Yamaska.[3] His parents were Nicolas Urbain Cadrin and Marianne Modore. (The name Cadran may also appear as Cadreau, Cadrin, Catrin or Cadron, among others.) The date and location of their marriage are still unknown.

Michel and Sophie had at least eight children:

1. A baptism for their first-born son, Michel, has not been located, but a birth date was found in his military records as 20 July 1847.[4] He enlisted as a Private in Company K, 7th Michigan Cavalry on 14 March 1864 and discharged on 10 March 1865.[5] He married Mary Contine on 3 October 1869 in Sault Ste. Marie, Michigan.[6] He died in Grand Rapids, Michigan, at the Old Soldiers Home on 10 June 1921. His remains were returned to Mackinac Island and buried in Ste. Anne's Cemetery.[7]
2. Joseph was born 20 October 1849.[8] He died 3 September 1910 on Mackinac Island.[9]
3. Marie was born 14 April 1852.[10] She married Theodore Reithes on 19 May 1870 on Mackinac Island.[11]
4. Antoine Alfred was born 6 July 1854.[12]
5. Jean Baptiste was born 4 July 1856.[13] He married Grace Decatur on 28 September 1898.[14] He died 29 August 1930.[15]
6. Remi Joseph was born 1 March 1860.[16]
7. Alfred Edmund was born 7 April 1864.[17] He married Therese Bennett (daughter of Charles Bennett and no. 6 Angelique Sagitondaway) on 27 August 1889.[18] His occupation was listed as lighthouse keeper.
8. Louis Edmund was born 1 June 1867.[19]

Joseph and Alfred Cadran happened to be fishing near the Bois Blanc Lighthouse in early April of 1883 and became prominent figures in a dramatic rescue of the Spectacle Reef Lighthouse keeper, William Marshal, first lighthouse keeper, Edward Chambers, and third lighthouse keeper, Edward Lasley. For their bravery, they were awarded gold medals by the United States Life Saving Service.[20]

Michel Cadran's military marker in Ste. Anne's Cemetery.

COURTESY OF THE AUTHOR.

Standing, left to right: Edward Lasley, William Marshall; *seated, left to right*: Alfred Cadran and Joseph Cadran.

COURTESY OF *LIGHTHOUSE DIGEST*.

The death of Michel Cadran appeared in the *Detroit Tribune and Advertiser*, 26 February 1869:

> Two deaths on the morning of the 10th, Mr. Cadran started from his home with an ax on his shoulder on his way to Bois Blanc for wood, but when about halfway across the channel, he went down suddenly and disappeared under the ice. Those who heard them described his momentary screams as terrible. He was quite an old man, one of the old French voyageurs of the fur trade 40 years ago. He leaves a large family in destitute circumstances. The marks in the ice showed that the unfortunate man had examined the ice along his path with his ax, but the current wears under the surface very unequally at different points. His body has not been found and probably the current has carried it miles away.[21]

Sometime later, Sophie married Frank Cadotte in 1881. Frank Cadotte was the son of Louis Cadotte and no. 8 Marie Louise LaVerdure.[22] They had no children.

Sophie was well known on the island as a nurse and a midwife. The priest made comments at her funeral about how trusted she was for providing care to the island residents.[23] Sophie died on 1 August 1921 and was buried in Ste. Anne's Cemetery.[24] After death, Sophie's spirit continued to live on the island in the village (Harrisonville). Many of the island's year-round residents who live in the village are of Native descent. She is known as "Old Lady Bandana," and island residents remember her well. The following are firsthand stories that were shared with the author from some of those who have seen her.

The first is from Darlene Gallagher Olson:

> Boy do I remember how we were all afraid of 'ol lady bandana and the burners is a place where all the garbage went to be buried and all horses that died were burnt in the big furnace there along with paper trash, located behind [a local resident's] house down a small path to the right of the house walk about a quarter of a block and there it is. I wish it were summer I would show you the spot.[25]

From Lois Cadotte Maki:

> We had what we called a ghost in the old house on the island, she would stand at the head of the stairs and just look at my brothers in the night, she was called old lady bandana because she was dressed in a long dark cloak with a large bandana draped over her face and head. My brothers would hollar down the

Sophie Cadran Cadotte.
COURTESY OF THERESA WASHBURN CARR.

stairs to our mom that she was there again, and mom would turn on the light to chase her away.[26]

From John Cadotte:

Old burners is where she is. Kept us away from playing back there as kids. The parents all told us the old lady bandana stories. I never knew I was related to her. The old burners is where [the] dump used to be, [in the] Village area. I believe they cremated the dead horses there also. Used to be an old building standing there when I grew up. Now a cement slab, the whole area is overgrown with vegetation now. Used to be trails all through there. We would ride bikes there, catch snakes, pick strawberries and raspberries. The building was a big concern, as it was falling down. The story was she lived in that building, to try keeping us kids out. But kids will be kids and we played in there anyway.[27]

From Dawn Clayton:

My mom (Phyllis Cassibo Schmidt) remembered seeing her as a spirit in Harrison-ville during her childhood. They called her old Lady Bandana![28]

With the old building demolished, hopefully Sophie's spirit now rests in peace.

58. Mrs. Mary LaDuke (Mary Bruneau, Mrs. Jeremie LeDuc)

Michilimackinac, July 22, 1839,

Mary Le Duc [claims] for herself and her five children, of Michilimackinac, applies by Jeremiah LeDuc her husband. She is 35 years old, was born on the American side of Lake Superior near Isle Royal where she lived till [*sic*] she was ten years old. She then went to Red River where she staid [*sic*] 4 years, then to the Sault de Ste Marie where she staid [*sic*] a year, and the remainder of her life has been spent at Mackinac. She is a half-blood Chippewa and has been married 21 years. Her children are Louison 18, Mary 16, Genevieve 14, Adelaide 9, & Catherine 19 months. Mr. LeDuc says application was made under the Treaty of 1836, but nothing allowed.

No connexion [*sic*] with the Indians of the ceded country. Rejected.[1]

Jeremie LeDuc was an engagé in the fur trade. The earliest record in which he appears was a North West Company ledger from 1812. From 1819 to 1821, he was listed in Servant Accounts; in 1820 he appears in the English River equipment book.[2] His name appears on a list of men who were married at the Red River Colony (Manitoba) by a Catholic missionary. Unfortunately, the missionary only saw fit to list the grooms and left off the brides. According to this record, Jeremie was married in 1823.[3]

Mary and Jeremy had the following children:

1. Louison was born circa 1821. He married Marie Josette Closs (daughter of Louis Closs and Catherine Plaunte) on 24 May 1844 at St. Ignatius Loyola, St. Ignace, Michigan.[4] After she died, he married Lucy Beaugrand (daughter of Joseph Beaugrand) at Ste. Anne's on 21 February 1848.[5]
2. Marie was born circa 1823. She married Michel Plante (son of Pierre Plante and Josette Bouillette) on 19 March 1842 at Ste. Anne's on Mackinac Island.[6]
3. Genevieve was born circa 1827. She married François Plante on 8 January 1842 at Ste. Anne's.[7] After he died, she married Joseph Meunier on 8 February 1853.[8]
4. Adelaide was born 25 July 1830 and baptized at Ste. Anne's.[9] She married Andrew Rapin on 30 July 1849 at Ste. Anne's.[10] Andrew died in Cheboygan on 10 November 1899.[11] Adelaide died 21 November 1903 and was buried with her husband in Calvary Cemetery, Cheboygan.[12]
5. Edmund was born 23 August 1832 on Mackinac Island and was baptized at Ste. Anne's.[13]

Old Mackinac Lighthouse nearing completion in 1892. COURTESY OF MACKINAC STATE HISTORIC PARKS.

6. Pierre was born on Mackinac Island on 11 December 1834 and baptized at Ste. Anne's.[14]

7. Catherine was born 9 March 1838 and baptized at St. Ignatius.[15] She married Octave Toulouse (son of Basile and Sophie Toulouse) at Ste. Anne's on 21 January 1856.[16] By 1860, they were living on Beaver Island, Michigan.[17]

8. Isabel was born 2 February 1841 and baptized at St. Ignatius.[18]

9. Christine was born 13 December 1843 and baptized at St. Ignatius.[19] She married Edward St. Antoine. Edward died 29 October 1916 and was buried in Calvary Cemetery, Cheboygan.[20] Christine died 14 April 1923 and was buried next to her husband in Calvary Cemetery.[21]

10. Monique Eliza was born 5 March 1846 on Mackinac Island and baptized at Ste. Anne's.[22] She died 28 January 1858 at was buried in Ste. Anne's cemetery.[23]

There is a notation in the *Liber Defunctorum* at Ste. Anne's of the death of "Leduc," no first name recorded, on 1 February 1871. At seventy-nine years of age at death, one could assume that this person was probably Jeremie.[24] Another death record for Jeremie LeDuc appears in St. Mary's in Cheboygan on 20 February 1871.[25] It is not known in which cemetery he is buried. After Jeremie's death, Genevieve left the island to live in Cheboygan with her children. She died 20 August 1880 in Benton Township, Cheboygan County.[26]

32. Mrs. Joseph Lalotte (Lozon) (Marie Boyd)

Marie Boyd was the daughter of Joshua Johnson Boyd and Pamichiwag or Pamishiganokwe. She was born in November of 1831 somewhere along Lake Superior and baptized at Mackinac on 21 July 1832.[1] Her father was the son of Colonel George Boyd, an early Indian agent at Mackinac and Green Bay, and Harriet Johnson. Joshua was born around 1805 and died 21 October 1832.[2] After a brief time in the navy, Joshua joined his father in Wisconsin and became a fur trader. He was killed by a hunter at Sturgeon Bay, Wisconsin, who claimed he was refused credit for trade goods.[3] No additional information is known about Marie's mother.

Joseph Lozon was the son of Joseph Lozon Sr. and Elisabeth Nancy Pelotte. According to their marriage record, Joseph was born 10 June 1816.[4] Elisabeth was the sister of Ignace Pelotte (see no. 11 Mrs. Ignace Pelotte). Joseph Jr. was the brother of Alex Lozon, (father of nos. 12a, 12b and 12c).

If a union was blessed by the church, any children were recorded as legitimate. Such was the case of Joseph Lozon Sr. and Elisabeth Nancy Pelotte. According to their marriage record, Joseph Jr. was born in 1816, and Joseph Sr. and Elisabeth Nancy were married ten years later on 9 October 1826.[5]

Joseph Lozon and Marie Boyd were married at Ste. Anne's on Mackinac Island on 9 August 1847.[6] This couple appears to have had only one child, Joseph Alfred, who was born 22 December 1848.[7] He married Julia Grant (daughter of William Grant and Marie Leblanc) on 11 February 1872 at Ste. Anne's on Mackinac Island.[8]

Joseph Lozon Jr. died 5 March 1900 and was buried on Mackinac Island.[9] According to his death certificate, he was a widower. Information about Marie Boyd's death was not found.

12a, b, and c. Sarah, Louisa, and Charles Lalotte (Lozon)

Sarah, Marie Louise, and Charles Lalotte were the children of Alexander (or Alex) Lalotte (Lauson, Lozon) and Mary Shedawin (Oshedawin, D'Achidowan). Alex was the son of Joseph Lozon and Elisabeth Nancy Pelotte. He was born 2 February 1824 and baptized at Ste. Anne's on Mackinac Island.[1] Alex was living with a woman enumerated as Mary Lozon on the 1850 census in Mackinac County. Since their first child was born in December 1850, Mary Lozon was probably Mary Shedawin.[2]

Mary Shedawin was baptized at St. Ignatius Church in St. Ignace, Michigan, on 15 July 1855. The church recorded that she was born in July of 1838 and her parents were Achidowan and Nibanokodokwe.[3] According to the same baptismal records, Mary had a younger sister named Julie, who was born 20 October 1854 of the same parents and baptized the same day.

A story about Alex Lozon was recorded in the Alice Poole papers found at the University of Michigan:

> Old Alex Lozon had a pet horse called "Smuggler." He fell in [a] crack in [the] ice between [Mackinac] Isle and St. Ignace. [He] nearly drowned. Finally [he was] rescued and brought into the summer kitchen of [the] Lozon house. Bill Sullivan sent whiskey in buckets for [the] horse to save him, to drink and to wash [the] horse in.[4]

It is not known from this story whether poor Smuggler survived or not.

Alex Lozon and Mary Shedawin were married on 20 February 1855 at St. Ignatius in St. Ignace, Michigan.[5] They had at least four children. Durant listed three who survived into adulthood:

1. Sarah Bridgett was born on 8 December 1851,[6] probably in Escanaba, Delta County, Michigan.
2. Marie Louise was born circa 1858.
3. Charles was born 4 December 1850.[7]
4. Guillaume was born 29 July 1855 and baptized in St. Ignace.[8] He died 1 February 1858 and was buried on Mackinac Island.[9]

Mary died sometime after the 1860 census was taken and before late 1863. On 29 December 1863, Alex married Rosalie Louisignan at Ste. Anne's on Mackinac Island. She was the daughter of Pierre Louisignon and no. 8 Marie Louise Laverdure (Mrs. Louis Cadotte).[10]

Sarah Adeline Lancour McGuire.
COURTESY OF DALE MAGOON.

12a. Sarah Lalotte (Mrs. Paul Lancour)

Sarah was listed as the "head of the [Lozon] family" by Durant on the Field Note.[1] She married Paul Lancour on 18 April 1870 at Ste. Anne's on Mackinac Island.[2] He was born 28 February 1849 in St. Ignace,[3] the son of Joseph Lancour and no. 51 Genevieve (Jane) Pond.

Sarah and Paul had the following children:

1. William Alexis was born 18 March 1871 and baptized at Ste. Anne's.[4]
2. Caroline was born 28 June 1872 and baptized at St. Mary's in Cheboygan, Michigan.[5]
3. Sarah Adeline (called Addie) was born 4 August 1874 and baptized at Ste. Anne's.[6] She died 6 May 1915 and was buried at Ste. Anne's Cemetery.[7] She married Ferguson McGuire on 5 November 1901 at Mackinac Island.[8] Ferguson was the brother of Chester McGuire.
4. Phoebe Anne was born 4 May 1876 and baptized at St. Mary's in Cheboygan.[9]
5. Olivier was baptized 4 March 1878 and died 29 July 1880 in Cheboygan.[10]
6. Marie Josephine was born circa 1879 and died 27 August 1881.[11]
7. Gertrude was born circa 1885. She married Chester Maguire on 26 October 1904 on Mackinac Island.[12]

8. Charles Albert was born 18 October 1883 in Cheboygan.[13] He married Rose Bray on 17 February 1909 in Cheboygan, Michigan.[14] Charles died 30 January 1939 in Detroit.[15]

9. Felix Arthur was born in February 1888.[16] He died 20 June 1889 at sixteen months of age.[17]

10. Alfred Roy was born around 19 December 1889 and died 7 November 1920.[18]

11. Virginia Elizabeth was born 5 April 1892 at St. Mary's in Cheboygan,[19] and she married Frank E. Beachett on 24 September 1914 in Cheboygan, Michigan.[20]

12. Eva was born 16 July 1894 and baptized at St. Mary's in Cheboygan.[21]

Sarah Lozon Lancour died at Mackinac on 4 August 1914 and was buried on Mackinac Island.[22]

12b. Marie Louise Lozon (Mrs. John Poupard)

Marie Louise Lozon was the youngest child of Alexis Lozon and Mary Shedawin. She was born 4 August 1862. Marie Louise married John Baptiste Poupor (Parper, Poupard, Poupart) the son of Peter Poupor.[1]

Marie Louise and John had the following children:

1. Jean Roy was born 14 February 1885 and baptized at St. Mary's in Cheboygan, Michigan.[2] He died 27 August 1885.[3]

2. Peter Alexander was born 28 February 1886 and baptized at St. Mary's.[4]

3. Marie Olive was born February 1888 and baptized at St. Mary's.[5]

4. John Elmer was born 28 June 1890 and baptized at St. Mary's.[6]

5. Marie Josephine was born 1 May 1892 and baptized at St. Mary's.[7]

6. Louis Charles was born 16 July 1894 and baptized at St. Mary's.[8]

John and Marie Louise died and were buried in Flint, Michigan. John died 11 October 1926,[9] and Mary died 16 January 1929.[10] They were buried in All Saints Cemetery, in Flint, Michigan.

Left to right: Alex Lozon, Charles Lozon, Mary Lozon, and Mrs. Edward (illegible).
COURTESY OF A DESCENDANT OF THE AGATHA BIDDLE BAND.

12c. Charles Lozon

Charles Lozon (or Lalotte) was the eldest child of Alexander Lozon and Mary Shedawin. He was born 4 December 1850 and baptized at Ste. Anne's on Mackinac Island.[1] He first married Helen Hamlin (daughter of James Hamlin and Rosa Gendron) on 18 April 1878 at Ste. Anne's.[2] She died less than a month later, on 13 May 1878.[3] He then married Mary Satigo on 9 February 1880 at St. Ignace, Michigan.[4]

Mary Satigo was the daughter of Joseph Chevallier Satigo/Mesautego, or Pabish-ka-kezhick, and Esther Martin (daughter of Antoine Martin and Suzanne Kinokwe). She was born 26 September 1853,[5] and lived at the Satigo Settlement, a farming community just north of St. Ignace. Here Mary and Charles had a farm and raised crops. They had one son, named Alexis, who was born in 1898. Only after Charles's death did Mary report on the census that Alex was her adopted son.[6]

Charles was famous for his basket-making and added local color as a "stop" on the sightseeing carriage tours operated by Felix Paquin and his son-in-law, Harvey Clarke, in St. Ignace. The carriages "with the fringe on top" met tourists at the docks.

From there they visited several locations, including Father Marquette's grave and Castle Rock. "Among other points of interest, they stopped at the wigwams on the North Shore . . . where Chas. Lozon (also called Charlie Lalotte) . . . made and sold baskets in a picturesque Indian setting."[7]

Charles died at the Satigo Settlement on 24 May 1928 and was buried in the St. Ignatius Cemetery.[8] Mary died 28 May 1931 and was also buried in St. Ignatius Cemetery.[9]

51. Mrs. Jane Lancour (Genevieve Pond)

Michilimackinac July 22, 1839

Wm Laencourt of Pointe Ste. Ignace, applies for his wife and three children. The name of his wife is Genevieve. She is the daughter of Peter Pond and has the same claims as said Ponds other children. She is a half-blood Chippewa, 27 years old, was born at Vermillion Lake in the Fond du Lac country and was brought from there soon after. She has been married 8 years. Her children, Genevieve 6 years, Agatha 3 and Justin one month old were all born at Pointe St. Ignace. Application made under the Treaty of 1836, but nothing allowed, as they say. No connection with the Indians of the ceded Territory. Rejected[1]

The application for monies comes from the 1837 Treaty of St. Peters that ceded parts of the western Upper Peninsula of Michigan and parts of northern Wisconsin. All persons who felt they were entitled to payment derived from the treaty could apply through an agent. At this time, Genevieve "Jane" Pond was already married to Joseph William Lancour. They were married on 1 February 1833 at Ste. Anne's.[2]

Genevieve's parents were Augustin Peter Pond and Marie Louise Boucher. Genevieve ("Jane") was born circa 1812 in the Wisconsin Territory of Vermillion Lake, and then she came to the Mackinac area. Her father was born circa 1780 and died July 1844 at St. Ignace, Michigan.[3] Her mother, Louise Boucher, was born around 1797 and died 6 May 1871 at St. Ignace.[4] The elder Pond's application to the St. Peter's Treaty reads:

Michilimackinac July 22, 1839

Peter Pond of Pointe St. Ignace in the county of Michilimackinac, a half blood of the Chippewa Nation applies for himself. He is 59 years old, was born in the region of Fond du Lac and remained in that country till [*sic*] he was 23 years old. He then went to Montreal and remained in that vicinity 17 years when he came to St. Mary's [Sault Ste. Marie] where he was employed as blacksmith in the Indian Department and has resided there and at his present residence for the last 16 years. He also claims for his seven children, Marian 16, Augustin 14, Cyril 12, Louis 10, Pierre 6, Julia 4 and Isabelle 2 years of age. His wife, their mother is 42 years old, was born at Point au Blondish south of Fond du Lac and is a half-blood Chippewa with the same claims as himself. Her name is Louise and her father's name was Boucher. Application was made in behalf of the above under the Treaty of Washington in 1836 and disallowed as Pond says because he came from too far up country.[5]

Augustin Peter's father was Peter Pond, who was a traveler. He was known to have gone as far as the Athabaska country (approximately ninety miles north of Edmonton, Alberta) where he discovered a large, fur-rich district in the late 1780s.[6] Augustin Peter Pond retraced his father's footsteps in 1798 when he was posted at Fort Chipewyan. Peter Pond scholar Harry Duckworth of the University of Manitoba writes:

The name of Pond did appear in the Athabasca again. One Augustin Peter Pond of Sorel, was hired by McTavish, Frobisher and Company on 11 January 1798 to go to the northwest and was posted to Fort Chipewyan, where he witnessed several hiring contracts signing his own name, during the season of 1798–9. He signed his own two-year contract on 26 April 1799, to work as 'milieu & forgeron' (oarsman and blacksmith) at Fort Chipewyan or Rivière de la Paix...Augustin Pond remained in the North West Company's employment in the Athabasca through the period of 1811–1821, . . . He was taken over by the Hudson's Bay Company . . . in 1821. . . . he was retired to Canada . . . in 1822. Thereafter he disappears.[7]

The documents recorded for the 1837 Treaty, federal censuses, and church records prove that Augustin Peter Pond did not disappear but created a home and raised a family in the Mackinac area.

According to the Peter Pond Society,[8] the Northern Michigan Ponds, of which Augustin Peter Pond was the patriarch, used the surname Robescar or Robesca, believed to be a corruption of the word Athabaska as well as a badge of honor for the patriarch's accomplishments. He died in St. Ignace during the month of July 1844.[9]

Marie Louise Boucher was the daughter of François Boucher. In the 1850 Federal Census for Mackinac County, the last individual enumerated in Louise Pond's home was François Bouise. He was ninety years old in 1850.[10] Is it possible this was her

278	284	Louisa Pond	57	F.			
		Louisa Cadotte	11	F.			Mich.
		Harriet "	9	F.			"
		Emily "	7	F.			"
		Catharine "	15	F.			"
		Francis Bonice	90	M.		100	Canada

Partial image of 1850 Michilimackinac census, page 46/94 (Pond).

father and he was buried somewhere in St. Ignace? Marie Louise Boucher Pond died on 6 May 1871. Her death record at St. Ignatius Loyola indicates she was born at Lake Robesca, British Possession.[11]

Available voyageur contracts for Augustin Peter Pond can be reviewed at the St. Boniface of Manitoba Centre du Patrimonie web site https://archivesshsb.mb.ca/en. A contract dated 15 November 1802 stated his position was rudder (*gouvernail*) and he would "*hyverner dans les limites des postes de Robeska*." (He would winter within the boundaries of the posts [forts] at Robeska [Athabaska]).[12]

All Our Relations names the wife of François Boucher as Wassauque and states that she was a relation of Chief Buffalo at LaPointe. Witnesses to the treaty reported François Boucher at Mackinac but Wassauque stayed in the north at the time of the application (affidavits were taken in 1839).[13]

Augustin and Marie Louise Pond had the following children:

1. Genevieve was born circa May 1813 at Vermillion Lake, and married William Joseph Lancour.[14]
2. Rachel was born circa 1816 and married Charles St. Andre on 30 January 1837.[15]
3. Louise was born circa 1819. She married Achille Cadotte (son of Joseph and Angelique Cadotte) on 24 September 1837 in Sault Ste. Marie, Ontario.[16] She died 8 May 1847 and was buried in the St. Ignatius Cemetery.[17]
4. Marian was born circa 1823 and married Charles Mincier on 22 January 1849 at St. Ignatius in St. Ignace, Michigan.[18]
5. Augustin was born 16 July 1825 and was baptized 2 August the same year.[19] He married Marie Beaudoin, on 4 February 1845, in St. Ignace.[20]
6. Cyril was born circa December 1827 and baptized 18 August 1828.[21] He married Susan Grondin, 7 February 1853.[22] Cyril was enumerated in the Durant Roll on page 15, no. 22.
7. Louis was born circa 1829 and married Catharine Mincier on 9 January

Augustin Pond Jr., wife
Marie Beaudoin, and
daughter Mary.
COURTESY OF ROBERT BLOOMFIELD.

1850.[23] She died 28 March 1860 at St. Ignace.[24] He then married Marianne
Lessard on 13 May 1864.[25]

8. Pierre was born 3 September 1833,[26] and married Josette Perrault at St. Ignace
   on 26 December 1857.[27]
9. Julia (see no. 64) was born 11 February 1836,[28] and married Peter Closs on 4
   May 1857 at St. Ignace.[29]
10. Isabelle/Elisabeth was born 28 February 1838 and baptized 11 March 1837 at
    St. Ignace.[30]
11. Simon was born 12 April 1840 and baptized 24 April 1840 at St. Ignace.[31]

Joseph Guillaume Lincourt and Genevieve Robescar (Pond) were married 6
June 1834.[32] Guillaume/William was born about 1806, probably in Canada, and
died 3 May 1852, in St. Ignace.[33] He was a boat-builder.[34] From this marriage, there
were at least nine children:

1. Genevieve was baptized on 2 February 1834,[35] and married Theophile
   Fountain on 29 January 1851.[36]
2. Victor was born 9 July 1835.[37]
3. Agatha was born circa 1837. She was married to George Vincent Bourassa on
   26 February 1854 in Mackinac County by the justice of the peace.[38]

4. Justine was born 25 June 1839.[39] She first married Elie Bouchard (son of Oliver Bouchard) who was part of Company K, 7th Michigan Cavalry. He went missing in action at Front Royal, Virginia, on 16 August 1864.[40] Justine applied for her widow's pension on 5 June 1865.[41] Later, she married Joseph Therrien in Cheboygan on 8 October 1875.[42] She died 9 January 1897 and was buried at St. Ignace.[43]

5. Phebe/Flavia was born about 1840 and married Alexander Charbonneau on 28 April 1857 in St. Ignace, Michigan.[44] She died 23 July 1880.[45]

6. Maria was born 5 December 1845,[46] and died the next year on 16 September 1846.[47]

7. Cecelia was born 10 July 1847.[48]

8. Paul was born 28 February 1849 at St. Igance,[49] and married no. 12a Sarah Brigitta Lozon, 18 April 1870.[50]

9. Adeline was born 3 May 1851 at St. Ignace.[51]

Genevieve Pond Lincourt was last seen on the 1880 St. Ignace Census living in the household of her daughter Justine Therrien.[52]

Descendants of Augustin Peter and Louise Pond still live in the Mackinac area, but no longer use the Robescar/Robesca name.

62. Josephine LaPierre (Unknown)

The data on the worksheet 14/62 listed two children—Sarah and John Lafond; however, no connection to Josephine LaPierre was established. A search was also conducted under the name Stone, the English translation of LaPierre, with no results. Durant made a note on the worksheet that he could not locate her.

4. Mrs. Edward Lasley (Therese Bennett)

Mrs. Edward Lasley was born Therese Bennett on 1 March 1826. Her parents were Louis Bennett (Bennett-Beaubin, Beauben, or Beaubien) and Christine Outapitakawinam (see no. 38 Mrs. Louis Beaubin). At the time of Therese's birth, according to her baptism, her parents were, "vivant ensemble sans etre marié," (living together without being married). Louis and Christine were later married on 28 October 1827.[1]

Therese is part of the largest family in the Biddle band. In addition to her mother, Christine, there are four additional sisters: no. 2 Mrs. Louis Maishtaw, no. 6 Mrs. Charles Bennett, no. 13 Mrs. Francis Rastoul, and no. 19 Mrs. David Kniffen. Members of this family were enumerated on the Half Breed Census of the 1836 Treaty of Washington, and they appear as nos. 220 through 227.[2]

Edward was the son of Samuel Lasley and Rachel Abitigawinan. He was born during the month of August 1825 and baptized the day he married Therese Bennett, 26 October 1848.[3]

From this marriage several children were born:

1. Therese Julia was born 18 December 1848 and baptized at Ste. Anne's.[4] She later married Frank Plaunt.
2. Louis was born 13 July 1850.[5] He married Louise Robinson on 18 April 1871 (niece of no. 33 David Robinson and no. 59 Mrs. Angel Robinson) and died 24 June 1918 at Cross Village, Michigan.[6]
3. Katherine was born 19 April 1852.[7]
4. Christina Helena was born 3 March 1855.[8]
5. Edward was born 15 November 1857.[9]
6. Marie Mathilda was born 18 January 1860.[10]
7. Samuel was born 12 July 1863.[11] He married Hattie McCaulic/McCulloch.[12] Samuel died 8 April 1920.[13]
8. John was born 4 March 1870 at L'Arbre Croche, Michigan.[14]

Edward supported his family as a fisherman and was later enlisted in the Civil War serving in Company K, 7th Michigan Cavalry. He survived the war and applied for veteran's benefits in 1882.[15] Between the years 1883 and 1896 he worked as the lighthouse keeper at Spectacle Reef and Beaver Island.[16] He died 17 July 1896 and was buried at St. James Township, Beaver Island, Michigan.[17]

Some personal information about Therese was found in the Helen Collar Papers from Beaver Island.[18] She was described as a midwife, with a "dark, Indian face," who "went out in the woods and gathered herbs and made medicine for the patient[s]." She also "saved Barney Martin's frozen feet by immersing them in a box of fresh horse manure."[19] To date, Therese's death information has not been located. She may rest next to her husband in the Beaver Island Cemetery.

40. Mrs. Joseph Laslin (Julia Lesieur Aslin)

Julia Victoria Lesieur was born 19 February 1836 and baptized at Ste. Anne's on Mackinac Island.[1] She was the daughter of Edward Lesieur from Yamachiche, Quebec, and Angelique Peltier, from Drummond Island. Angelique was the sister of no. 46 Catherine St. Onge and no. 65 Victoire Bellaire and the daughter of Jean Pierre Peltier and Angelique Okichebanoque.

Julia's father, Édouard Lesieur, was probably the son of Jean Baptiste Lesieur dit LaPierre and Marie Josephe Miville dite Deschenes.[2] On 27 April 1825, Édouard Lesieur from Yamachiche, Quebec, signed a three-year voyageur contract with the Hudson's Bay Company for service at the Lake Huron post located at La Cloche, Ontario, near Manitoulin Island.[3] After serving his contract, Edward went to Mackinac Island. Here he most likely met Angelique Peltier. Angelique and Edward were married by a justice of the peace on 24 November 1829.[4]

Their daughter Julia married Joseph Aslin. He was the son of Joseph Aslin dit Chevreau and no. 39 Marie Charlotte Dejadon. He was born 30 January 1830 and baptized 13 January 1833 by Fr. Samuel Mazzuchelli at Ste. Anne's.[5]

Both Julia and Joseph were enumerated on the Half Breed Census of the 1836 Treaty of Washington, DC. Julia was no. 521 and was enumerated with her mother and sisters. Joseph was no. 375 and enumerated with his family under the surname Chevreau.

They were married at Ste. Anne's on 21 January 1853.[6] From this marriage at least fourteen children were born.

1. Alexis was born 1 March 1855 on Bois Blanc Island and baptized at Ste. Anne's.[7]
2. Angelique Elisabeth was born 16 November on Mackinac Island and baptized at Ste. Anne's.[8] She married Charles Johnson from Denmark, in Newton Township on 29 November 1883.[9] She died 3 November 1909 and was buried in St. Ignace.[10]
3. Isabella was born 18 December 1857 and baptized at Cross Village, Emmet County, Michigan.[11]
4. Peter Julius was born 17 December 1859 and baptized at Cross Village.[12] He married Agnes Peck on 20 May 1882 in Orville, Michigan.[13] She was the daughter of Paymekezhickwayskung (Henry Peck) and Margaret Labelle. He appears on the Durant roll (no. 5/32). Peter Aslin died 28 March 1927 and was

Peter Aslin and Agnes Peck.
COURTESY OF THE E. J. BLANCHARD COLLECTION.

buried in St. Ignatius Cemetery, St. Ignace.[14] Agatha died 12 June 1934 and was buried with her husband in St. Ignatius.[15]

5. Esther was born 18 November 1860 and baptized at Cross Village.[16]

6. Marie Joanna "Jane" was born 18 July 1862 on Bois Blanc Island and baptized at Ste. Anne's.[17] She married Edward Landry (son of J. Napoleon Landry and Marie Louise Arsenault of Carleton, Bonaventure, Quebec) on 29 August 1885 in Newton Township.[18] He died 24 June 1932.[19] Marie Jane died 28 May 1836 and was buried with her husband in Newton Township.[20]

7. Joseph Edward was born 17 September 1864 at Scott Point and baptized at Ste. Anne's nearly two years later.[21] His death was recorded in the Holy Cross (Cross Village) records as July 1874.[22]

8. Marie Henriette was born 7 September 1865 and baptized at Cross Village.[23] No additional information has been found on her.

9. Julie Henriette "Harriet" was born 7 September 1866 at Scott Point and baptized at Ste. Anne's 15 July 1867. She married Antoine Martin on 25 October 1883.[24] Harriet died 29 October 1916 and was buried in Manistique, Schoolcraft County, Michigan.[25] Antoine died 2 February 1919 and was buried with his wife.[26]

10. William was born 7 April 1869 and baptized at Cross Village.[27] He married Myrtle Bush (daughter of George Bush and Catherine Smith) on 5 June 1894 in Newton Township, Mackinac County.[28] William died 8 September 1842 and was buried in Detroit.[29]

The Agency House where annuities were paid out. POSTCARD FROM THE AUTHOR'S COLLECTION.

11. Joseph Rubin was born 12 March 1871 and baptized at Cross Village.[30] He died 3 December 1901 and was buried in St. Ignatius.[31]

12. Edmond was born circa 1875. He married Josephine Levalley (daughter of Joseph Leveille) on 2 September 1911 in St. Ignace.[32] Josephine died 11 June 1917 and was buried in Cedarville, Michigan.[33] After her death, Edmond married Roseanne Bosley (daughter of Louis Norton and Harriet Valkenburg) on 5 June 1919 in St. Ignace,[34] and lived on Drummond Island.[35] On 4 July 1922, he drowned near Johnswood, Drummond Island, and was buried there two days later.[36]

13. George was born 25 April 1874 and was baptized in Cross Village.[37]

14. Paul Joseph was born 23 March 1879 and was baptized at Ste. Anne's.[38]

After at least fourteen babies, Julia died 25 March 1879 and was buried in Ste. Anne's Cemetery.[39]

45. Mrs. Samuel LeBlanc (Elizabeth Belonga)

Elizabeth Belonga (Belonzhay, Belanger) was the daughter of Louis Belanger and Genevieve Montreuil (see no. 43 Mrs. Louis Belonzhay), and sister to no. 44 Mrs. Joseph Menasaw. Elizabeth was born 8 February 1836 and baptized at Ste. Anne's.[1]

Anselm "Samuel" LeBlanc (Lablanc, White) was born in the parish of St. Jacques L'Achigan, Quebec, on 19 February 1831 to Paul LeBlanc and Marcelle Guyon.[2] According to the 1850 Mackinac Census, the LeBlancs were settled at Mackinac Island. When they arrived in Michigan is unclear. Father and son earned a living as fishermen.[3]

Elizabeth and Samuel were married 30 December 1852 on Mackinac Island at Ste. Anne's Catholic Church.[4] From this marriage at least nine children were born:

1. Louis was born 27 October 1853.[5]
2. Justine was baptized on 3 June 1855, at one month old.[6] She married James Henry Wachter, date and location unknown. He was a lighthouse keeper at several lights including Beaver Island (1909–1912).
3. Paul was born 22 November 1857.[7]
4. Alexander Bernard was baptized on 9 May 1860.[8] He married Mary Anne Fountain on 7 July 1882 at Scott Point, Michigan.[9]
5. Ludger was born 24 July 1864.[10]
6. Samuel was born 31 August 1866 at Farnswell Point (location unknown).[11]
7. William was born around 1871 and died 5 March 1931 in Marquette, Michigan.[12] He married Henrietta Lapeer in Cheboygan, Michigan, on 25 September 1895.[13]
8. Eugene was born 25 July 1865.[14] He died 5 August 1927 and was buried in Gros Cap Cemetery.[15]
9. Joseph was born 10 December 1874 on Beaver Island, Michigan.[16] He married Minnie Josephine Davenport on 3 July 1897.[17]

Elizabeth died 7 August 1898 at Newton Township and was buried at Scott Point (Newton Township Cemetery).[18] Samuel died 24 April 1908 at Cheboygan, Michigan and was buried there.[19]

35. Mrs. Alixse Lelone (Marie Louise Cadotte)

There are no notes on the worksheet for Mrs. Alixse Lelone other than "do not know of any children." One child and one adult were recorded for payment to this individual in the 1870 annuity. The most logical candidate for Mrs. Alixse Lelone is Marie Louise Cadotte.

Marie Louise Cadotte was the daughter of no. 8 Mrs. Louis Cadotte (Marie Louise Laverdure). She was born 27 October 1842 and baptized at Ste. Anne's on Mackinac Island on 27 November 1842.[1] Alexander was born 22 July 1843 and baptized Alexis at Ste. Anne's.[2] He was the son of François Lalonde and Marie Augé (Ojee) who were married at Ste. Anne's 20 September 1836.[3]

Marie Louise Cadotte married Alexander Lelonde in a civil ceremony 5 March 1862.[4] From this marriage there was one child: Charles Alexander Lelonde, who was born 21 May 1862 and baptized 25 May 1862 at Ste. Anne's.[5] No additional information was found on Charles.

Alexander enlisted in the army at Marquette and mustered in 10 October 1862 in the 27th Michigan Infantry, Company H. He was wounded in the Battle of the Wilderness on 6 May 1864. There is no additional information regarding Alexander's service. He probably died from those wounds.[6]

Marie Louise then married James DeLaurier (Deloria) and was listed as the *Veuve* (Widow) Lalonde in the marriage record dated 31 March 1872.[7] Marie Louise (Mary Deloria) died 3 June 1914 and was buried on Mackinac Island.[8]

54. Mrs. Angeline Louisignon (Angelique Aslin)

Angelique Aslin was born 10 December 1834 at Mackinac Island, the daughter of Joseph Aslin dit Chevreau and no. 39 Marie Charlotte Dejadon.[1] She was the niece of no. 23 Mrs. Hyacinthe (François) Dufina, no. 26 Mrs. Paul Belonzhay, and no. 43 Mrs. Louis Belonzhay.

Angelique was the youngest member of her family listed on the 1836 Half Breed Census (as Angelique Chevreaux[2]). Angelique and her siblings were listed as quarter-blood Chippewa. Under the remarks column, it reads, "Of Mississippi origins. B. Jellee [Basile Jolie] says she [Marie Charlotte Dejadon] is from Fond du Lac." The family was rejected in council.

Joseph Aslin applied for funds under the treaty made with the 1837 Chippewa of Lake Superior.

Joseph Aslin, Louis Belonger, Paul Belonger, Francois Daufine apply for their wives and children and the same evidence applies to all, as they married four sisters. Joseph Aslin's wife is named Maria the daughter of Henry De Jourdain [and] is ½ breed Chippewa, 24 yrs of age, was born on Red Cedar lake, left there 7 years since and resides now at Mackinac, has 4 children the eldest is named Joseph 7 yrs of age, Angelique 5 yrs., Isabelle 4, Peter 2 mos. All born at Mackinac, was married to her husband who was in the employ of the American fur Company at Red Lake.[3]

Additional information follows: "Joseph Aslin was among a group of voyageurs who were brought out to Mackinac in 1822 to work for the American Fur Company. He was in the Fond du Lac outfit."[4] None of the families listed above were awarded funds from this treaty.

Marie Charlotte died 10 November 1869,[5] and Joseph died 22 July 1887 on St. Helena Island. He was buried next to his wife in Ste. Anne's Cemetery.[6] Excerpted from his obituary comes the following: "He came to Mackinac Island in 1812 and was one of the early voyageurs for the American Fur Co., during its life here at this place. He is without doubt the last surviving employee which was with that noted company while here on the Island."

Their daughter Angelique Aslin first married Alexis Martile Therrien at Ste. Anne's of Mackinac Island on 11 October 1850.[7] He died sometime before the 1860 Mackinac County census was taken because Angelique was listed as a widow.[8]

Angelique then married Charles Louisignon on 2 March 1862 at Ste. Anne's on Mackinac Island.[9] He was born 9 November 1827, the son of François Louisignon and Agathe Langlade.[10] He was enumerated on the 1836 Half Breed Census with his family. He was listed as half-Odawa and had lived all his life on Mackinac Island.[11] Prior to his marriage to Angelique, Charles was married to Mary Davenport (daughter of Ambrose and Susan Davenport), on 9 May 1850, by a justice of the peace in Mackinac County.[12] She died July of 1855.[13]

From the marriage of Angelique Aslin and Charles Louisignan, the following children were born:

1-2. Jeanne Angelique and twin Jacques Charles were born 29 January 1863.[14] Jeanne Angelique died 15 January 1869.[15]
3. Marie Isabelle was born 8 September 1868.[16] She married William Chapman on 29 November 1889 at St. Ignace, Michigan.[17]
4. Helene Agatha was born 4 March 1870 at McGulpin's Point, Emmet County, Michigan.[18] She died 27 May 1872 on Mackinac Island.[19]

St. Helena Lighthouse and outbuildings. COURTESY OF THE GREAT LAKES LIGHTHOUSE KEEPERS ASSOCIATION.

5. Ida Anna was born 26 October 1873.[20] She died 8 March 1886.[21]

6. Lucy was born 16 March 1875.[22] She married Fred L. Bailey in St. Ignace on 14 November 1894.[23]

Charles Louisignan was a lighthouse keeper in the Mackinac area. He began his career as the keeper of the McGulpin Point Lighthouse in Emmet County, Michigan, on 8 June 1869.[24] He stayed at this light until 1875 when he swapped positions with the keeper of the St. Helena light. Charles and his family stayed at St. Helena until he resigned from the US Lighthouse Service on 30 May 1888.[25] After retiring from the Lighthouse Service, Charles and Angelique moved back to Mackinac Island. Here he earned a living as a painter.[26] Charles died 8 April 1903 on Mackinac Island and was buried there.[27] Angelique died 17 November 1906 on Mackinac Island and was buried next to her husband.[28]

47. Miss Rosalie Louisignan (Lusignan)

Rosalie Louisignan (pronounced Loo-ee-zin-aw) was born 2 December 1809 according to her parent's marriage record, in Green Bay, Wisconsin. François Louisignan and Agatha Langlade were married 9 October 1826 at Ste. Anne's Catholic Church on Mackinac Island.[1] The marriage record indicates the couple had been married earlier in May 1800, by a civil magistrate. Once a Catholic priest had come to Mackinac, they were able to be married in the Catholic Church. All children born prior to this marriage were recorded and seen as legitimate by the church. Rosalie's birth date was recorded along with several other siblings.

Agatha Langlade was the daughter of Charles Langlade Jr. and granddaughter of the famous Charles Langlade and his first wife, an Odawa woman named Agathe (or Oo-la-te).[2] Agathe's father, Charles Langlade Jr., followed in his father's footsteps by taking up a military career. He was part of the British outfit that captured the fort at Mackinac Island during the War of 1812. Later, after the British left Mackinac, he followed them to Drummond Island and to Penetanguishene, Ontario. Little is known about Agathe's mother.[3]

The Louisignons were at Mackinac as early as 1820, where François appeared on the census in a household with five boys and one little girl.[4] In 1823, Rosalie, Mary, Paul, and Benjamin were enrolled in the Ferry Mission School.[5]

Agatha Louisignon and her children were listed on the 1836 Half Breed Census (nos. 258–267). Agatha was listed at three-quarters-Odawa. Her children, including Rosalie (no. 260), were listed as half-Odawa and had lived their entire lives at Mackinac.[6] Agatha was buried in Ste. Anne's Cemetery on 5 August 1852.[7] François Louisignon joined her on 20 July 1863.[8]

Rosalie is one of the few women in this band who never married and had no children. Consequently, there is little information about her life. According to the 1860 Michilimackinac Census she still lived with her father.[9] Later, in 1870, she was living with her brother, Joseph, Joseph's family, her sister, Ursula Rice (no. 48), and Ursula's children.[10] In the 1880 census, she was found still living with brother Joseph Louisignon and his family.[11] Rosalie Louisignon died 10 July 1891 and was buried on Mackinac Island.[12]

53. Mrs. Moses Maillet (Angelique McClure)

Angelique McClure (or Maclure) was born around 1828. She was eight years old when listed on the 1836 Half Breed Census. She was listed as half-Chippewa and awarded second-class funds of $305.89 that were "retained."[1] In the "Remarks" column it reads, "Abandoned by father, mother dead." Angelique was an orphan. It is not known who cared for her until she married.

On 19 October 1844, Angelique married Moses Maillet.[2]

The marriage register shows that both the bride's and the groom's fathers were named Jean Baptiste; their mothers' names were not recorded. Moses was born in Canada and Angelique was born on Mackinac Island. The number 2 represents the number of times banns were called.

A marriage for Jean Baptiste McClure and "an Indian woman" took place in

Ste. Anne's marriage record of Moses Maillet and Angelique McClure, 1844.

1828 (the year Angelique was probably born), performed by John Drew, justice of the peace.[3] This couple was probably Angelique's parents.

François Moses Maillet (Mayotte) was born and baptized on 23 April 1809 at St. Denis sur Richelieu, Quebec. His parents were Jean Baptiste Maillet, an artisan potter, and Marie Françoise Cadieux.[4] Marie Françoise died 17 May 1809, less than a month after Moses's birth.[5]

"Baptiste Maillet" appeared in the Michilimackinac County 1821 census and "Jean Baptiste Mayotte" was recorded annually until 1825. It is not clear exactly where he lived in the county and if this is Moses's father. It is known that Moses and Angelique were married 19 October 1844 and that they had several children. Some of their children had baptismal records; others were known from the census. Information about this family is scarce. In addition to the family data provided, the family was found in only the 1860 and 1870 Mackinac County censuses. Angelique was head of the family in 1870, therefore, Moses either died or left the area after Jeremie was born and before 1870.

1. Francis Moses was born 5 July 1845 and baptized at Ste. Anne's of Mackinac Island.[6]
2. Xavier was born circa 1848.
3. Rosina was born circa 1853.
4. Joseph Raphael was born in July of 1855 and baptized at Ste. Anne's.[7]
5. Effa was born circa 1856.
6. George Napoleon was born circa 1857.
7. Andrew Jean Baptiste was born 24 January 1858 and baptized at Ste. Anne's.[8]
8. Joseph Remi (Jeremie?) was born 4 January 1862 and baptized at Ste. Anne's.[9]

No other information about this family has been found to date.

2. Mrs. Louis Maishtaw (Marie Bennett-Beaubin)

Marie Bennet-Beaubin was the daughter of Louis Bennett-Baubin (also known as Bennet and Bauben) and Christine Outapitakewinam. She was born on 22 March 1821 on Mackinac Island.[1]

Marie married Louis Maishtaw (Masta); however, a record of the marriage was not found. It is possible that they were married by Isaac Handorn, justice of the peace, on 4 February 1841.[2] The baptismal record of their first child, Louis, says he is legitimate, indicating this couple was already married. This couple had at least a dozen children:

1. Louis was born 15 November 1841 and baptized at Ste. Anne's.[3]
2. Charles was born 5 February 1845, at old Fort Mackinac (current-day Mackinaw City in Cheboygan County).[4]
3. Marie Amabilis was born 11 June 1846.[5] She married Amab LaQuea (Lecuyer) on 2 May 1871, in Emmet County, Michigan.[6] She died 18 December 1915 and was buried in Mackinaw City.[7]
4. Christina was born 18 March 1848.[8] She was first married to Laverin Kagedjiewan (also known as Sam Kagetchiwan) on 3 March 1862.[9] After he died, she married Joseph St. Peter in Cross Village, Michigan.[10]
5. Jean Baptiste Napoleon was born 13 June 1850 and baptized at Ste. Anne's.[11]
6. Jean Baptiste was born 11 April 1852.[12] He married Harriet Cadotte in a double ceremony with his twin sister Marie Matilda.
7. Marie was born 11 April 1852 and went by the name Matilda.[13] She married three times. The first marriage was with Charles Cadotte at Mackinac Island on 27 June 1873.[14] This was a double ceremony with her brother John, who married Charles' sister Harriet.[15] After he died, she married Louis Cadotte.[16] After Louis died, she married Alfred Kinctel in Sault Ste. Marie, Canada.[17] She died 22 April 1922 and was buried in Mackinaw City, Michigan.[18]
8. Joseph Florimont was born 29 March 1854.[19] He married Rosalia Kosequat on 8 June 1880, in Emmet County, Michigan.[20] Joseph died 11 July 1931 at Middle Village, Emmet County, Michigan.[21]
9. Julie was baptized on 16 November 1856 at nine months of age.[22]
10. Antoine was baptized on 23 September 1858 at three months of age.[23]
11. Margaret was baptized 19 July 1861 at the age of eleven months at Ste. Anne's on Mackinac Island.[24]
12. Ruben was born 15 June 1865 and was baptized at Ste. Anne's.[25]

Sometime during the late 1860s, Louis moved his family to Inverness, Cheboygan County.

21. Mrs. Francis Martin (Agatha Fountain)

Agatha Fountain was the daughter of no. 14 Angelique Fagnant and Joseph Fountain, and the sister of no. 20 Angeline Fountain (Mrs. Vital Bourassa). She was born 9 September 1840 and baptized at Ste. Anne's.[1]

Francis Martin was born in Canada (probably at Manitoulin Island, Ontario). He was baptized at St. Mary's, Sault Ste. Marie, Michigan, on 23 June 1841,[2] and was the son of Simon Martin and Marie Lisette Leveille. Simon and Marie Martin and their family were first enumerated in the 1850 Mackinac census. Marie is listed in a separate household with the surname LaValley (Leveille) as are the children. She lived next to the Farlan (Feurtin, Fertia) home where her husband, Simon Martin, was enumerated.[3]

Agatha Fountain and Francis Martin were married on 4 May 1858 at Ste. Anne's on Mackinac Island.[4] Agatha and Francis had at least six children.

1. Angelique was born on 6 December 1860 and baptized at Ste. Anne's.[5]
2. François was born on 8 March 1863 and baptized at Ste. Anne's.[6] He married Mary Lozon (daughter of Joseph Alfred Lozon and Julia Grant) on 9 June 1897.[7]
3. Joseph Antoine was born 1 December 1865 and baptized at Cross Village.[8] He married Ellen Delaurier (daughter of David Delaurier and Catherine Perault) on 17 March 1891 by a justice of the peace on Mackinac Island.[9] She died 21 September 1920,[10] and Joseph died 2 September 1941.[11] They were buried on Mackinac Island.
4. Agatha was born 12 April 1868 and baptized at Cross Village.[12] She was married to Antoine Nicholas Perault (son of Antoine Perault and Philomene Cadran) on 1 September 1885 by a justice of the peace on Mackinac Island.[13] Agatha died 28 September 1927,[14] and Antoine died on 18 December 1931.[15] They were buried on Mackinac Island.
5. Mary Jane was born 2 May 1871 and baptized at Cross Village.[16] She first married Joseph Thomas Bazinet (son of Jean Baptiste Bazinet and no. 56 Mary Dufina) on 3 November 1889 on Mackinac Island.[17] After his death, she married Julius Andress (son of David Andress and Maggie (Marguerite)

Mrs. Francis Martin (Agatha Fountain).

COURTESY OF A DESCENDANT OF THE AGATHA BIDDLE BAND.

Aslin) on 7 November 1897 on Bois Blanc Island.[18] He died 24 May 1832 and was buried in the Protestant Cemetery on Mackinac Island.[19] Mary Jane died on 3 May 1934 and was buried on Mackinac Island.[20]

6. Eugene William was born on 6 April 1875 and baptized at Ste. Anne's.[21] He does not appear in a later census.

Francis, along with four other sailors, died when a steam valve burst opened and burned the men while working aboard the tugboat *Bennet* on 14 November 1876 near Moran, Michigan.[22] He was only thirty-four years old and as mentioned in the article, "Martin the mate, leaves quite a large family in Mackinaw." He has his own page in the Durant Roll, no. 38/15. All the children were listed on Agatha's page.

By 1880, Agatha and her family were living on Mackinac Island, but no additional information was found about Agatha's death or where she was buried.

55. Miss Lizzette Martin (later Mrs. Antoine Truckey)

Lizzette or Isabelle Martin was the daughter of Charles Martin and Marianne Ayabins. She was born 1 January 1842 and was baptized on 11 February 1842 at St. Ignatius Church in St. Ignace, Michigan.[1] Her father, Charles Martin, was the son of Antoine Martin, Sr. and Suzanne Kinokwe.[2] Marianne Ayabins was the daughter of Ayabins and an unknown Indian woman.[3]

She married Antoine Truckey who was the son of Augustin Truckey (Troquier, Trottier) and Marguerite Plante. He was born 13 May 1852 and baptized at St. Ignatius Loyola, in St. Ignace.[4] They married 7 May 1874 at Ste. Anne's on Mackinac Island.[5]

From this marriage there were at least six children.

1. Peter was born 30 September 1876 in Moran, Michigan.[6]
2. Augustin Henry was born on 8 November 1878 and baptized in St. Ignace, Michigan.[7] He died 19 August 1902 in Marquette, Michigan.[8]
3. Joseph Henry was born on 20 March 1879 and baptized in St. Ignace.[9] He died 7 April 1934 at Gros Cap and was buried there.[10]
4. Charles was born 2 March 1880 and baptized in St. Ignace.[11]
5. Marianne was born 8 September 1881 and baptized in St. Ignace.[12]
6. Agnes was born in October of 1882.[13] She married Samuel Guerney from Ireland on 10 July 1907 in St. Ignace.[14] She died 13 May 1910 and was buried in Gros Cap Cemetery.[15]

Antoine Truckey died 3 January 1917 of exposure and was buried in Gros Cap Cemetery.[16] Isabelle died 26 March 1924.[17]

49. Mrs. Benjamin McGulpin (Elizabeth Boyd)

Elizabeth Boyd was born sometime during 1832 and baptized on 8 April 1833, at Ste. Anne's on Mackinac Island.[1] She was the daughter of Thomas A. B. Boyd and Catherine Yarns, who did not marry.[2] Thomas Boyd was the son of George Boyd, whose family was from the Washington, DC, area and influential in national politics and international business. George Boyd was appointed the Indian agent at Mackinac under President Monroe in 1818. George's wife, Harriet Johnson Boyd, was the niece of the governor of Maryland and the sister-in-law of President John Quincy Adams. George Boyd moved his family to Mackinac Island in 1820, where they lived until he was appointment Indian agent at Green Bay, Wisconsin, in 1832.

Thomas Alexander Brooks Boyd was born around 1812 in Washington, DC, and came to the Mackinac area with his parents. As a young adult, he formed a relationship with Catherine Yarns. They had at least two children. Alexander was

Anna McGulpin (*left*) and her mother, Mrs. Boyd McGulpin.
COURTESY OF EMILY REDMAN MILLS.

born circa 1834,[3] and Eliza was born in 1832.[4] Eliza was baptized Elisabetha at Ste. Anne's on 8 April 1833 by Father Samuel Mazzuchelli.[5]

Catherine Yarns was probably the daughter of George Yarns, a voyageur and trader, who worked for the Mackinac Company from 1800 to 1810, wintering at Lac Courte Orielle, Wisconsin.[6] The *F. V. Malhiot Journal* that chronicled his year at Lac du Flambeau mentions George Yarns several times in connection with his position at the post. One mention stated that Malhiot was sending Yarns to his father-in-law, the old chief "La Chouette" (the Owl).[7] Perhaps La Chouette's unnamed daughter was Catherine's mother.

According to the Half Breed Census of the Treaty of Washington (1836), both of Boyd's children with Catherine were awarded first-class status payments in the amount of $1,812.50 each. The payments were given to their father.[8] Following the two Boyd children on the census was Susan Yarns, who was fifteen years old at the time. She received a second-class payment. Her funds were retained because both her parents were dead.[9] Perhaps she was Catherine's sister.

Found in the Mackinac County Courthouse, dated 11 February 1834, was the deed for a plot of land on Mackinac Island given by William and Nancy Sylvester to Catherine Yarns. The lot measured 134 feet in length by 112 feet wide and bordered Lake Huron."[10] There is no house in the description, so it must have been built later. An interesting note to this deed is that Thomas A. B. Boyd was one of the witnesses.

Thomas Boyd left the Mackinac area in 1838, when he was appointed Indian agent at Prairie du Chien, Wisconsin. He married Martha Mayfield and had several children with her. He later died in Detroit and was buried there on 9 October 1854.

Benjamin McGulpin was born 9 April 1827 and baptized in October of the same year at Ste. Anne's.[11] He was the son of William McGulpin and Madeleine Bourassa. Through his mother's line, Benjamin's family had continuously lived on Mackinac Island for nearly one hundred years at the time of his birth. He lived a busy life working in the fur trade, in the lighthouse service,[12] and at one time he served as the island's township treasurer.[13] He married Elizabeth Boyd on 3 January 1854 at Ste. Anne's.

From this marriage there were at least ten children:

1. Benjamin was born 3 June 1854 on Mackinac Island.[14] He married Mary Jane Lapine on 24 May 1878 at Newton Township in Mackinac County. She divorced him on 23 January 1911.[15] He died 12 August 1914 in Cross Village, Michigan.[16]
2. Mollie Mary was born in 1856. On 22 September 1878,[17] she married Louis Boulanger (son of Paul Boulanger and no. 26 Angelique Montreuil). She died at Cross Village, Michigan, 13 February 1943.[18]
3. William Julius was born 4 March 1858 on Mackinac Island.[19] He died at Cross Village, Michigan, on 11 February 1926.[20] According to his death certificate, he was single.
4. Anna (Helen) was born 26 December 1859.[21] She first married Patrick Tobin on 19 May 1878.[22] Patrick was from Ireland and a soldier at Fort Mackinac. Later, she married Henry Perault,[23] son of Antoine Perrault and Catharine Cadran. She died 15 October 1940 in Wyandotte, Michigan, and was buried on Mackinac Island.[24]
5. Elizabeth Ursule was born 12 January 1862 on Mackinac Island,[25] died in Kingsley, Michigan, on 3 November 1933, and was then buried in Ste. Anne's Cemetery on Mackinac Island.[26] She married Charles Wehrner, a soldier from Germany, stationed at Fort Mackinac, on 17 May 1881 at Ste. Anne's.[27]
6. Jacques George or James George was born 25 March 1864 on Mackinac Island,[28] and he died on 30 March 1945.[29]
7. Catherine Helene was born 17 April 1866.[30]
8. Madeleine was born 14 January 1869.[31]
9. Mary Jane was born 8 October 1871.[32]
10. William Sellew was born 2 July 1876.[33] He married Lenora Chapman on 20 October 1900 at Ste. Anne's.[34]

Benjamin McGulpin
by William H.
Gardiner.
COURTESY OF MACKINAC STATE
HISTORIC PARKS.

Benjamin McGulpin died on 12 July 1910,[35] and was buried at Ste. Anne's Cemetery. Elizabeth died on 27 January 1916,[36] and was buried next to her husband.

52. Miss Mary McGulphin (later Mrs. Mary Garrison)

Mary McGulpin was fourteen years old when the 1870 annuity was recorded. Her father was Jerome McGulpin, and her mother was Angelique St. Onge, (daughter of no. 46 Catharine Peltier). Mary McGulpin's paternal grandparents were William McGulpin and Madeleine Bourassa.

Mary McGulpin was born on 23 June 1856 and baptized the same day at Ste. Anne's.[1] She married John O. Garrison (son of Peter Garrison and Mary Jane Dingman) of Lyme, New York, on 15 October 1877.[2] He worked for the Coates & Arnold Company (later the Arnold Line ferry service).[3]

Mary and John's children were:

1. Minnie, born 29 December 1877.[4] She died before the 1880 census.
2. Mary Madora, born 14 March 1879.[5] She married W. M. Newton in Grand Rapids, Michigan, on 26 March 1904.[6]
3. John Peter Garrison, born 25 May 1880.[7] He married Rose M. Francis in St. Ignace on 17 November 1904.[8] He filed for divorce, which was granted on 7

April 1908. He then married Dena Demmink (from Holland) on 26 June 1913.[9] He died on 9 May 1916 in Grand Rapids.[10]

4. Catharine Elisabeth, born 11 June 1882.[11] She married Delos K. Sayles on 7 November 1905 in Grand Rapids, Michigan.[12] She died in Florida during April of 1966.[13]

5. Louis Frederick Garrison was born 16 February 1885.[14] He married Josephine Nelson of Sweden on 16 September 1905 in Chicago.[15] He died in Cascade, Michigan, on 20 November 1948.[16]

Durant's worksheet indicates that Mary and her husband remained on Mackinac Island, while the children went to Grand Rapids, Michigan. Son John first appears in Grand Rapids in 1891 as a gardener/caretaker of one of the city's public parks. In 1903, brother Fred (Louis Frederick) joined him there working as a tile-setter. Sister Catherine joined them in 1904. At that time, they all lived at the same residence,[17] until she met and married her husband.

John and Mary later joined their children in Grand Rapids where they both died. John died in Grand Rapids on 7 April 1910. His remains were returned to Mackinac Island where they were buried in the Protestant Cemetery.[18] Mary died 30 March 1932 and was buried in Woodlawn Cemetery in Grand Rapids, Michigan.[19]

41. Miss Nancy McGulpin

Nancy McGulpin was probably born 24 November 1808, daughter of George McGulpin and Françoise Gébéosé,[1] and baptized on 3 July 1831. George and Françoise were married at Ste. Anne's on 22 February 1836.[2] Françoise was baptized the same day.[3]

Not much is known about Nancy's life. From the 1836 Treaty of Washington, Nancy was awarded a third-class payment along with the rest of her family.[4] Nancy never married and had no known children. She moved from Mackinac Island to Inverness in Cheboygan County and was enumerated there on the 1870 census.[5] She died 21 October 1873 in Cross Village, Emmet County.[6]

44. Mrs. Joseph Menasaw (Mary Belanger)

Mary Belanger (Belonga) was baptized 12 October 1834 at Ste. Anne's Catholic Church. Her parents were Louis Belanger and Genevieve Montreuil (see no. 43, Mrs. Louis Belonzhay).[1] The Belangers lived in St. Ignace, Michigan.

Joseph Hercule Menançon (Melanson, Monosso) was born 7 February 1833 in the parish of Saint-Hugues, Quebec, and baptized there the following day.[2] His parents were Joseph Menançon and Lucie Lefebvre dite Boulanger (sister-in-law of no. 26 Mrs. Paul Belonzhay).

Mary Belanger and Joseph Menançon were married at Ste. Anne's on Mackinac Island on 8 August 1853.[3] They had at least eight children:

1. Louis was born 30 March 1855 in Mackinac County, Michigan.[4] He married Mary Sanville on 28 December 1876 in Door County, Wisconsin.[5] He died 8 September 1824 and was buried in Sturgeon Bay, Wisconsin.[6]
2. Rose Delima was born in Green Bay, Wisconsin, circa 1856, and married Michael Gorman on 21 September 1872, at Ste. Anne's on Mackinac Island.[7] He died 6 November 1898 and was buried in St. Ignatius Cemetery, St. Ignace, Michigan.[8] Rose died in Everett, Washington, 11 March 1923.[9]
3. Genevieve "Jennie" was born 10 May 1858 in St. Ignace, Michigan.[10] She married Leon Michael Wertz. "Mike" was the son of Jacob Wertz and Marie Rose Lefebvre Boulanger (also sister-in-law of no. 26 Mrs. Paul Belonzhay). She died 6 August 1917 in Antigo, Wisconsin.[11]
4. Jean Baptiste "John" was born circa 1860. He married Anna Elizabeth Stamnitz on 15 Aug 1887.[12] He died early October 1889 while hunting in Michigan.[13]
5. Louis William was born circa 1862 in Wisconsin.
6. Mary was born circa 1864 in Wisconsin. She married Burton Whaples on 24 February 1878,[14] and later sued him for divorce.[15]
7. Joseph was born circa 1867 in Wisconsin. He married Anna Elizabeth Stamnitz, widow of his brother, John.[16] After she died, he married Marie Peterson.[17]
8. Lucie was born circa 1869 in Wisconsin.

Joseph Sr. served in Company F, commonly known as the Depere Rifles, of the 14th Wisconsin Infantry during the Civil War. He was mustered 23 January 1864 and mustered out 9 October 1865.[18] On 18 June 1887 he applied for an invalid pension.[19]

Louis Monosso.
COURTESY OF JIM WELCH.

Prior to serving in the war, Joseph was a farmer. In 1858 he purchased eighty acres of land in Clay Banks, Wisconsin. The family was enumerated here in the 1870 and 1880 Wisconsin federal census.

Mary died 10 October 1911 in Oshkosh, and Joseph died in Sturgeon Bay, 26 April 1915. His obituary follows.

JOSEPH MONOSSO DIES SUDDENLY

Joseph Monosso, Sr. died suddenly and unexpectedly on Monday morning, from an attack of epilepsy. [The] Decedent was subject to epileptic fits but for some time past he had been in the best of health apparently. Monday morning when he got up he remarked that he was feeling better than he had for many days, and signified his intention of going fishing. His daughter, Mrs. M[ike] Vertz, with whom he made his home suggested to him that he wait until after dinner and she would accompany him. He sat down in an armchair and she went about her housework. A few minutes after she heard him making an unusual noise in the room and going from the kitchen found he was suffering one of the fits to which he was subject.

Applying the usual remedies without effect, she summoned Dr. Kreitzer, who upon his arrival pronounced the man dead.

Mr. Monosso was among the early settlers of the county. He was born in Canada in 1820, making him 80 years of age at the time of his death. In 1852, he was married to Mary Balanger [Belanger], seven children being born of the union, of which 5 survive. These are Mrs. Jennie Vertz, with whom he lived; Mrs. Mary Whopples; Mrs.

Rosa Gorman of St. Ignace, Mich.; Louis of Pembine, Mich; and Joseph, keeper of the Seul Choix Point Light. In 1867, the family moved to this county, settling in the town of Clay Banks, which was their home until some years ago, when the deceased moved to this ward to spend the remaining days of his life. After the death of his wife his daughter moved here to look after him.

In 1862, Mr. Monosso enlisted in the war, joining Company F, 14th Wis. Regiment, 17th corps. He served for about two and a half years, when he was honorably discharged. He was a member of the local G.A.R. post, which had charge of the funeral services.

The funeral took place on Wednesday morning from the house and the remains were interred at Bayside.[20]

18. Mrs. Daniel Moore (Louise Charbonneau)

Louis Charbonneau (also known as Provençalle) was born 25 February 1772 at Saint-Ours, Quebec, son of Jean Baptiste Charbonneau and Genevieve Sans Chagrin.[1]

Louis Charbonneau's first wife was most likely a Sioux woman named Therese Archange. A record of their marriage has not been found and may have been a "country" marriage. Children from this union were Marie Louise and Paul, who appear in the marriage record of Louis and Susanne Godin. The sacrament states, *"Susanne Godin reconnait et prend pour ses enfants adoptifs, Marie Louise agée denviron dix sept ans, Paul né le treizieme jour de Novembre mil huit cent trieze."*[2] (Susanne Godin acknowledges and takes for her adoptive children, Marie Louise around age 17, Paul born the 13th day of November 1813.) The following children of Louis Charbonneau and "a savage woman of the Sioux nation" were baptized at St. Ignace de Michilimackinac on 4 August 1821: Louis, born 13 April 1814; Antoine, born 12 December 1816; Archange, 29 October 1818; and Joseph, 22 December 1819.[3]

Louis and Susanne Godin (daughter of François Godin and Josette Wouabigandam) were married 29 January 1827 at L'Arbre Croche by Father Vincent Badin.[4] Four children were recognized as their legitimate children in the sacrament: Therese, born 12 July 1815; Archange, born 22 January 1817; Jean Baptiste, born 11 July 1821; and Basile, born 29 February 1824.[5] If the dates were recorded correctly, Louis was having relations with both women simultaneously.

Marie Louise Charbonneau married Joseph Biron Lapine in a civil ceremony performed by John Drew at Mackinac Island on 20 February 1828.[6] From this marriage at least five children were born:

Military marker of Isaac Lapine in Ste.
Anne's Cemetery, Mackinac Island.
COURTESY OF THE AUTHOR.

1. Joseph was baptized 20 March 1831.[7] He first married Marie Anna Visnaut
   on 21 May 1851.[8] After her death, he married Isabelle Aslin on 31 March 1856
   (daughter of no. 39 Mrs. Joseph Chevreau [Aslin]).[9]
2. Louis was baptized at Ste. Anne's on 23 December 1831.[10] He married May
   Brunette (daughter of Peter Brunette and Archange Charbonneau) on 4 April
   1858.[11]
3. Pauline was baptized 5 April 1834.[12] She married Felix Martineau at Ste.
   Anne's.[13]
4. Victor was born 6 October 1837 at St. Ignace, Michigan.[14] He married
   Armine Archambeau on 6 March 1859 (daughter of Francis and Lisette
   Archambeau).[15]
5. Isaac was born 10 April 1840 at St. Ignace, Michigan.[16] He enlisted in
   Company K of the 7th Michigan Cavalry on 14 March 1863. He mustered in
   29 April 1864 and was discharged on 23 June 1865.[17] Formed in 1863, one of
   Company K's first engagements was the battle at Gettysburg and was headed
   by (newly promoted) General George Armstrong Custer. Isaac survived the
   war and came home to marry Angelique Pelotte (daughter of no. 11 Mrs.
   Ignace Pelotte) at Ste. Anne's on 2 February 1866.[18] Isaac died 17 January
   1887.[19] Angelique died six months later, on 13 June 1887.[20] They were buried in
   the Ste. Anne's cemetery.

Joseph Lapine died before 1848[21] leaving Marie-Louise the responsibility of a large family. She later married Daniel Moore; however, a record of the marriage has yet to be located.

Despite her marriage to Moore, Durant labeled Louise "the head of the Lapine family" on her Field Note page (no. 18, p 13). Louise died 23 December 1884 on Mackinac Island and was buried in Ste. Anne's Cemetery.[22]

3. Mrs. Andrew Moran (Mary Kekematiwain)

Mary Kekematiwian was born 23 April 1834 and baptized at Ste. Anne's on Mackinac Island.[1] Her parents were Joseph Kekematiwain and Mary Ann Kelegekwanebe. Joseph died, and Mary Ann married Joseph Caron Jr. on 2 July 1840.[2] (See no. 29 Mary A. Karrow). Mary grew up in the Caron household with her mother and later married Andre (Andrew) Moran (Morin, Morrow).

Andre Morin was born 24 February 1797 in Montreal, Quebec.[3] Andre had outlived two previous wives, Marianne Naawandago and Marie Louise Beaubin, when he married Mary. They were married 7 June 1867 at St. Mary's in Cheboygan, Michigan.[4] Since all three women were named Mary/Marie, only the children listed on Mrs. Andrew Moran's worksheet will be discussed.

1. Oliver was born 22 September 1865 on Bois Blanc Island and baptized at Ste. Anne's.[5] He was married to Elizabeth Clark on 30 June 1891 in St. Ignace.[6]
2. Mary Margaret was born 26 February 1868 in Duncan, Cheboygan County.[7] She married Edward "Ned" Davis on 3 August 1907.[8]
3. Angeline was born 5 August 1874 and died 12 October 1931.[9] She was first married to Henry Demers on 22 November 1902 in Cheboygan.[10] Then she married Charles Shampine on 6 December 1911 in the same place.[11]
4. Narcisse was born in 1880, well after Andre's death. It is not known who his father was.

Andre died on 22 August 1878 in Benton, Cheboygan County.[12] According to the 1880 Cheboygan census, Mary was listed as a pauper.[13] Mary died on 24 March 1886 and was buried the same day. She was forty years old.[14]

11. Mrs. Ignace Pelotte (Rosalie Boucher)

Rosalie Boucher was born 5 May 1812 in Green Bay, Wisconsin.[1] According to Rosalie's 1869 marriage to Ignace Pelotte at Ste. Anne's, her parents were Xavier Bushy (Boucher?) and Charlotte Bushy.

Ignace Pelotte was the son of Ignace Pelotte Sr. and Lisette, an Odawa woman from L'Arbre Croche.[2] He was born 25 December 1803 and baptized 7 October 1826 at Ste. Anne's on Mackinac Island. From the Alice Poole Papers comes this description of Ignace parents' wedding:

> Jim Doud said in October 1938, Ignace Pelott told him that when a boy [he] saw his father and mother married in a group marriage in the open by the Perry Cannon. Missionary priests came seldom, and he often married a couple and baptized their children at the same time. It was a custom. Ignace, his bro[ther] Pete [Alexis?] and sister [Elisabeth Nancy] were baptized at this time their father and mother were married.[3]

This description is perhaps a bit fanciful in the Pelotte's case, but no doubt it happened regularly until a priest was permanently stationed at Ste. Anne's. Ignace's actual baptism occurred two years before his parents' wedding. Baptisms for Ignace Jr. and Elisabeth were found at Ste. Anne's dated 7 October 1826.[4] No record for a Pelotte named "Pete" has been found.

The elder Pelottes were first married on 3 January 1807 by Samuel Abbot, justice of the peace.[5] They were later married in a religious service at Ste. Anne's, dated 17 August 1828.[6] The bride was Lisette *La Sauteuse*.[7] The record states Ignace Sr. was then *bien malade* (very ill). He died two days after the marriage.[8] Death information for Lisette comes from a second hand but valuable source since death records are scarce during this early period. In a letter dated 6 December 1841, from Mary Anne Fisher to her daughter Elizabeth Baird, she writes, *"La vieille Pilate a etois enterez aujourd'hui"* (Old Mrs. Pilate was buried today).[9]

Ignace and Rosalie were first married in a civil service performed by William Scott, justice of the peace, on 22 June 1837.[10] From this marriage, there were at least ten children.

1. Alexis was born probably in Wisconsin. He married Marie Kanodnishikan at Ste. Anne's on 31 October 1836.[11]

Military marker of Gabriel Pelotte in Ste. Anne's Cemetery, Mackinac Island.
COURTESY OF THE AUTHOR.

2. Angelique was born circa 1838. She married Isaac Lapine (son of Joseph and Marie Louise Lapine) on 29 January 1866, at Ste. Anne's.[12]

3. Marie Elisabeth was born 22 August 1839.[13] She married Charles Fountain (son of Theophile and Agatha Fountain) on 14 January 1856 at Ste. Anne's.[14]

4. Harriett was born 8 April 1841,[15] and she married Levi Gabriel Chapman (son of no. 30 Mrs. Bela Chapman) on 14 November 1861 at Ste. Anne's.[16]

5. Ignace Gabriel was born 15 February 1843.[17] He was one of several Mackinac men who were part of Company K of the Michigan 7th Cavalry.[18] Known as the Wolverine Brigade, this brigade was commanded by the newly promoted General George A. Custer. The company mustered in 20 February 1863, and in just a few short months they were involved in the Battle of Gettysburg. They were largely engaged in scouting and reconnaissance duty. After the conclusion of the war, the company was sent out west. Ignace was mustered out 10 March 1866 at Salt Lake City, Utah.[19] He died 13 June 1876 and was buried in Ste. Anne's cemetery with a military marker.[20]

6. Catharine Rosalie "Rosie" was born 7 June 1847.[21] She married John Gallagher (son of John and Sarah Gallagher) on 17 January 1878 in Mackinac County.[22]

7. Marie Madeleine was born 13 March 1849.[23]

8. William was born 5 October 1851.[24]

9. Edward Alfred was born 28 October 1853.[25]

10. Christine was baptized 30 March 1855.[26] She married Samuel O. Decatur (from England) on 3 May 1874.[27]

Ignace and Rosalie Pelotte.
COURTESY OF A DESCENDANT OF THE AGATHA BIDDLE BAND.

After thirty-two years together and at least ten children, Ignace and Rosalie were married a second time on 6 April 1869 in Ste. Anne's on Mackinac Island. The groom was sixty-five years old and the bride was fifty-seven. They stood at the altar with the priest who blessed their union and repeated the sacred vows that cemented their marriage in the eyes of the church.

According to her tombstone in Ste. Anne's Cemetery, Rosalie died 24 June 1890.[28] At her death, the couple had been married fifty-three years. Ignace died a few years later in 1897.

Five months after his death, the St. Ignace Enterprise published a souvenir "women's edition" that included information about flora and fauna, curiosities for tourists, and stories about local personalities. One of those personalities was Ignace Pelotte. Because of the great length of the story, it is limited to biographical information here:

> Ignace Pelotte was not, properly speaking, a "voyageur," for he never made any of the long journeys of the fur traders into the far west and north; but he had made summer cruises in the bateaux and canoes of the company to Green Bay and Sault

Ste. Marie, and he had many very interesting reminiscences of the fur trade and the war of 1812.

The Record correspondent called on him one day in last October [of 1896] and found him living in a little house facing the water on the southernmost point of Mackinac Island. Around it were [*sic*] the gay cottages and hotels of a fashionable summer resort, but Pelotte's house was low and old-fashioned and stood well back from the street, sheltered by a row of plumb [*sic*] trees. In front of it and across the road lay the broad, white beach where the Indians used to set up their wigwams when they came to receive the money which was given them annually by the government in payment for their lands. Beyond were the Straits of Mackinac, where Pelotte used to see the long, narrow boats of the voyageurs pass in and out of the harbor, or the bark canoes of the Indians. . . .

Grandpere Pelotte has been growing feebler for a long time and when I entered, he was lying upon a bed in an adjoining room, but he came out to meet me and gave me a cordial greeting when I introduced myself, for he had known my father forty years before. He was bent and shrunken, and his hair was very thin and gray, but his mind and memory seemed as bright and clear as those of a man of 60. In his manner was something of the courtesy, almost courtliness of the French nobility from whom some of the Island people are said to be descended.[29]

The *St. Ignace News* dated 6 February 1897 ran his obituary: "Ignace Pelotte, better known as Grandpere Pelotte, who celebrated his 93d birthday anniversary Christmas, died on Monday [1 February 1897] at his home on Mackinac Island. Grandpere Pelotte was the only inhabitant left who had witnessed the capture of the Fort Mackinac by the British in 1814."[30]

65. Victoire Peltier (Mrs. David Bellaire)

Victoire Peltier, of Mackinac, a half blood Chippewa, applies through her Brother in Law, Edward Lesuir. She is 20 years of age, was born in the vicinity of White fish Point in Lake Superior, has resided at Mackinac for two years past and has never received an allowance for half breeds, not having applied under the Treaty of 1836. Her relations live principally at Saut [*sic*] de Ste Marie. None of them live higher up Lake Superior than Grand Island. No connexion [*sic*] with the Indians of the ceded Territory. Rejected.[1]

Excerpt from the 1850 Michilimackinac County census, page 73/94 (Granger).

Victoire was the sister of no. 46 Catharine Peltier St. Onge. In the Remarks column of the Half Breed Census of the 1836 Treaty of Washington, DC, for her sister, Catharine, it notes that the family was "Relations of Sault Ste. Marie Indians."[2] While Catharine St. Onge and her four children received third-class allotments of $94.14 each,[3] another sister, Angelique Lesieur, was awarded second-class payment, and her three daughters were awarded third-class payments.[4] Yet another sister, Julia Pelkey (Peltier), also received a second-class payment.[5] Victoire, for some reason, did not apply for funds from the 1836 treaty.

Victoire married David Bellaire at Ste. Anne's on Mackinac Island on 3 October 1841.[6]

At least five children were born to David and Victoire during the first decade of their marriage. Four of those children appear in the baptismal records of Ste. Anne's of Mackinac Island. David, born in August 1842, and Louisa, born January of 1846, died from cholera in September of 1849. Two other children, John Paul and Juliane, were also lost probably because of cholera. All these children were born in the 1840s but do not appear on a later census.

To prevent the loss of their last living child from the cholera epidemic, it appears the Bellaires placed Alfred, born circa 1848, with the Lyman Granger family who lived an isolated life at the Bois Blanc Island lighthouse.[7] It was a prudent strategy, as Alfred was still living in 1909 on Bois Blanc Island when Durant recorded him on his mother's page. Another son, Theodore (born 28 November 1851),[8] also lived to adulthood and was enumerated along with his brother. He made his home on Mackinac Island, where he died on 14 June 1932.[9]

Victoire died 10 May 1874,[10] at the age of fifty-three, cause of death listed as "old age." At the time of her death, she was a widow. No data was found regarding David Bellaire's death.

13. Mrs. Francis Rastoul (Christine Bennet-Beaubin)

Christine Bennet-Beaubin is the daughter of no. 38 Christine Otapitakewinam and Louis Beaubien (Bennet, Baubin, Beaubin, etc.) and the sister of no. 15 Mrs. Francis Johnston, no. 19 Mrs. David Kniffen, no. 4 Mrs. Edward Lasley, and no. 2 Mrs. Louis Maishtaw. She was born in September 1834 and baptized 8 October 1834 at Ste. Anne's on Mackinac Island.[1]

Christine married Francis Rastoule. He was born in 1833 and baptized 28 June 1838 at St. Ann's in Penetanguishene, Ontario.[2] His parents were Michel Rastoule and Marie Anne Parisien.

Christine and Francis were married 27 April 1859 at Ste. Anne's on Mackinac Island. From this marriage at least a dozen children were born:

1. Mary Elizabeth (Elizabeth Isabell, Lisabella) was born in 1860. She married Nils Anderson from Sweden on 8 February 1882 in Cheboygan, Michigan.[3]
2. Thomas was born circa 1861. He appeared on the 1880 Cheboygan County Census.[4]
3. Joseph was born circa 1862. He appeared on the 1870 Cheboygan County Census.[5]
4. Francis Florimante was born 17 December 1862 and baptized at Ste. Anne's on Mackinac Island.[6]
5. Charles was born circa 1864. He died 25 September 1884 in Cheboygan County, Michigan.[7]
6. Marie Matilda was born 14 November 1865 in Mackinaw City and baptized 8 May 1866 at Ste. Anne's on Mackinac Island.[8] She died in Beaugrand, Cheboygan County, on 10 April 1882.[9]
7. Margaret was born circa 1868. According to the Durant Roll worksheet, she married a Mr. Drumwald. No marriage record was located.
8. Mary was born on 28 December 1875 in Beaugrand.[10]
9. Eliza was born 20 January 1876 (date from death certificate) and died 9 November 1945 in Saginaw, Michigan.[11]
10. Jennie was born 26 November 1876.[12] She married Milton Morse (son of Albert Morse and Mary Steward) in Mackinaw City on 7 December 1895.[13] Milton died 22 December 1951 and was buried in Saginaw.[14] Jennie died on 26 June 1964 and was buried with her husband in Oakwood Cemetery.[15]
11. Unnamed Baby Boy was born 25 December 1877 in Cheboygan County, Michigan.[16]

12. Frank Louis was born 24 December 1879.[17] Frank enlisted in the army on 30 October 1901 at Mackinaw City,[18] and then went to the Philippines and served at Corregidor and Malahi Islands.[19] He was discharged for disability at Fort McDowell, California, 3 April 1911.[20] He married Anna Reck (daughter of Ferdinand Reck and Pauline Lichtenburg of Germany) on 10 November 1913 in Petoskey, Michigan.[21] They moved to Lansing, Michigan, where Anna died 16 February 1920 from influenza. As of 1940, Frank Jr. was living with his son, Donald, in Lansing.[22]

Christine died sometime after the birth of Frank Louis in 1900. Frank Sr. is listed as single in the 1900 census,[23] where he is a lumber man living in Carp Lake, Michigan. Frank Sr. moved to Lansing with Frank Jr., where Frank Sr. died 16 February 1920 and was buried in the Mount Hope Cemetery in Lansing, Michigan.[24]

48. Mrs. Benjamin A. Rice (Ursula Lusignan)

Ursula Lusignan was the daughter of François Louisignan and Agatha Langlade. She was baptized on 20 October 1832.[1] (See her sister no. 47, Rosalie Louisignan). She was married to Benjamin A. Rice on 26 September 1851 by US chaplain John O'Brien.[2] From this marriage there were four daughters:

1. Helene Isabelle was born 23 May 1852 on Mackinac Island.[3] She married Thomas Sharp 5 Jan 1874.[4] He was a lifelong soldier rising to the rank of lieutenant colonel.[5] She died 18 November 1884 and was buried on Mackinac Island.[6]
2. Rosalie Louise was born 12 April 1854 on Mackinac Island.[7] She married Louis Joseph Joli on 1 February 1874.[8] She died 3 April 1890.[9]
3. Ursula was born in March 1856 and died 1 October 1856.[10]
4. Harriet "Hattie" was born 5 May 1858.[11]

Ursula and Benjamin were either divorced or had their marriage annulled since both individuals later remarried. These documents have yet to be located. She married Alexis Lozon (father of nos. 12a, b, and c) on 26 April 1879.[12] The ceremony was performed by Felix Cadieux, justice of the peace in Mackinac County. She died 23 September 1901,[13] and was buried in Ste. Anne's Cemetery on Mackinac Island.
Benjamin A. Rice was from Lebanon, New York. His parents were Abner and

Thomas Sharp.
COURTESY OF SARAH CLARK.

Helen Rice Sharp.
COURTESY OF SARAH CLARK.

Keziah (Buck) Rice.[14] There was at least one brother and one sister with Benjamin on Mackinac Island, and all three married Lusignan siblings. His brother James C. Rice married Isabelle Lusignan, and sister, Anna L. Rice, married Joseph Lusignan. Later, Anna's son, Joseph Francis Luisignan, married Eliza Rice, daughter of another Rice brother, Ezra W., living in Wisconsin.

Sometime between 1858 and 1861, Benjamin left Michigan and went to Minnesota. He enlisted 1 October 1861 in Company C of the 4th Minnesota Infantry, serving the duration of the Civil War. He mustered out 19 July 1865.[15] After the war he went to Wisconsin where his brother Ezra lived. Here, he met and married Sarah E. Dunlap on 4 July 1869 in Crawford County, Wisconsin.

According to the Minnesota Soldier's Home records, Benjamin moved to Minneapolis, Minnesota, around 1889,[16] where he entered the Minnesota Soldiers Home. He died there on 19 September 1907.[17] He was buried in Lakewood Cemetery in an unmarked grave.[18] Sarah died in Chicago, Illinois, 18 July 1929.[19]

59. Angel Robinson (Mrs. George Lamyott)

Angel (Angele, Angeline) Robinson was the sister of no. 33 David Robinson. She was born 12 November 1840,[1] and was the daughter of François Robinson (Robertson) and Josette Chibayabos (Leaving Phantom).

No children were listed on her worksheet. She married in 1861 but was still listed with her maiden name of Robinson.

George Lamiott and daughters, probably Anna and Octavia, circa 1885.
FROM THE COLLECTION OF STEPHEN J. LAJOICE.

George Lamiott (Amiot, Lamyotte) was born in Penetanguishene, Ontario on 4 June 1837,[2] and baptized there at St. Ann's. He was the son of Colbert Amiot and Julie Solomon.

Angel married George Lamiott on 2 Jan 1861 at St. Ignatius Church in St. Ignace.[3] They had at least nine children

1. Georges was born 27 May 1862 and baptized at St. Ignatius.
2. Anne was born 5 August 1865 and baptized at St. Ignatius.[4] No additional information was found about her.
3. Georges Edmond was born 8 July 1867 in Epoufette, Michigan.[5] He married Elizabeth Paquin (daughter of Antoine Paquin and Suzanne Levake) on 7 July 1890 at St. Ignatius, St. Ignace, Michigan.[6] He died 27 May 1948 in St. Ignace, Michigan.[7]
4. Mary Philomene was born 8 June 1868.[8] She first married Noel Lajoie (son of Louis Lajoie and Mary Lavake) on 30 November 1888 in St. Ignace.[9] After his

death, she married Joseph Therrien (son of Joseph Therrien and Julie Fortier) on 12 October 1899 in St. Ignace, Michigan.[10] She died 14 April 1937 in Port Huron, Michigan,[11] and was buried in St. Ignace.

5. Agnes was born circa 1872. She married Oliver Therrien (son of Antoine Therrien and Rose Lajoice) on 19 May 1896 at St. Ignace, Michigan.[12] She died 27 January 1898.[13]

6. John Ruben was born circa 1871. He married Therese Ance on 9 April 1894 at St. Ignatius.[14] He died 7 April 1956 and was buried in St. Ignatius Cemetery.[15]

7. Octavia was born 15 April 1873 in Moran, Michigan.[16] She married Joseph B. Levake (son of John B. Levake and Katherine Plant) on 16 February 1901, in St. Ignace.[17] She died 4 August 1937 and was buried in St. Ignace.[18]

8. Anna Eustasia was born circa 1877. She first married Henry Vallier (son of James Vallier and Frazine Lajoice) on 11 June 1896 in St. Ignace.[19] After he died, she married Antoine Fournier on 4 October 1919.[20] She died 1 June 1951 in St. Ignace, Michigan.[21]

9. Frank Paul was born 16 March 1881 in St. Ignace.[22] He died 3 October 1918.[23]

Angeline Robinson Lamiott died 25 September 1900,[24] and George died 6 May 1920.[25] They were buried in St. Ignatius Cemetery, St. Ignace.

33. David Robinson

David Robinson was one of the few men in the Agatha Biddle band. He was the brother of no. 59 Angel Robinson Lamiott.

David was the son of François Robinson (Robertson) and Josette Chibayabos. François was born in Berthier, Quebec, on 4 November 1797.[1] Josette Chibayabos was born about 1795 in Minnesota according to the 1860 Mackinac County Census.[2] Josette was also known by the surnames of Boullionmore and Jacobs.

His grandfather on his mother's side was Chibayabos or "Leaving Phantom" and was the chief of Iroquois Point (now Graham's Point of St. Ignace). He was listed in the Tenth Article in the 1836 Treaty of Washington, DC, as a chief of the second class and was awarded $200.[3]

François and Josette were married 11 September 1826, in St. Ignace.[4] David was born 22 February 1846, at St. Ignace.[5] It appears he never married and had no children. He died 4 September 1927 on Mackinac Island and was buried there three days later.[6]

27. Mrs. Charles Roussain (Rousseau) (Charlotte Martin)

Charlotte Martin was the daughter of Salomon Martin and Lisette Duperais. Salomon and Lisette were married 21 July 1832 by Father Samuel Mazzuchelli.[1] On the same day, Lisette, or Louise, was baptized by Father Samuel Mazzuchelli. Lisette was born somewhere along Lake Superior,[2] and her parents were N. Duperias and N. Pashikishigokwe.[3]

Salomon Martin was probably born 13 March 1797 at Saint-Jacques-de-L'Achigan, a parish of Montreal,[4] son of Joseph Martin and Therese Maugre. A voyageur contract was found for Salomon Martin from Saint-Jacques, Montreal, dated 1823.[5] His *métier* for the company was that of a *cultivateur* or farmer. He would serve "*tout le haut Canada*," including specific locations of "*Michilimackinac, ou ses dependances et le Pays sauvages . . . la dite Isle Drummond*" (all of upper Canada, Michilimackinac or the sub-units [forts] and the savage country . . . [and] the said Drummond Island).

Census records in the Mackinac area for Salomon Martin begin as early as the 1820 Michilimackinac Census. According to subsequent censuses, he earned his living as a grocer. Unfortunately, no spouse was recorded. The Mortality Schedule of 1870 indicates Salomon, who was seventy-four, died in June 1869,[6] and that he was married but, again, no spouse was listed. In the records of St. Ignatius Loyola in St. Ignace, Michigan, there is a death record in 1841 for a Lisette Martin, no age or spouse listed. Without additional information, it is impossible to know if this is Mrs. Salomon Martin or another woman with a similar name.[7]

Salomon and Lisette had at least four children:

1. Charlotte was born during 1831 along Lake Superior and was baptized 13 July 1833 at Ste. Anne's on Mackinac Island.[8]
2. Marie was born on 12 March 1834 and baptized at Ste. Anne's.[9]
3. Susan was born circa 1837.
4. Joseph Michael was baptized 10 Dec 1839 at St. Ignatius Loyola in St. Ignace.[10]

Charlotte and Marie were listed on the 1836 Half Breed Census (nos. 304–305) as half-Chippewa and received third-class payments of $95.14 each. The Remarks column indicated they had lived in St. Ignace since birth.[11]

Charlotte first married Antoine Babineau (from Detroit) 28 October 1850 at Ste. Anne's on Mackinac Island.[12] There was one child from this marriage. Antoine was born 22 April 1851,[13] and baptized at St. Ignatius Loyola in St. Ignace, Michigan.

John Jonas Rousseau and
daughter, Mary Jane, circa 1915.
COURTESY OF DELAYNE DUHAIME.

During his lifetime, Antoine Jr. also used the surname of Rousseau. Charlotte then married Charles Rousseau, but the record has yet to be found.

At least six children were born to this couple:

1. Charles was born 24 November 1854 and baptized at Ste. Anne's on Mackinac Island.[14] He died young.
2. Charles was born 27 March 1857 and baptized at St. Ignatius in St. Ignace, Michigan.[15]
3. Maceala Isadore was born 23 April 1859 and baptized at St. Ignatius.[16] He died 3 November 1860 and was buried at St. Ignatius Cemetery in St. Ignace, Michigan.[17]
4. Joseph Michael was born 8 May 1867.[18] He died 21 February 1882 and was buried in the St. Ignatius Cemetery in St. Ignace.[19]
5. Charlotte Josephine was born 12 August 1868 and baptized at St. Ignatius.[20] She died 29 August 1871 and was buried in the St. Ignatius Cemetery.[21]
6. John Jonas was born 17 May 1875 on Beaver Island, Charlevoix County,

Tombstone of Charles
Rousseau at the Old Soldiers'
Home, Grand Rapids, MI.
COURTESY OF CRYSTAL KIMBLE.

Michigan.[22] He married Susan Morrison and died in Duluth, Minnesota, on
25 January 1950.[23]

Charles Rousseau served in the Civil War in the 23rd Michigan Infantry,
Company I. He enlisted at Houghton, Michigan, for a three-year term beginning 9
August 1862. At the time of his enlistment he was thirty-two years old. By the end
of the war he had risen to the rank of sergeant and was mustered out in Salisbury,
North Carolina, on 28 June 1865.[24]

In 1894, Charles appeared on the St. Ignace roster of Civil War veterans. On 5
September 1895, he was admitted to the Soldiers Home in Grand Rapids, Michigan.
His application listed that he was deaf in one ear and had rheumatism in his
shoulders, hips, and limbs that prevented him from earning a living.[25] Charles died
on 5 November 1900 and was buried in the cemetery at the Old Soldiers' Home with
a military marker.[26]

According to a private, local register kept by James Blanchard of Gros Cap,
Michigan, Charlotte Martin Rousseau died 19 August 1884.[27] No burial information
was located.

46. Mrs. Louis St. Onge (Catharine Peltier)

Catharine Peltier was born in January 1809. Her parents were Jean Pierre Peltier and
Angelique Okichibanoque or Angelique Peau de Chat (Cat Skin) from Drummond
Island.[1] She was the sister of no. 65 Victoire Peltier.

Louis St. Onge was possibly the son of Jean Baptiste St. Onge and Angelique Panneton. A baptismal record for Louis St. Onge was found at L'Assomption, Quebec, with a birth date of 13 February 1798.[2] Also, two voyageur contracts were found for Louis St. Onge dated 1819 and 1820. The second contract was for three years of service at Drummond Island signed by company representative David Mitchell.[3]

Catharine married Louis St. Onge in a double ceremony with sister Angelique and Edward LeSieur on Mackinac Island by justice of the peace, Michael Dousman, on 24 November 1829.[4]

The four eldest children (Angelique, Louis, Theophile, and Catherine) and their mother were listed on the 1836 Half Breed Census and were awarded $95.14 each.[5]

The St. Onge's had at least eleven children:

1. Angelique was born circa 1832. She married Jerome McGulpin (son of William McGulpin and Madeleine Bourassa) on 23 May 1845.[6] (See their daughter, no. 52 Mrs. Mary McGulpin [Garrison].)
2. Theophile was born 31 October 1833.[7] He married Elise Plaunt on 28 February 1859.[8]
3. Joseph was born circa 1834. He married Mary Misweninimi (of Petite Traverse) on 26 April 1859 at St. Ignatius in St. Ignace, Michigan.[9] Mary was the daughter of Ignatius Misweninimi and Mary Sagitoo.
4. Catharine was born 18 December 1835.[10]
5. Catharine was born 24 December 1837.[11] She married Wellington Force on 11 August 1856.[12]
6. Louis was baptized 1 January 1832.[13] He first married Margaret Derusha on 14 February 1857.[14] After her death, he married Eleanore Archambeau.[15]
7. Sophia was born 26 May 1840.[16]
8. Edward was born 30 November 1842.[17] He married Margaret Derusha's sister, Sophie, on 4 November 1861.[18]
9. Jean Baptiste was born 14 May 1845.[19] He first married Mary Ance circa 1873. After she died, he married Josephine Jingwan.[20] He died 6 September 1920 in St. Ignace, Michigan.[21]
10. Rosalie was born 23 April 1848.[22] She married Alexander Paquin 10 January 1875 at St. Ignatius in St. Ignace, Michigan.[23]
11. Marie Louise was born 4 August 1850.[24] She first married Oliver Labutte on 13 May 1873 at St. Ignatius.[25] After Oliver died, she married Alphonse "Peter" Cody.[26]

Louis St. Onge died 27 Apr 1880 in St. Ignace. Catharine died on 21 April 1892, and was buried with her husband in St. Ignatius Cemetery, St. Ignace, Michigan. Louis and Catharine's descendants still reside in the St. Ignace area today.

37. Miss Martha Tanner

Martha Tanner was the daughter of the "White Indian" John Tanner and Therese Akwemikons.[1] She was baptized April 17, 1831 by Father Samuel Mazzuchelli at Ste. Anne's on Mackinac Island.[2] The record is unclear, but it appears that Mazzuchelli recorded her age at the time of her baptism as 18, which would make her birth year 1813. However, the Reverend Florimond Bonduel sent a certificate to Martha at the St. Clare Convent School in Detroit that she was born in 1823 on Lake Superior.[3]

Martha's mother, Therese Akwemikons, was probably from L'Arbre Croche in the northern Lower Peninsula of Michigan. According to John McDowell, Therese "was taught by the Schindler women to work as a housekeeper, and as such made her living on Mackinac for a dozen years."[4] She died 28 November 1850,[5] and, according to Alice Poole, she was buried in Ste. Anne's Cemetery.[6]

Martha first attended the Presbyterian Mission school started by Reverend William Ferry on Mackinac Island. According to Martha's records from the Mission School, the earliest date of her attendance was August 1825.[7]

When Martha was around seventeen years old and living in Sault Ste. Marie, Henry Rowe Schoolcraft engineered her removal from her father's care by legislative process.[8] She then became the ward of Captain Benjamin K. Pierce, commander of Fort Mackinac on Mackinac Island.[9]

Benjamin K. Pierce was the son-in-law of Madeleine LaFramboise, a religious and wealthy Indian woman, with a large stately home on Mackinac Island. Pierce had married LaFramboise's only daughter, Josette, who died four years after their marriage, after giving birth to a son who died at the same time.

While living on Mackinac Island, Martha was enumerated on the 1836 Half Breed Census for the Treaty of Washington. She was given second-class status and awarded $305.89.[10]

From Mackinac Island, she went to Detroit to attend the St. Clare Convent School.[11] After she completed her studies, she went to western Kentucky to attend Vincent's Academy. Later, she stayed with the Sisters of Loretto at Cape Girardeau, Missouri, who were dedicated to the education of poor children. The Sisters were a

John Tanner, an engraving from the frontispiece of the original 1830 edition of *A Narrative of the Captivity and Adventures of John Tanner.*

religious order, which Martha considered joining, but she apparently changed her mind because she did not become a nun.[12] She returned home and was hired to teach Indian and mixed-blood children in the Mackinac area under the direction of the Indian agent. She gave a start to many children, both Native and non-Native, sharing a single classroom. She taught school on Mackinac Island for several years then went to St. Ignace.

Martha lived a very interesting life and took on many challenges single-handedly. In 1858, she was hired to teach English, reading and writing by "Mr. Hamlin and Mr. Smith" in St. Ignace. Mr. Smith gave her the following instructions, "He told me not to teach Catechism or pray during school hours, also the priest had no business in my school."[13] Letters from Martha received by the Mackinac Agency between 1858 and 1860, indicated she had considerable trouble with the local priest, Father Piret, in the establishment of the school. The priest offered the Catholic school house for her use, but it required extensive repair. Father Piret also wanted to choose the books with which she was to teach and insisted she teach catechism.[14]

Disregarding Father Piret's offer of the Catholic school house, Martha determined to find something more suitable for her school. She found a rental house and fitted it with a new stove for heat. After the priest discovered Martha had no intention of renovating the Catholic school, he told the Native community they were "strictly forbidden" to send their children to her school. Martha, lamenting the situation to Indian Agent Fitch, wrote, "I see plainly he is my inveteret [*sic*] foe."[15] In another letter to Fitch she wrote, "The chief has not fulfilled one single promise he made when he petitioned for me to come and Teach their children, he has given me much abusive, insulting language, poor man I forgive him, as I know he is being influenced by the Priest."[16] At the end of the school year, she wrote to Mrs. Therese Baird, "And Oh! My dear friend you cannot imagine how relieved, how light, how happy I feel since I quit this school. Not that I dislike the occupation, no indeed, but the knowledge of, and suffering such impositions and injustices from Priest and Bishop made my life and employment an insupportable burden to me, but now I am once more free."[17]

The following year, relations improved with Father Piret. She writes, "The Rev.d Mr. Piret is very friendly and kind to me, regrets having opposed me last year, consequently most of his parishioners appear to be my friends."[18]

Martha's role in the community went well beyond that of a teacher. It appears that the local Anishinaabeg respected her and depended on her as a trusted mediator between the Native/Métis and European communities.

> Each head of family like so many naughty children comes to me with their stories against each other. I try to be like a patient Mother, hear all calmly, and endeavor to pacify as well as I can. Whenever I find a difficult case or when white people are concerned, as they are all Roman Catholics, I take them to the Revd. Mr. Piret and get him to use his authority which generally succeeds for the moment, but they always conclude by telling me I must tell all to their good father the Agent when he comes.[19]

It was probably during this time of her troubles with Father Piret that the old Ste. Anne's Cemetery on Astor Street on Mackinac Island was closed to additional burials.[20] Martha's sister, Lucy, and her mother were buried there. The following notation comes from the Alice Poole papers:

> Martha Tanner's sister Lucy and her mother were buried in the Old Catholic Cemetery (Ste. Anne's) on Astor Street. Martha had [the] remains removed to the Protestant Cemetery because of some trouble with [the] local priest. Later when that priest left [the] Island she had [the] bodies moved again to the present (1935) Catholic Cemetery. Martha's grave has a slab marker—[the] 2 other graves are unmarked.[21]

As evidenced by numerous letters in the Henry S. Baird Collection of the Wisconsin Historical Collections, there was a life-long relationship between Martha and the LaFramboise-Schindler-Fisher households. Martha was frequently mentioned in letters between Mary Anne Fisher and her daughter Elizabeth Baird (Therese Schindler was Madeleine LaFramboise' sister, and the mother of Mary Anne Fisher).

Cemetery marker of Martha Tanner in
Ste. Anne's Cemetery, Mackinac Island.
COURTESY OF MIKE CRANK.

A true demonstration of love and concern for Martha's welfare is shown in the free lease of Mary Anne Fisher's home. Found in the Mackinac County Register of Deeds, dated 21 November 1870, the agreement indicated that Martha could live there "to have and to hold for the term of her Natural life."[22] The home was owned by James Bennett, who purchased it from Henry and Elizabeth Baird, who owned it after Mary Anne Fisher's death. Clearly Mr. Baird, an attorney, made sure of Mrs. Fisher's promise in the sale of the house to Bennett.

An acquaintance of Martha's, Fanny Dunbar Corbusier, recorded in her diary that Martha had been treated by her father for breast cancer.[23] Martha died 25 July 1887 and was buried on Mackinac Island next to Therese Schindler in Ste. Anne's Catholic Cemetery. Her tombstone reads, "She has gone to worlds above where saints and angels meet to realize her Savior's love and worship at His feet."[24]

This woman, a half-blood Odawa, made quite a life for herself. She was the best educated person in Agatha Biddle's band and one who gave so much by educating a generation of white, Native, and Métis children in the Mackinac area. She was truly loved by many and their generosity saw her through to her life's end. She was the epitome of the Métis struggle—how to walk equally in two worlds. Others like her (mostly male), who were mixed-blood and educated, generally had the luxury of a European father who made way for them in a tough world. Martha pulled herself up on her own, shared her gifts and inspired many.

24a, b & c. Hester Terrien, sister, and Peter

Hester, Genevieve, and Peter Terrien (Therrien, Therriant) were children of Olivier Therrien and Isabelle Lozon. Olivier was the son of Peter Isaac Therrien and Angelique Majibinokwe. He was born 24 February 1829 and baptized at Ste. Anne's on Mackinac Island.[1] Isabelle was the daughter of Joseph Lozon and Nancy Elizabeth Pellotte. She was born 1 August 1832 and was baptized at Ste. Anne's.[2] Isabelle and Olivier were married 31 January 1853 at Ste. Anne's.[3]

Olivier and Isabelle had at least four children. Durant enumerated three who lived to adulthood:

1. Esther Elizabeth was born 27 October 1853 and was baptized at Ste. Anne's.[4]
2. Peter Isaac was baptized 29 March 1855.[5]
3. Genevieve, who went by Jennie or Jane, was baptized on 1 January 1857 at Ste. Anne's.[6]
4. Joanna Anna was born 21 November 1858.[7] She died young and did not appear on the Durant Roll.

Oliver Therrien died 12 March 1860.[8] Isabelle then married her brother-in-law, Noel Leveille. Noel was first married to Isabelle's sister, Magdeleine, who died giving birth on 16 March 1865.[9] Isabelle and Noel were married 25 December 1865 at St. Ignatius Loyola Catholic Church in St. Ignace, Michigan.[10] Isabelle died 29 July 1902 and is buried with her second husband, Noel Leveille.[11]

24a. Hester Terrien

Ester (Esther) Elizabeth was born 27 October 1853.[1] She was married to William Hildreth on 4 May 1874, on Mackinac Island, by a justice of the peace.[2] From their marriage there were at least five children:

1. Clarence Gabriel was born 26 March 1876 and baptized at St. Bernard's in Alpena.[3] He married Anna Parks on 9 June 1929 in Alpena, Michigan.[4] He served in the Spanish-American War, died 27 June 1933, and was buried in Leesburg, Florida.[5]
2. Isabella Joan was born on 16 July 1877,[6] and she died 1 October 1878 in Alpena, Michigan.[7]

3. Mary Agnes was born 22 March 1879 in Alpena and baptized at St. Bernard's there.[8] She married Harry Otto Beu. Mary Agnes went by the name Mae. She died 10 June 1933 in Erie, Pennsylvania.[9]

4. Joseph William was born 12 October 1881 in Alpena.[10]

5. Ellen was born 20 March 1885 and baptized at Ste. Anne's in Alpena.[11]

Ester died on 14 July 1906 and was buried in Holy Cross Cemetery in Alpena, Michigan.[12] No death information for William has been located.

24b. Genevieve Terrien

Genevieve, or Jane as she was called, was born 20 November 1857 on Mackinac Island. She worked as a servant before marrying Don Cheeseman on 1 June 1903, at St. Ignace.[1] They had no children. She died 21 June 1921 in Moran, Michigan.[2] Donald Cheeseman was the son of Alonzo Cheeseman and Amy Thorne, who were Mormon. Alonzo was from New York state and came to Beaver Island, Michigan, with Jesse James Strang, who was "king" of the Mormon church. The Cheeseman family still lives in the St. Ignace area.[3] Members of the family are buried together in Gros Cap Cemetery in Moran, Michigan.

24c. Peter Isaac Terrien

Peter Isaac was baptized on 29 March 1855 at Ste. Anne's on Mackinac Island.[1] He married another islander, Angeline Boulanger (Belonzhay, Beloungea) on 2 November 1886 in Newton Township, Michigan.[2] She was the daughter of no. 26 Angelique Montreuil and Paul Boulanger.

Peter and Angeline had at least seven children:

1. Eva Marie was born 13 September 1887 in St. Ignace, Michigan.[3] She does not appear on the 1900 census and no additional information was found.

2. Oliver Scott "Scotty" was born on 1 May 1890, according to his draft registration.[4] He married Lillian Chapman on 1 May 1926 in Crown Point, Indiana.[5]

3. Roma Elizabeth was born 5 June 1892. She married Dr. Clinton Bernard Brake in Jackson, Michigan, on 7 March 1916.[6] She died 7 September 1962.[7]

Adults in this picture: *top*, Angeline Boulanger Therrien, *left*, Roma Therrien Brake, and *right*, Florence Therrien.

4. Florence Angeline was born circa 1895. She married Bert Squires (son of Stephen Squires and Kitty Leightener) on 23 November 1913 in Detroit, Michigan.[8]
5. Laurence was born 5 Aug 1896,[9] and died 26 August 1896.[10]
6. Herbert Arthur was born circa 1897. He married Katherine Martin (daughter of Joseph Martin and Katherine Deloria) on 31 May 1916 at Mackinac Island.[11]
7. Peter was born in 1900 and died 9 August 1900.[12]

Peter Isaac Terrien Jr. died on 3 November 1911 and was buried on Mackinac Island.[13] Angeline died 25 July 1929 and was buried next to her husband in the Protestant Cemetery on Mackinac Island.[14]

The Mackinac Island fire brigade circa 1900. *Left to right*: Darius Bunker, John Francis, Augustin "Gus" Bazinaw, Mackinac Island superintendent B. Frank Emery, Pete Therrien, and unknown. COURTESY OF ROGER HORN.

Bert Squires and Florence Therrien.
COURTESY OF ROGER HORN.

Anthony Thompson military marker in the Old Soldiers' Cemetery, Grand Rapids. COURTESY OF CRYSTAL KIMBLE.

61. Mrs. Margueritta Thompson (Margaret Pouillat)

Marguerite Pouillat (Bouillat, Poulliotte) was born 10 February 1853 at L'Arbre Croche.[1] Her parents were Pierre Pouillat and Josette LaRiviere (Weshebenase), who married on 01 August 1842.[2] Josette died and was buried in Ste. Anne's Cemetery on Mackinac Island on 18 December 1862.[3] Later, Peter married Margarethe Kinikwe and lived with her at Cross Village. He died 14 June 1893 at Cross Village.[4]

Marguerite married Anthony Thompson on 11 January 1870 by Justice of the Peace, Peter Hombach,.[5] Anthony was a soldier at Fort Mackinac and was a son of Joseph Thompson, from Scotland, and Sarah or Jane Nightengale. He was born 29 October 1845 in St. Clair, Michigan.[6] He enlisted in the Army on 28 September 1868 and served his enlistment at Fort Mackinac. He was discharged 28 September 1871.[7]

From this marriage there were at least 5 children:

1. Edwin was born 16 December 1871.[8] He died single on 19 June 1920 in Escanaba, Michigan.[9]
2. Louisa was born 2 March 1874.[10] She first married John B. Levack on 7 December 1889 in Harbor Springs, Michigan.[11] He was the son of Narcis Levack and Josette Seguin. He later sued Louisa for divorce. It was granted 06 February 1900.[12] She then married Emory Welch.[13] She died 18 September 1931 in Lansing, Michigan.[14]
3. Lucy was born 05 March 1874 at Cross Village, Michigan.[15] She died 18 October 1884.[16]

4. Harriet Joanna was born 20 May 1875.[17] She died 24 September 1877.[18]
5. Elizabeth was born 24 October 1876 at Cross Village, Michigan.[19] She died 05 November 1876.[20]

Marguerite died 23 July 1885 in Cross Village.[21] Anthony went back to St. Clair county where he married Emily Hazen on 24 December 1887 in Wayne, Michigan.[22] After she died, he married Emma Drone on 14 December 1892 in East China, St. Clair county, Michigan.[23] As of the 1910 Census, he was an "inmate" of the Old Soldiers' Home in Grand Rapids.[24] He died on 31 December 1915[25] and was buried there with a military headstone.

66. William Valier

William Valier was the son of Antoine Valier and an unknown Native woman. He was born circa 1825 in Canada. He first appears in the Mackinac area on the 1850 Mackinac County census in the household of Louis Claus. He does not appear on the 1836 Half Breed Census, nor in any application in the 1837 Treaty of Lake Superior Chippewa. He was not found in a voyageur contract. He was not found in the *Programme de recherche en démographie historique* (Research program in historical demography). No relation to the Damase/Thomas Vallier family was found.

William married Rosalie Paquin (daughter of Joseph Paquin and Marianne Aslin of St. Cuthbert, Quebec) on 17 February 1851, at St. Ignatius Loyola Church in St. Ignace.[1] She was born 30 January 1835 and baptized at St. Cuthbert, Quebec.[2]

There were at least seven children born to this couple:

1. Antoine was born 10 April 1852 and was baptized at St. Ignatius.[3] He married Lucy Martineau (daughter of Oliver Martineau and Marie McGulpin) on 10 May 1872.[4]
2. Rosine was born 5 January 1854 and was baptized at St. Ignatius.[5]
3. William was born circa 1855. He married Julianna Martineau, sister of Lucy Martineau, on 8 May 1876 at St. Ignatius.[6]
4. Josephine was born 26 November 1857 and baptized at St. Ignatius.[7] She married Robert Johnson. Josephine died 29 November 1940 and was buried at St. Ignatius cemetery.[8]
5. John Benjamin was born 25 October 1859 and was baptized at St. Ignatius.[9]

6. Thomas Leander was born 8 December 1861 and was baptized at St. Ignatius.[10] He died 6 October 1922,[11] and was buried in Engadine, Michigan.

7. Joseph was born 14 December 1863 and was baptized at St. Ignatius.[12] He married Mary Gallagher.

William died 9 April 1895,[13] and was buried in the St. Ignatius Cemetery in St. Ignace. Rosalie died 13 October 1910 and was buried at St. Ignatius Cemetery.[14]

50. Mrs. Henry Vaillancourt (Catherine LaCroix)

Catherine LaCroix was the daughter of Pierre Isidore LaCroix. She was born 2 March 1806 and baptized 15 August 1823 by Father Gabriel Richard.[1] Catherine's baptism record from Ste. Anne's on Mackinac Island states that her mother was Angelique of the Osage Nation;[2] however, she appears on the 1836 Half Breed Census of Ottawa and Chippewa as Catherine Vincencourt who was half-Chippewa.[3] Both Catherine and her daughter, also Catherine, were awarded second-class status and received $305.89 each.

Henry Vaillancourt was born on Mackinac Island on 29 September 1802.[4] At nine years of age, on 1 March 1812,[5] he enlisted into military service as a musician at Fort Michilimackinac where his father, Joseph, was a sergeant: "Henry brother of Marie, was a drummer boy at the Fort 9 years old when the British under Captain Roberts, captured Mackinac July 17, 1812. Henry Vaillancourt was enlisted by Lieutenant Porter Hanks, March 1, 1812."[6] As a part of the drumming corps, a description of his duties may have been: "transmitting orders . . . regulate camp duties and to help with morale. It kind of takes your mind from the arduous task of long-distance marching if you hear something."[7] Additional duties for drummer boys included the following: "During the 18th and 19th centuries, the term 'boy' often meant apprentice, and that many drummer boys were just that to older Army musicians and officers. Their duties could include acting as servants to the officers or as assistants to the unit surgeons."[8]

War was declared between the United States and Great Britain on 18 June 1812. On 17 July 1812, the British took Fort Mackinac from the Americans without firing a shot. Henry, along with his father and two brothers, were among the men taken as prisoners of war.[9] From Mackinac, the prisoners were shipped to Detroit and then on to Fort Fayette near Pittsburgh. According to Henry's enlistment register, he was paroled by the British from Fort Fayette in November of 1812.[10] Records of his whereabouts begin again in 1815, where he spent time at Fort Niagara in Captain Benjamin K. Pierce's Artillery unit. The war ended in March 1815 with the final defeat of Great Britain. Henry's artillery unit returned to Fort Michilimackinac, where he served the remaining two years of his enlistment. Here, he continued to serve under the command of Captain Benjamin K. Pierce until 28 February 1817 when he was discharged at the age of fourteen.[11]

After life in the army, records indicate Henry became engaged in the fur trade. He appears on the American Fur Company roster for the Upper Mississippi Outfit for 1829.[12] In 1833, he was listed on a roster of fishermen who requested Henry Schoolcraft retain "the right and privaledge [sic] which they have heretofore had enabling them to fish at the fishing grounds known by the name of Roufett Island and Mill O Coquin and its vicinity."[13] In 1839, he was granted a license by Henry Schoolcraft to trade on Goose Island.[14]

Catherine LaCroix and Henry Vaillancourt were married at Ste. Anne's on 21 May 1838.[15] They made their home on Mackinac Island. From this marriage, there were at least nine children:

1. Catherine was born 21 September 1834 on Mackinac Island.[16] She married David William McGulpin at Ste. Anne's on 13 September 1852.[17]

2. Henry was born 27 March 1839 and baptized at Ste. Anne's.[18] He married Salomée Delaurier (daughter of David Delaurier and Catherine Perrault), at Ste. Anne's on 11 April 1864. Henry enlisted in Company K, 7th Michigan Cavalry on 20 March 1864,[19] and mustered in on 28 April 1864.[20] He went missing in action at Front Royal, Virginia, 16 August 1864.[21] His widow applied for benefits 5 June 1865.[22]

3. Marie-Therese was born 17 May 1841 and baptized at Ste. Anne's.[23] No additional information was found on her.

4-5. Peter and Paul, twins, were born 26 September 1842.[24] No additional information was found on the twins.

6. Andrew (Andre) was born 31 March 1844 and baptized at Ste. Anne's.[25]

7. Timothy Vincent was born on 10 June 1847 and baptized at Ste. Anne's.[26] He first married Marie Beaudoin on 12 September 1869 at Ste. Anne's.[27] After she died, he married Grace Bourisaw on 30 January 1911.[28] He died 28 April 1917 and was buried on Mackinac Island.[29]

8. Joseph Edward was born 4 July 1849 and baptized at Ste. Anne's.[30] No additional information was found on him.

9. David Henry was born 3 August 1853 and baptized at Ste. Anne's.[31] No additional information was found on him.

Henry and Catherine spent their lives on Mackinac Island. He died there on 8 December 1877 and was buried in Ste. Anne's Cemetery. Catherine died 4 November 1881 and was buried in Ste. Anne's Cemetery. Currently, they do not have a marker.

28. Mrs. Thomas Valliere (Josette Thibault)

Josette Thibault was born around 1810 in Wisconsin. To date, her parents remain unknown.

Damase Leandre Valliere was born 9 December 1797, son of Jean Baptiste and Marguerite Cornellier dite Grand Champ.[1] Born in Quebec, the family emigrated to York (Toronto) around 1798.[2] Later, Leandre and his brother, Angus, settled in Penetanguishene where they worked for the Naval Establishment.[3]

Where Josette and Damase were married remains unknown. Judging by the births of the earliest child, they were probably married around 1825. Damase/Thomas worked in a civilian position as a carpenter for the Naval Establishment in Penetanguishene until at least 1829. The local Catholic church did not begin recording sacraments until 1835.

Damase/Thomas and Josette had at least a dozen children.

1. Marie Louise was born circa 1826. She married Amable Goudreau (son of Louis Goudreau and Marguerite Robitaille) on 25 May 1847 at St. Ignatius in St. Ignace.[4] According to the marriage records, Marie Louise's family name was Brouillard, but in other records, it is listed as Vallier.

   The Goudreaus were a hard-working fishing family that established the village of Epoufette on the northern shore of Lake Michigan in Mackinac County. Amable and Marie became the in-laws of Genevieve Derusha when she married their son, Louis. Genevieve described her father-in-law and their connection to the Valliers in the following paragraph:

   Amable Goudreau, whose fish business was booming, had a large warehouse in Epoufette in one corner of which these festive occasions took place. The barrels and crates were shunted aside to allow the celebrants plenty of room and music was supplied by the village's two most accomplished fiddlers, Aunt Jane's father,

Right: Damase Valiere and Josette Thibault Valiere. *Left*: Unknown.
TINTYPE COURTESY OF JANE DEVOTA.

Joseph and Jim Vallier. Jim Vallier, a brother-in-law of Amable Goudreau (his sister Marie married Amable), was married to Frazine LaJoie, Aunt Jane's maternal aunt. . . . Jim and Frazine Vallier had four sons, Henry, John, Oliver and Joseph of whom John and Oliver still survive and reside in St. Ignace.[5]

2. The first child of this couple, Marie, was born 4 October 1844. She was baptized in February of the following year, and her godparents were Leander Vallier and Josepha Tibeau.[6] In 1849, William Vallier and Margaret Vallier were godparents for Abraham Goudreau. In 1853, Joseph Blanchett (Blanchard) and his wife, Isabelle Vallier, were the godparents for Caroline Goudreau. In 1859, Marianne Vallier was godmother to Josette Bernadine Goudreau. While not primary source evidence, the honor of being a godparent usually goes to closely related family members. Amable died 19 August 1882,[7] and Marie Louise died 24 December 1895; they were buried together in St. Ignatius Cemetery.[8]

3. Margaret Genevieve was born 25 December 1826.[9] She was married to John Wagley (son of Abraham Wagley and Polly Henson) 5 February 1846 on Mackinac Island by Judge Shurtleff.[10] Captain Wagley died 28 May 1888 and was buried in Cross Village.[11] Margaret died 7 November 1904. Her life, and that of her husband, was summed up in Margaret's obituary describing some of their adventures:

Cross Village 1890s. COURTESY OF MARY SHURTLEFF COLLECTION, BENTLEY HISTORICAL LIBRARY, UNIVERSITY OF MICHIGAN.

Mrs. Margaret Wagley, wife of Captain John Wagley, passed away at her home in Cross Village at the age of 80 years. The Captain and Mrs. Wagley were among the earliest settlers of this region, coming here about 60 years ago. They were married in 1846 by Judge Shurtlefff at Cross Village. Captain Wagley built the first dock at Cross Village, and as boat owner and captain was closely identified with the early fishing and lumbering of this lake region. His boat, the *Abel*, carried 60 men to Beaver Island when the attempt to drive King Strang and the Mormons out of the country was made. The funeral of Mrs. Wagley was held Friday afternoon. She is survived by eight children.[12]

Mrs. Wagley is listed in the Durant Roll under no. 103/22. Her mother was identified as "Indian and named Vallier."[13]

4. Elizabeth/Isabelle was born 30 July 1832.[14] She married Joseph Blanchard (son of Isaac Blanchard and no. 36 Mary Babeau) circa 1851. He died 28 April 1880,[15] and Isabelle died 18 May 1903 and was buried with her husband in Gros Cap Cemetery.[16]

5. Sophia was born 27 March 1836 in Penetanguishene, Ontario.[17] She married Frank Sawyer. No marriage record was found for this couple. In the 1850 Mackinac County census, Frank Sawyer was living with the Wagleys. In the 1870 census, Sophie is in the Mackinac area with two children, Marie and François. She is listed as married, but Frank Sawyer is not enumerated with her. She died 1 July 1900.[18]

6. Samuel was born 2 April 1838 in Sault Ste. Marie.[19] He married Margaret Abbott (daughter of Samuel Abbott and Bridget St. Cyr) on 12 December 1858

Left: Frazine Lajoie Vallier.
COURTESY OF MARION KING.

Right: Frank O. Sawyer.
COURTESY OF THE VERMONT HISTORICAL SOCIETY.

at St. Ignatius in St. Ignace, Michigan.[20] He died 19 May 1892,[21] and Margaret died 14 October 1894.[22] They were buried together in Gros Cap Cemetery.

7. Marianne was born 7 January 1841 and baptized at St. Ignatius in St. Ignace.[23] She married Jean Baptiste Champagne on 5 May 1867 at St. Ignatius.[24]

8. James was born 6 March 1843. He married Frazine Lajoie (daughter of Louis Lajoie and Marie Levake) on 13 May 1868 at St. Ignatius.[25] She was born 11 December 1846 on Owen Sound, Georgian Bay, Ontario.[26] Frazine died 29 November 1905,[27] and James died 6 October 1915.[28] They were buried together in Gros Cap Cemetery.

9. Jane was born circa 1845.

10. Alice was born circa 1847. She married Frederick Lavake (son of Isaac Lavake and Susan Iyabins) on 5 August 1893.[29] Alice died 13 March 1896 in Moran, Michigan.[30]

11. Celestina was born 11 April 1849 in St. Ignace, Michigan.[31]

12. Thomas Leander was born 28 February 1849 and baptized at St. Ignatius.[32] He married Marianne Martin (daughter of Antoine Martin and Marie Louise Paquin) on 18 April 1873 at St. Ignatius.[33] He died 3 October 1916 and was buried in Manistique, Michigan.
13. Caroline was born in December 1851 and baptized at St. Ignatius on 7 March 1852.[34]

Thomas died on 30 April 1882,[35] and Josette died 24 March 1889 and was buried in Gros Cap Cemetery.[36]

60. Mama Walsh

There is no data on the worksheet to determine who she was. She was not on the 1868 annuity payment roster, so she was a late addition. The only Walsh or Welch family found in the area was from Ireland.

Durant Correspondence to the Commissioner of Indian Affairs

The Honorable

Commissioner of Indian Affairs.

Sir:

According to a long established law and custom of our tribe our half-breed or mixed-blood relatives do not share in payments made to the tribe without consent of the chiefs and headmen, who designate by name what mixed-bloods, and how many of their children, should participate.

Such was the custom and practice in 1870 and prior thereto and this has never been changed. Sufficient and conclusive proof of such law and custom can be had by an examination and investigation of all the rolls of the tribe.

Therefore, we, the undersigned chiefs and headmen of the various bands and sub-bands of the Ottawa and Chippewa Tribe of Indians of Michigan following the traditions and customs of the tribe hereby designate the persons who were enrolled with the tribe in 1870 as mixed-bloods or half-breeds, and, while agreeing that they may be enrolled on the roll now in preparation by Special Agent Horace B. Durant, and participate in the distribution of funds awarded to us by the judgment of the Court of Claims, if living,- at the same time we do most solemnly and earnestly protest against the enrollment of such of the children or other descendants of the within named half-breeds or mixed-bloods as were not enrolled with the tribe in 1870,-

Mixed-bloods of the _Mackinac_ Band.

Number and page on the roll of 1870.	Name
20 - 11	George La Belle
24 "	Leon Belonghay
25 "	Paul Aelin
26 "	Modor Dophena
27 "	Alex Dophena
28 "	Thomas Ward
29 "	Louis Belonghay
30 "	Mrs Mary Walkertin's children

3	12	John B. Cadotte	26	13	Mrs. [illegible] Belonghay
5	12	[illegible] Cadotte	27	13	Mrs. Chas. [illegible]
8	12	Mrs. Hyacinthe Deplanje	28	13	Mrs. Thomas Villaire
12	12	" Francis "	29	13	Mrs. Mary A. Karrow
14	12	" Mary A. Parrow	30	13	Mrs. Bela Chapman
20	12	Joseph Paul	31	13	Mrs. [illegible] Lampson
25	12	Mrs. Philemon Barton	32	13	Mrs. Joseph Lelotte
1	13	Mrs. Agathe Biddle	33	13	D[illegible] Karrow
2	13	Mrs. Louis Michler	34	13	Mrs. Sarah Champaign
3	13	Mrs. Andrew Moran	35	13	Mrs. Alice Lalone
4	13	Mrs. Edward Cooley	36	13	Mrs. Lena Blanchard
5	13	Mrs. Joseph Karrow	37	13	Miss Martha Turner
6	13	Mrs. Charles Bennett	38	13	Mrs. Louis Bauvais
7	13	Mrs. Wm Karrow	39	13	Mrs. Joseph Chevron
8	13	Mrs. Louis Cadotte	40	13	Miss Nancy McGulphin
9	13	Mrs. Alice Cushing	41	13	Mrs. Joseph Leslie
10	13	Mrs. Henry Karrow	42	14	Mrs. Wm Davenport, Sr
11	13	Mrs. Ignatius Pelotie	43	14	Mrs. Louis Belonghay
12	13	Mrs. Jane & Louise [illegible]	44	14	Mrs. Joseph Menard, Sr
13	13	Mrs. Francis Restoul	45	14	Mrs. Samuel Le Blanc
14	13	Mrs. Joseph Fountain	46	14	Mrs. Louis St Onge
15	13	Mrs. Francis Johnson	47	14	Mrs. Rosalie Louisignore
16	13	Mrs. Mary Hudson [illegible]	48	14	Mrs. Benjamin Rice
17	13	Mrs. Betsey Champaign	49	14	Mrs. Benj. McGulphin
18	13	Mrs. David Moran	50	14	Mrs. Henry Valmore
19	13	Mrs. David Karrow	51	14	Mrs. Jane Lareau
20	13	Mrs. Vieln Bauvais	52	14	Miss Mary McGulphin
21	13	Mrs. Francis Martin	53	14	Mrs. Moses Maceedo
22	13	Mrs. Peter Jacobson	54	14	Mrs. Angelica Louisignore
23	13	Mrs. Hyacinthe Deplan	55	14	Miss Lizzie Martin
24	13	Miss Kate Fleming & Sister & Bro.	56	14	Mrs. Mary Bazinet
25	13	Mrs. Michael Karrow	57	14	Edward Karrow

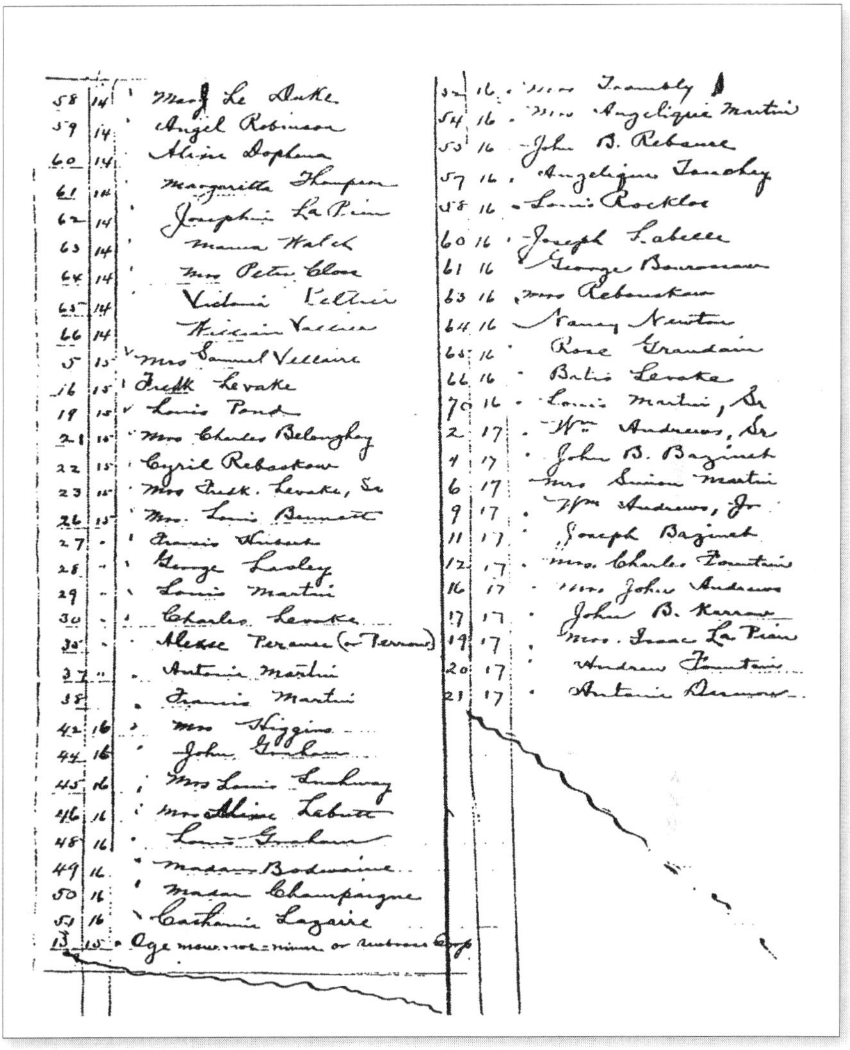

58	14	Mary Le Duke
59	14	Angel Robinson
60	14	Aleine Doplena
61	14	Margaritta Thompson
62	14	Josephine La Pine
63	14	Maria Walch
64	14	Mrs Peter Close
65	14	Victoria Vellier
66	14	William Vallier
5	15	Mrs Samuel Velliare
16	15	Fredk Levake
19	15	Louis Pond
21	15	Mrs Charles Belongley
22	15	Cyril Rebaskow
23	15	Mrs Fredk. Levake, Sr
26	15	Mrs. Louis Bennett
27	"	Francis Hinault
28	"	George Lasley
29	"	Louis Martin
30	"	Charles Levake
35	"	Alexse Peranee (or Perron)
37	"	Antoine Martin
38		Francis Martin
42	16	Mrs Higgins
44	16	John Graham
45	16	Mrs Louis Lashway
46	16	Mrs Aleine Labutte
48	16	Louis Graham
49	16	Madam Bodwaine
50	16	Madam Champaigne
51	16	Catharine Lazaire
13	15	Age more - not - nine or sixteen [illegible]
52	16	Mrs Trombly
54	16	Mrs Angelique Martin
55	16	John B. Rebanse
57	16	Angelique Tanchey
58	16	Louis Rocklos
60	16	Joseph Labelle
61	16	George Bonneman
63	16	Mrs Rebaskaw
64	16	Nancy Newton
65	16	Rose Grandain
66	16	Batis Levake
70	16	Louis Martin, Sr
2	17	Wm Andrews, Sr
4	17	John B. Bazinet
6	17	Mrs Simon Martin
9	17	Wm Andrews, Jr
11	17	Joseph Bazinet
12	17	Mrs. Charles Fountain
16	17	Mrs John Andrews
17	17	John B. Kerrau
19	17	Mrs. Isaac La Pine
20	17	Andrew Fountain
21	17	Antoine Desnoer

I, Louis La'Sage, hereby certify, that I have this day read the foregoing petition to the undersigned chiefs & headmen of the Mackinac Band, and have duly explained the same to them in the Indian language; & that they fully understand the same, and that they signed the same in my presence.

Louis Lasage

In witness whereof we have hereunto affixed our signatures this _9th_ day of _August_ 1909.

In behalf of the _Mackinac_ Band.

Witness to signatures by mark
Homer B. Drouach
spl agent

Louis Lasage   Amable   his X mark   Acc. Chief

Edl. Boucha   Joseph   his X mark   Mesowitego headman

                Francis   his X mark   Graham headman

_____ headman

_____ headman

_____ headman.

I hereby certify to the correctness of the above petition, that the same is fully understood by the signers who sufficiently understand the English language to comprehend the meaning thereof and its effect.

Homer B. Drouach
Spl Ind. Agent

Aug. 9. 1909
St. Ignace, Mich.

Notes

Preface

1. The data in this book is organized alphabetically based on the annuity list of 1870 for the Mackinac Island band.

2. For a discussion of Anishinaabeg social order, see Charles E. Cleland, "A Sense of Time, a Sense of Place," *Rites of Conquest: The History and Culture of Michigan's Native Americans* (Ann Arbor: University of Michigan Press, 1992).

3. Treaty of Detroit, 1855, Clark Historical Library, Central Michigan University, https://www.cmich.edu/library/clarke/ResearchResources/Native_American_Material/Treaty_Rights/Text_of_Michigan_Related_Treaties/Detroit_1855/Pages/Ottawa-and-Chippewa.aspx. For a comprehensive account of the history of both the 1836 Treaty of Washington, DC, and its supplement, the 1855 Treaty of Detroit, see Charles Cleland, *Faith in Paper: The Ethnohistory and Litigation of Upper Great Lakes Indian Treaties* (Ann Arbor: University of Michigan Press, 2014).

4. "Correspondence, Field Notes, and the Census Roll of All Members or Descendants of Members who Were on the Roll of the Ottawa and Ojibwe Tribes of Michigan in 1870, and Living on March 4, 1907 (Durant Roll)," National Archives Microcopy 2039, reel 4, file 45533-08-053, 3 of 7.

38. Mrs. Louis Beaubien (Christine Otapitakewinam)

1. *Liber Matrimonium*, in *Mackinac Register, 1695–1888* (Mackinac Island, MI: Ste. Anne Church, [2000?]), p. 6, compact disc. This CD contains the following: "Baptismal Register," *Liber Matrimonium, Liber Defunctorum,* and "Indexes and Miscellaneous."

2. "Baptismal Register," *Mackinac Register, 1695–1888,* 6. The Beaubins had this child before the priest was available to bless their union. She was made "legitimate" by this marriage. This practice was common at the time. The community recognized the couple as more or less married, and it was not deemed inappropriate. This family went by several names: Beubin, Beauben, Bennet, or Bennet-Beaubin. Some family members are listed in Ste. Anne's registers under Binnet.

3. "Baptismal Register," *Mackinac Register, 1695–1888,* 22. See under "Beaubien."

4. Michigan State Archives, "Death Records, 1897–1920," *Michiganology*, entry for Mary Kniffen, 1911, https://michiganology.org.

5. "Baptismal Register," *Mackinac Register, 1695–1888*, 36.

6. "Baptismal Register," *Mackinac Register, 1695–1888*, 42.

7. Larry Wyckoff, trans., "Mixed-Blood Census Register, Ottawas and Chippewas of Michigan, Treaty of March 26, 1836," *Roots Web*, http://www.rootsweb.ancestry.com/~mimacki2/annuities/1836mb.pdf, n.d., no. 220.

8. St. Ignatius Loyola (St. Ignace, Michigan), "Marriages, 1838–1893," pp. 20–21, parish office. The groom's name in this case was listed as Barrette instead of Bennett. A single child was recorded at Ste. Anne's under the name Benette from these parents. A death record for "Rachel Bennett" was recorded at Ste. Anne's, 12 June 1880.

9. *Durant Census Roll of the Ottawas and Chippewas of Michigan and the 1908 Supplemental Census Roll* (Washington, DC: National Archives and Records Service, 1969), under Leon Belanger, microfilm publication M2039, roll 1, p. 11, no. 24.

10. *Liber Defunctorum, Mackinac Register, 1695–1888*, 102.

11. "Baptismal Register," *Mackinac Register, 1695–1888*, 52.

12. "Baptismal Register," *Mackinac Register, 1695–1888*, 72.

13. "Baptismal Register," *Mackinac Register, 1695–1888*, 89.

14. "Baptismal Register," *Mackinac Register, 1695–1888,* 103. See "Joseph Bobin."

15. *Liber Defunctorum, Mackinac Register, 1695–1888*, 90. See "Ludivicus Beaubin dit Bennet."

16. "Michigan Deaths and Burials, 1800–1995," *Family Search,* database, https://familysearch.org/, under Daguinan Bennet, 9 December 1876, citing Beaugrand, Cheboygan, MI, reference vol. 1 p. 7; Family History Library (FHL) microfilm 964,407. I strongly believe this is Christine Otapitakawinam Bennet. The first name listed on the death register is probably a derivation of her Indian name; this person is also listed as a half-breed.

43. Mrs. Louis Belonzhay (Genevieve Montreuil)

1. *Mackinac Register, 1695–1888,* Baptismal Register, 44–45. See Genevieve Montri.
2. "Québec, registres paroissiaux catholiques, 1621–1979," *Family Search,* database with images, https://familysearch.org, "Saint-Michel-d'Yamaska," image 683 of 710, *Nos paroisses de Église Catholique, Québec* (Catholic Church parishes, Quebec).
3. *Liber Matrimonium, Mackinac Register, 1695–1888,* 10.
4. "Baptismal Register," *Mackinac Register, 1695–1888,* 52.
5. "Baptismal Register," *Mackinac Register, 1695–1888,* 62.
6. "Baptismal Register," *Mackinac Register, 1695–1888,* 85.
7. "Baptismal Register," *Mackinac Register, 1695–1888,* 92.
8. Michigan State Archives, "Death Records, 1897–1920," *Michiganology,* entry for Louis Belanga, 1923, https://michiganology.org.
9. "Baptismal Register," *Mackinac Register, 1695–1888,* 101.
10. "Baptismal Register," *Mackinac Register, 1695–1888,* 131. See Bellanger.
11. St. Ignatius Loyola (St. Ignace, MI), "Deaths, 1838–1893," p. 15 (Montreuil [Belanger], 1879), parish rectory. The church listed her first name as Joanna although her name was Genevieve and went by Jane.
12. "Michigan Deaths and Burials, 1800–1995," *Family Search,* database, https://familysearch.org/, under Louis Belonga, 10 March 1895, citing St. Ignace, Mackinac, MI, reference years 1873–1899, p. 87, Family History Library (FHL) microfilm 1,007,364. Please note Louis's death is recorded under the name "Belonga," which is the current spelling.

26. Mrs. Paul Belonzhay (Angelique Montreuil)

1. Theresa M. Schenck, *All Our Relations: Chippewa Mixed-Bloods and the Treaty of 1837* (Winnipeg, Manitoba: The Center for Rupert's Land Studies at the University of Winnipeg, 2010), 24.
2. Schenck, *All Our Relations,* 60–61.
3. "American Fur Company," vertical file, n.d., Petersen Library, Mackinac State Historic Parks (MSHP), Mackinaw City, MI.
4. "American Fur Company," vertical file, MSHP.
5. Marriage record of Paul Belanger and Angelique Montraine, "Port of Mackinac Records," Office of the Register of Deeds, St. Ignace, Mackinac County, MI, p. 84, no. 95.
6. "Québec, registres paroissiaux catholiques, 1621–1979," *Family Search,* database with images, https://familysearch.org, "Sainte-Anne-d'Yamachiche," image 577 of 618, *Nos paroisses de Église Catholique, Québec* (Catholic Church parishes, Quebec). This baptism is for Paul LeFebvre. Documenting that this person was indeed the spouse of Angelique Montreuil was determined through Paul's brother Benjamin. There were three marriages

in the Mackinac area for Benjamin Belanger in which Paul and his wife stood witness. One of those marriages (to Catherine Plante, 2 June 1857 [under Bellanger]) listed his parents and home parish in Quebec. After locating the parents and their children, the data proved that Benjamin and Paul's true surname was LeFebvre dit *Boulanger*, not Belanger, and that they were born of the same parents in Yamachiche, Quebec.

7. *Liber Matrimonium, Mackinac Register, 1695–1888*, 33.

8. Daughters of the American Revolution, Louisa St. Clair Chapter, *Vital Records from the Detroit Free Press/Michigan Works Progress Administration/Vital Records Project, 1831–1868*, 17 vols. (Detroit: *Detroit Free Press*, [1939?]), 4:70. *Detroit Free Press*, 4 June 1853, p. 2, col. 1, follows: "Accident at Birch Point–A correspondent at Mackinac informs us that an accident occurred on Wednesday Morning last at Birch Point in that county, which resulted in the death of Lucy, wife of Wm. Davenport, Jr. of the Island. Mr. D. was at Birch Point with his family, engaged in fishing. On the morning stated he took down his gun (a double barreled one) from its place in his house, for the purpose of going out hunting. Whilst examining the gun to see if the caps were adjusted properly, one of the barrels went off, lodging the whole charge in the head of his wife, killing her instantly. Her remains were brought down to Mackinac on Wednesday, and a coroner's jury being summoned, returned a verdict in accordance with the facts above state. Mrs. D. was only about 18 years of age and leaves a child only four months old."

9. *Liber Matrimonium, Mackinac Register, 1695–1888,* 48–49, under the name "Bellanger." Some marriages have two pages because the groom's information is on one side and the bride's is on the other.

10. "Leon Belongia," obituary, *St. Ignace Enterprise,* 4 March 1915, p. 6, col. 1.

11. *Liber Matrimonium, Mackinac Register, 1695–1888*, 58–59.

12. *Liber Matrimonium, Mackinac Register, 1695–1888*, 58–59.

13. *Liber Matrimonium, Mackinac Register, 1695–1888*, 72

14. "Baptismal Register," *Mackinac Register, 1695–1888*, 88. See Belange.

15. *Liber Matrimonium, Mackinac Register, 1695–1888*, 48–49.

16. "Baptismal Register," *Mackinac Register, 1695–1888*, 113.

17. *Liber Matrimonium, Mackinac Register, 1695–1888*, 56–57.

18. "Baptismal Register," *Mackinac Register, 1695–1888*, 153.

19. *Liber Matrimonium, Mackinac Register, 1695–1888*, 70–71.

20. "Baptismal Register," *Mackinac Register, 1695–1888*, 172.

21. "Michigan Deaths and Burials, 1800–1995," *Family Search,* database, https://familysearch.org/, under Louis Belonger and Mollie M. Mcgulpin, 22 September 1878, citing Family History Library (FHL) microfilm 1,007,362.

22. *Durant Census Roll of the Ottawas and Chippewas of Michigan and the 1908 Supplemental*

Census Roll (Washington, DC: National Archives and Records Service, 1969), microfilm publication M2039, Louis Belonzhay, 29/11.

23. "Baptismal Register," *Mackinac Register, 1695–1888*, 184.

24. "Baptismal Register," *Mackinac Register, 1695–1888*, 190.

25. "Michigan Marriages, 1822–1995," *Family Search*, database, https://familysearch.org, under Joseph Belonga and Bridget Gallagher, 15 October 1886, citing FHL microfilm 2,342,479.

26. "Baptismal Register," *Mackinac Register, 1695–1888*, 194. See Clement Bellangier.

27. "Michigan Marriages, 1868–1925," *Family Search*, database with images, https://familysearch.org, under Clement Belonga and Libby Fountain, 31 August 1889, citing "Marriage: Mackinac, Michigan," Michigan Secretary of State, Department of Vital Records, Lansing, FHL microfilm 4,207,809.

28. "Find a Grave Index," *FamilySearch*, database, https://familysearch.org, under Mary Boulanger Wachter, 1893, Burial: Mackinac, Michigan, United States of America, Gould City Township Cemetery, record ID 69445577, *Find a Grave*, http://www.findagrave.com.

29. Paul Belonga and wife to Walter Donovan, indenture, 6 December 1893, Office of the Register of Deeds, St. Ignace, Mackinac County, MI, Deed Record, bk. 10, p. 68.

6. Mrs. Charles Bennett (Angelique Antoine)

1. Antoine was her father's given name. Taking the father's first name as a surname was a common Anishinaabe practice. Edward Heidcan, *Social Anthropology: Canadian Perspectives on Culture and Society* (Toronto: Canadian Scholars Press, 2012), 213:

> "Personal names are another symbol of identity. In Euro-Canadian society the child takes the surname of his or her father, but this is not a universal pattern. In my research among the Anishenabe (Ojibwa) of Northern Ontario, when I was constructing people's genealogy, I discovered that some families used at least two surnames, one English and the other Aboriginal. For example, one family was known among the local residents as 'Shawahamish,' but used the name 'Slipperjack' for treaty and other outside purposes. When treaties were signed, most Anishenabe did not use a surname, perhaps thinking that a surname was the same as the name of their clan. When asked for their name when signing a treaty, they might have said, 'Peter Wolf,' and that surname stuck. Others, unsure of what to do when asked for a surname, gave the name of their local Hudson's Bay factor. Another form of identification was the Aboriginal trapping territory, so one might have identified himself or herself with this location when asked for a surname. Once these names were written down, and outsiders asked on repeated occasions for a surname, it became a routine matter to use the same one over and over, thus making such names more or less permanent."

2. Charles Joseph Kappler, ed. and compiler, "Treaty with the Ottawa, etc., 1836," in *Indian Affairs: Laws and Treaties*, vol. 2, *Treaties* (Washington, DC: Government Printing Office, 1904), p. 455, https://dc.library.okstate.edu/digital/collection/kapplers/id/26296/rec/1.

3. *Ste. Anne's Church Registers: 1704–1842*, microfilm, 3 rolls (Detroit, MI: St. Anne's of Detroit). See roll 3, *Chapelle du nordest: Baptisms, Marriages, Burials, 1810–1838*, p. 109.

4. *Ste. Anne's Church [Detroit] Registers: 1704–1842*, 117. See Saquitandawoué.

5. *Ste. Anne's Church [Detroit] Registers: 1704–1842*, 110. See Thérèse Sanguitandowé.

6. *Ste. Anne's Church [Detroit] Registers: 1704–1842*, 113. See Louis Sakitandowé.

7. *Ste. Anne's Church [Detroit] Registers: 1704–1842*, 119. See Louis Saguitandawoue Wabinini.

8. *Ste. Anne's Church [Detroit] Registers: 1704–1842*, 119. See Louis Saguitandawoue Wabinini.

9. *Ste. Anne's Church [Detroit] Registers: 1704–1842*, 119. See Louis Saguitandawoue Wabinini.

10. *Ste. Anne's Church [Detroit] Registers: 1704–1842*, 119. See Louis Saguitandawoue Wabinini.

11. "Baptismal Register," *Mackinac Register, 1695–1888*, 72. See Charles Beaubin.

12. *Holy Cross Church Records* (Cross Village, MI), microfilm publication, one roll (Ann Arbor, MI: Bentley Historical Library, University of Michigan), roll 1, arranged mostly alphabetically; see family 13, "Carolus Bennet."

13. Emmet County, *Vital Records Search*, searchable database, http://apps.emmetcounty.org/clerk/marriagerecords.aspx, under William Onenagons and Joanna Benett, 22 February, 1876, liber 1, folio 9.

14. "Baptismal Register," *Mackinac Register, 1695–1888*, 196. See Lucy Benett.

15. "Michigan Marriages, 1822–1995," *FamilySearch*, database, https://familysearch.org, under Frank Dofinais and Lucy Bennett, 19 November 1883, citing Family History Library (FHL) microfilm 964,409.

16. *Holy Cross Church Records* (Cross Village, MI), roll 1, see family 13, "Carolus Bennet."

17. "Baptismal Register," *Mackinac Register, 1695–1888*, 205. See Benette.

18. *Holy Cross Church Records*, roll 1, see family 13, "Carolus Bennet."

19. *Holy Cross Church Records*, roll 1, see family 13, "Carolus Bennet."

20. *Holy Cross Church Records*, roll 1, see family 13, "Carolus Bennet."

21. *Holy Cross Church Records*, roll 1, see family 13, "Carolus Bennet."

22. *Holy Cross Church Records*, roll 1, see family 13, "Carolus Bennet."

23. *Holy Cross Church Records*, roll 1, see family 13, "Carolus Bennet."

24. *Holy Cross Church Records*, roll 1, see family 13, "Carolus Bennet."

25. "United States Census, 1910," *Family Search*, database with images, https://familysearch.org, under Charles Bennet, Mackinaw, Cheboygan, Michigan, United States, citing enumeration district (ED) 80, sheet 1B, family 9, NARA microfilm publication T624 (Washington, DC: National Archives and Records Administration, 1982), roll 641, FHL microfilm 1,374,654.

26. "Michigan Deaths and Burials, 1800–1995," *Family Search*, database, https://familysearch.org/, under Charles Bennett, 6 August 1916, citing Village of Mackinaw, Cheboygan, Michigan, reference vol. 3, p. 4, FHL microfilm 964,407.

27. "Michigan Deaths and Burials, 1800–1995," *Family Search*, database, https://familysearch.org/, under Angelina Bennett, 8 March 1919, citing Mackinaw City, Cheboygan, Michigan, reference vol. 3, p. 5, FHL microfilm 964,407.

56. Miss Mary Bezonette (Miss Mary Dufina, Mrs. Jean Baptiste Bazinet)

1. "Baptismal Register," *Mackinac Register, 1695–1888*, 92.

2. Theresa M. Schenck, *All Our Relations: Chippewa Mixed-Bloods and the Treaty of 1837* (Winnipeg, Manitoba: The Center for Rupert's Land Studies at the University of Winnipeg, 2010), 18.

3. Larry M. Wyckoff, trans. and compiler, "Mixed-Blood Census Register, Ottawas and Chippewas of Michigan Treaty of March 28, 1836," *Roots Web*, http://www.rootsweb.ancestry.com/~mimacki2/annuities/1836mb.pdf, nos. 383–385. The family was enumerated under the name Bazelette.

4. "Baptismal Register," *Mackinac Register, 1695–1888*, 28.

5. Schenck, All Our Relations, 18.

6. *Liber Matrimonium, Mackinac Register, 1695–1888*, 54–55.

7. Linda E. Bristol, St. Joseph Mission and Holy Family Catholic Church: Marriage Records 1835–1880 (Bayfield, WI: L. E. Briston, 1993), 6.

8. Bristol, St. Joseph Mission, 13.

9. "United States Census, 1850," *Family Search*, database with images, https://familysearch.org, image 2 of 11, citing NARA microfilm publication M432 (Washington, DC: National Archives and Records Administration, n.d.).

10. *Liber Matrimonium, Mackinac Register, 1695–1888*, 54–55.

11. "Baptismal Register," *Mackinac Register, 1695–1888*, 218. The baptismal register was written with the name Clemence Delia.

12. *Liber Matrimonium, Mackinac Register, 1695–1888*, 72–73. Married under the name of Julia Messwa.

13. "Burned in His Bed: Gus Bezineau Dead as a Result of a Fire Which Destroyed His Home Wednesday," *St. Ignace Enterprise*, 30 December 1915, p. 6, col. 1.

14. "Baptismal Register," *Mackinac Register, 1695–1888*, 197.

15. "Baptismal Register," *Mackinac Register, 1695–1888*, 207.

16. "Michigan Marriages, 1822–1995," *Family Search*, database, https://familysearch.org, under William Bazineau and Mary Andress, 3 Jun 1899, citing Family History Library (FHL) microfilm 1,007,362.

17. "Michigan Deaths and Burials, 1800–1995," *Family Search*, database, https://familysearch.org/, under William Bezine, 18 January 1913, citing Mackinac Island, Mackinac, Michigan, ref. yr. 1899–1946, p. 61, FHL microfilm 1,007,364.

18. "Baptismal Register," *Mackinac Register, 1695–1888*, 214.

19. "Baptismal Register," *Mackinac Register, 1695–1888*, 220.

20. "Baptismal Register," *Mackinac Register, 1695–1888*, 226. See Basinet. Mother's name says Mary Lusignan.

21. "Baptismal Register," *Mackinac Register, 1695–1888*, 231.

22. "Michigan Deaths and Burials, 1800–1995," *Family Search*, database, https://familysearch.org/, under Julius O. Bazinau, 19 October 1920, citing Mackinac, Michigan, ref. yr. 1899–1946, p. 100, FHL microfilm 1,007,364.

23. "Baptismal Register," *Mackinac Register, 1695–1888*, 237.

24. "Michigan Deaths and Burials, 1800–1995," *Family Search*, database, https://familysearch.org/, under Mary Bazina, 28 May 1909, citing Mackinac Island, Mackinac, Michigan, ref. yr. 1899–1946, p. 42, FHL microfilm 1,007,364.

1. Mrs. Agatha Biddle (Agatha Sarrasin)

1. "The Biddle Story" (1961), Biddle folder, vertical files, Petersen Library, Mackinac State Historic Parks (MSHP), Mackinaw City, MI.

2. Elizabeth T. Baird, *The Story of Mackinac: Reminiscences of Early Days on Mackinac Island*, vol. 14 (Madison, WI: State Historical Society of Wisconsin, 1910): 44, http://content.wisconsinhistory.org.

3. "The Biddle Story," MSHP.

4. Larry M. Wyckoff, trans. and compiler, "Mixed-Blood Census Register, Ottawas and Chippewas of Michigan Treaty of March 28, 1836," *Roots Web*, http://www.rootsweb.ancestry.com/~mimacki2/annuities/1836mb.pdf, 538.

5. Baird, *Reminiscences*, 14:44. Mrs. Baird writes that Agatha and Edward were married in the home of her stepfather, Joseph Bailly.

6. "Baptismal Register," *Mackinac Register, 1695–1888*, 49.

7. See "The Rose of Sorrow," a type-written paper from the Steere Collection, Bayliss Public Library, Sault Ste. Marie. Surely it is a fictional account, but Sophie's attachment to Pemberton was reportedly true. According to records, Pemberton was at the Upper Great Lakes and Fort Mackinac in 1840 and 1841. Sophia's death occurred seven years later. She died from consumption, not a broken heart.

8. "Find a Grave Index," *Family Search*, database, https://familysearch.org, under John Biddle, 1886, Burial: Protestant Cemetery, Mackinac Island, Mackinac County, MI, record ID 31541375, *Find a Grave*, http://www.findagrave.com.

The birth and death dates have been taken from his tombstone. Like other families with a European father and a native mother, the boys practiced their father's religion, while the girls were usually baptized in the Catholic faith of their mother.

9. "Find a Grave Index," John Biddle, *Find a Grave*, 31541375.,

10. "Baptismal Register," *Mackinac Register, 1695–1888*, 11.

11. "Baptismal Register," *Mackinac Register, 1695–1888*, 49.

12. *Liber Matrimonium, Mackinac Register, 1695–1888*, 41.

13. Larry M. Wyckoff, trans. and compiler, "Mixed-Blood Census Register, Ottawas and Chippewas of Michigan Treaty of March 28, 1836," *Roots Web*, http://www.rootsweb. ancestry.com/~mimacki2/annuities/1836mb.pdf, 538.

14. "Find a Grave Index," *Family Search*, database, https://familysearch.org, under Sarah Biddle Durfee, 1923, Burial: Ste. Anne's Cemetery, Mackinac Island, Mackinac County, MI, record ID 40319880, *Find a Grave*, http://www.findagrave.com.

15. Henry Rowe Schoolcraft, *The Papers of Henry Rowe Schoolcraft, 1782–1878* (Washington, DC: Library of Congress Photoduplication Service, 1966), roll 32, special file no. 156.

16. Schoolcraft, The Papers of Henry Rowe Schoolcraft.

17. Schoolcraft, The Papers of Henry Rowe Schoolcraft.

18. Biddle folder, vertical file, MSHP.

19. Frank Straus, "Biddle House Celebrates Almost 230 Years of History on Mackinac Island," *The Town Crier* (Mackinac Island, MI), 25 July 2009, p. 20.

20. James Silk Buckingham, *The Eastern and Western States of America,* vol. 3 (London, UK, 1842), 355.

21. Biddle folder, vertical file, MSHP.

22. John Read Bailey, *Mackinac: Formerly Michilimackinac*, 4th ed. (Lansing, MI, 1899), 180.

36. Mrs. Isaac Blanchard (Mary Babeau, Babbien)

1. Theresa M. Schenck, *All Our Relations: Chippewa Mixed-Bloods and the Treaty of 1837* (Winnipeg, Manitoba: The Center for Rupert's Land Studies at the University of Winnipeg, 2010), 25.

2. Henry Rowe Schoolcraft, Narrative of an Expedition through the Upper Mississippi to Itasca Lake, the Actual Source of This River; Embracing an Exploratory Trip through the St. Croix and Burntwood (or Broule) Rivers, in 1832, under the Direction of Henry R. Schoolcraft (New York, 1834), https://www.loc.gov/resource/lhbum.08794/?sp=1.

3. Joy Reisinger, "Baptismal Records, 1835–1887, Kept at LaPointe & Bayfield, Indian Missions, by Iraneus Frederic Baraga," *Lost in Canada? Canadian-American Journal of History & Genealogy for Canadian, French & Métis Study* 2 (Fall 1995): 77. See under "Kabimabi, Joseph."

4. Linda E. Bristol, *St. Joseph Mission and Holy Family Catholic Church: Marriage Records 1835–1880* (Bayfield, WI: L. E. Briston, 1993), 11.

5. Schenck, All Our Relations, 35.

6. Bristol, St. Joseph Mission and Holy Family Catholic Church, 4.

7. Reisinger, "Baptismal Records, 1835–1887," 26.

8. Linda E. Bristol, Liber Defunctorum: St. Joseph Mission and Holy Family Catholic Church; Death Registry, 1835–1900 (Bayfield, WI: L. E. Bristol, 1994), 9.

9. Bristol, St. Joseph Mission and Holy Family Catholic Church, 6.

10. US Congress, *American State Papers: Documents, Legislative and Executive, of the Congress of the United States in Relation to the Public Lands*, vol. 5, edited by Walter Lowrie (Washington, DC, 1823), 231–233. Joseph Babeu later moved to Bourbonnais, Illinois, with Suzanne LaJeuness (his sister) and Pierre Henri Boucher, her husband.

11. "Baptismal Register," *Mackinac Register, 1695–1888*, 5. See under Marie Babeu.

12. "Baptismal Register," *Mackinac Register, 1695–1888*, 5. See under Susanne Lajeunesse.

13. Marriage record for Pierre Sillier and Josette (an Indian woman), "Port of Mackinac Records," Office of the Register of Deeds, St. Ignace, Mackinac County, MI, no. 59.

14. Emerson Smith, *Before the Bridge: A History and Directory of St. Ignace and Nearby Localities* (St. Ignace, MI: Kiwanis Club of St. Ignace, 1957), 56.

15. US Congress, *American State Papers*, 5: 231–233. "On the same day and year aforesaid came also before me Simon Champaigne, who, being duly sworn, deposeth and saith that Louis Babbien occupied a cultivated the tract of land described in the preceding notice for some time previous to the late war [War of 1812] between the United States and Great Britain, and was in the peaceable possession of the same on July 1, 1812. The said Louis Babbien had a dwelling-house on said tract, and had a considerable improvement made thereon; that the said Louis Babbien died in the fall of 1821, and that the said Joseph Babbien and Mary Babbien mentioned in the annexed notice are the son and daughter of the said Louis Babbien, deceased, and are the only lawful heirs of him, the said Louis Babbien, as this deponent has been informed and verily believes. [signature] Simon Champaigne. County of Mackinac, Register of Deeds office, 8 October 1849."

16. "United States Census, 1830," *Family Search*, database with images, https://familysearch.org, under Isaac Blanchard, Michilimackinac, Michigan Territory, citing 201, NARA microfilm publication M19 (Washington, DC: National Archives and Records Administration, n.d.), roll 69, Family History Library (FHL) microfilm 363,348.

17. "Michigan, County Marriages, 1820–1940," *Family Search*, database with images, https://familysearch.org, under Isaac Blanchard and Mary Babcup, 9 December 1824, citing FHL microfilm 926,733.

18. Some sources say he was born in Plainfield, New Hampshire; others, say Concord, New

Hampshire. His birth date varies as well, but all agree on 1787 as his birth year.

19. Inspection Return of Capt. Benjamin K. Pierce, 1817, under Isaac Blanchard, Henry and Elizabeth Baird Papers, 1798–1937, Wis Mss V, box 5, folder 4, WIHV94-A1354, Wisconsin Historical Society, https://content.wisconsinhistory.org/digital/collection/baird/id/3956/rec/4.

20. "Biographies, Mackinac County, Michigan: Isaac Blanchard Sr. and Son Isaac Blanchard Jr.," Genealogy Trails, http://genealogytrails.com/mich/mackinac/bioblanchard.html.

21. Henry Rowe Schoolcraft, "Abstract of Licenses Granted by Henry R. Schoolcraft, Acting Superintendent of Michigan [Indian Affairs] during the Year Ending 30th September 1839," *The Papers of Henry Rowe Schoolcraft, 1782–1878* (Washington, DC: Library of Congress Photoduplication Service), roll 8.

22. "Baptismal Register," *Mackinac Register, 1695–1888*, 23.

23. Marriage record for John Shurtleff and Mary Blanchard, "Port of Mackinac Records," Office of the Register of Deeds, St. Ignace, Mackinac County, MI, no. 238.

24. "Find a Grave Index," *Family Search*, database, https://familysearch.org, under Mary Belle Blanchard Shurtleff, 1896, Burial: Gros Cap Cemetery, Gros Cap, Mackinac, MI, record ID 24160220, *Find a Grave*, http://www.findagrave.com.

25. "Baptismal Register," *Mackinac Register, 1695–1888*, 23.

26. "Baptismal Register," *Mackinac Register, 1695–1888*, 23.

27. *Liber Matrimonium, Mackinac Register, 1695–1888*, 36. See under Joseph Blanchette and Isabelle Valliere.

28. "Find a Grave Index," *Family Search*, database, https://familysearch.org, under Joseph Blanchard, 1880, Burial: Gros Cap Cemetery, Gros Cap, Mackinac, MI, record ID 23990527, *Find a Grave*, http://www.findagrave.com.

29. "Baptismal Register," *Mackinac Register, 1695–1888*, 34.

30. "Find a Grave Index," *Family Search*, database, https://familysearch.org, under Isaac Blanchard Jr., 1859, Burial: Gros Cap Cemetery, Gros Cap, Mackinac County, MI, record ID 19556021, *Find a Grave*, http://www.findagrave.com. Birth and death information was taken from the grave marker.

31. The murder of Isaac Blanchard by Augustus Pond was determined to be a legal defense of his home with deadly force against an intruder. See Larry Peterson, "Pond v. the People: Michigan Sets a Legal Precedent," *Michigan History* (Marc/April 2011): 37–41, https://www.michbar.org/file/programs/milestone/pdf/pond%27sdefensemhm2011.pdf; Augustus Pond v. The People, 8 Mich., 150, http://www.micourthistory.org/wp-content/uploads/verdict_pdf/pond/pond_decision.pdf.

32. "Michigan Deaths and Burials, 1800–1995," *Family Search*, database, https://familysearch.org, under John Blanchard, 10 October 1903, citing St. Ignace, Mackinac, MI, ref. yr.

1899–1946, p. 18, Family History Library (FHL) microfilm 1,007,364.

33. *Liber Matrimonium, Mackinac Register, 1695–1888*, 64–65. See under Isabelle Leveille.

34. "Michigan Deaths and Burials, 1800–1995," under John Blanchard, 10 October 1903.

35. "Find a Grave Index," *FamilySearch*, database, https://familysearch.org, under Phebe Blanchard Recolly, 1923, Burial: Maple Grove Cemetery, Mullett Lake, Cheboygan, MI, record ID 62830828, *Find a Grave*, http://www.findagrave.com. Birth and death dates taken from tombstone.

36. *Liber Matrimonium, Mackinac Register, 1695–1888*, 56–57.

37. "Michigan Death Certificates, 1921–1952," *Family Search*, database, https://familysearch.org, under Phoebe Recolly, 22 February 1923, citing Inverness, Cheboygan, MI, Division for Vital Records and Health Statistics, Lansing, FHL microfilm 1,973,214.

38. "Find a Grave Index," *Family Search*, database, https://familysearch.org, under William Henry Blanchard, 1879, Burial: Dayton National Cemetery, Dayton, Montgomery County, OH, record ID 374858, *Find a Grave*, http://www.findagrave.com.

39. Historical Data Systems, comp., *U.S., Civil War Soldier Records and Profiles, 1861–1865*, *Ancestry*, database, (Provo, UT: Ancestry.com Operations Inc., 2009), https://www.ancestry.com/search/collections/1555/.

40. *Historical Register of National Homes for Disabled Volunteer Soldiers, 1866–1938*, Records of the Department of Veterans Affairs, RG 15, Washington, DC: National Archives, microfilm M1749, 282 rolls.

41. Office of the Quartermaster General, Department of the Army, Department of Defense, *Burial Registers of Military Post and National Cemeteries, Compiled ca. 1862–ca. 1960*, ARC ID 4478151; Records of the Office of the Quartermaster General, 1774–1985, RG 92 (Washington, DC: National Archives and Records Administration).

42. St. Ignatius Loyola (St. Ignace, MI), "Baptisms 1838–1893," bk 3, p. 61 (Elvira Agnes Blanchard, 1850), parish rectory.

43. St. Ignatius Loyola (St. Ignace, MI), "Marriages 1838–1893," bk 1, p. 26–27 (Ambroise Corp and Agnes Elvire Agnes Blanchard, 1865), parish rectory.

44. "Michigan Death Certificates, 1921–1952," *Family Search*, database, https://familysearch.org, under Alvira Corp, 8 January 1924, citing Moran, Mackinac, MI, Division for Vital Records and Health Statistics, Lansing, FHL microfilm 1,972,852.

45. Keith Widder, Battle for the Soul: Métis Children Encounter Evangelical Protestants at Mackinaw Mission, 1823–1837 (East Lansing: Michigan State University Press), 70.

46. Prentiss M. Brown and Jennifer S. McGraw, comp., *The Reminiscences of David Corp, and other historic works regarding St. Ignace, Gros Cap, Pte. LaBarbe & St. Helena Island.* (St. Ignace, MI: Michilimackinac Historical Society), 14. There are many inaccuracies in this book. The authors state that Mrs. Blanchard's mother was Sioux; this was not the

case. Mary and her children appear on the Half Breed Census of 1836 clearly listed as Chippewa. He listed "Noko," or Josette LaJeunesse, as the sister of Chief Ance, local to the Mackinac area, but he also said Noko was from Saskatchewan (which is probably true). According to the research and genealogical information presented and documented here, no kinship relationship between Ance and Josette could be established. As a judge, Blanchard was a powerful man, no doubt friendly with Henry Rowe Schoolcraft. Schoolcraft manipulated this payment to the benefit of many families, headed by a European man, regardless of their spouse's blood affiliation. Blanchard's wife was from outside the treaty area, but because she was listed as a "relation of Aintz" from Oak Point, Mary and her children were given second class status and received $305.89 each.

47. John L. Hagen and Georgia M. Rhoades, comp., *Moran Township: When the Moon Is High* (St. Ignace, MI: Moran Township Board of Trustees, 1997), 2:165–66.
48. Hagen and Rhoads, *When the Moon Is High*, 2:166.
49. Hagen and Rhoads, *When the Moon Is High*, 2:166.

20. Mrs. Vital Bourassa (Angelique Fountain)

1. "Baptismal Register," *Mackinac Register, 1695–1888*, 11.
2. Larry M. Wyckoff, trans. and compiler, "Mixed-Blood Census Register, Ottawas and Chippewas of Michigan Treaty of March 28, 1836," *Roots Web*, http://www.rootsweb. ancestry.com/~mimacki2/annuities/1836mb.pdf, nos. 489–497. Listed under Boureseau, Vital is no. 494, listed as half-Ottawa and was awarded Second Class funds of $305.89.
3. *Liber Matrimonium, Mackinac Register, 1695–1888*, 30.
4. "Baptismal Register," *Mackinac Register, 1695–1888*, 134.
5. "Baptismal Register," *Mackinac Register, 1695–1888*, 152.
6. Lighthouse Friends, "Ile aux Galets (Skillagalee) Lighthouse," http://lighthousefriends. com/light.asp?ID=207. See "Keepers" heading at the end of the page.
7. *Liber Matrimonium, Mackinac Register, 1695–1888*, 72–73.
8. "Michigan Death Certificates, 1921–1952," *Family Search*, database, https://familysearch. org, Vital Bourisaw in entry for Frank Bourisaw, 29 June 1930, citing Mackinac Island, Mackinac, MI, Division for Vital Records and Health Statistics, Lansing, Family History Library (FHL) microfilm 1,972,852.
9. "Baptismal Register," *Mackinac Register, 1695–1888*, 171.
10. *Liber Matrimonium, Mackinac Register, 1695–1888*, 68–69.
11. Lighthouse Friends, "Ile aux Galets (Skillagalee) Lighthouse," http://lighthousefriends. com/light.asp?ID=207. See "Keepers" heading at the end of the page.
12. *Liber Defunctorum, Mackinac Register, 1695–1888*, 112.
13. "Baptismal Register," *Mackinac Register, 1695–1888*, 185.

14. "Baptismal Register," *Mackinac Register, 1695–1888*, 189.

15. "Baptismal Register," *Mackinac Register, 1695–1888*, 193.

16. "Michigan Deaths and Burials, 1800–1995," *Family Search*, database, https://familysearch. org, under Vetal Bourassan, 11 May 1875, citing Holmes, Mackinac, MI, ref. yr. 1873–1899, 4, FHL microfilm 1,007,364.

17. "Baptismal Register," *Mackinac Register, 1695–1888*, 197.

18. "Baptismal Register," *Mackinac Register, 1695–1888*, 210.

19. *Liber Defunctorum, Mackinac Register, 1695–1888*, 107.

20. *Liber Matrimonium, Mackinac Register, 1695–1888*, 72–73.

21. "Michigan Deaths and Burials, 1800–1995," *Family Search*, database, https://familysearch. org, under Vetal Bourisaw, 3 March 1904, citing Mackinac Island, Mackinac, MI, ref. yr. 1899–1946, 19, FHL microfilm 1,007,364.

8. Mrs. Louis Cadotte (Marie Louise Laverdure)

1. *Ste. Anne's Church Registers: 1704–1842*, microfilm, 3 rolls (Detroit, MI: St. Anne's of Detroit). See roll 3, *Chapelle du nordest: Baptisms, Marriages, Burials, 1810–1838*, arranged by date; see no. 78, "Baptême de Marie Leveque," p. 95.

2. Sally Ann Cummings, Correspondence, Field Notes, and the Census Roll of All Members or Descendants of Members Who Were on the Roll of the Ottawa and the Chippewa Tribes of Michigan in 1870, and Living on March 4, 1907 (Durant Roll) (Washington, DC: National Archives and Records Administration, 1996), p. 13. See Mrs. Louis Cadotte, no. 8.

3. "Baptismal Register," *Mackinac Register, 1695–1888*, 65.

4. *Liber Matrimonium, Mackinac Register, 1695–1888*, 54–55. See under Alexis Lauson.

5. "Baptismal Register," *Mackinac Register, 1695–1888*, 85. See under Peter Louzignan.

6. *Liber Matrimonium, Mackinac Register, 1695–1888*, 64–65.

7. Marriage record for Louis Cadotte and Louise Laverdure, "Port of Mackinac Records," Office of the Register of Deeds, St. Ignace, Mackinac County, MI, no. 226.

8. John P. DuLong, "Jean Baptiste Cadotte's Second Family: Genealogical Summary; Part 1," *Michigan's Habitant Heritage* (MHH) 36, no. 4 (October 2015).

9. "Baptismal Register," *Mackinac Register, 1695–1888*, 105.

10. Marriage record for Alexander LaLonde and Mary Cadotte, "Port of Mackinac Records," Office of the Register of Deeds, St. Ignace, Mackinac County, MI, no. 542.

11. *Liber Matrimonium, Mackinac Register, 1695–1888*, 1823–1888, 66–67.

12. "Baptismal Register," *Mackinac Register, 1695–1888*, 115.

13. *Liber Defunctorum, Mackinac Register, 1695–1888*, 1823–1891, 89.

14. "Baptismal Register," *Mackinac Register, 1695–1888*, 128.

15. *Liber Matrimonium, Mackinac Register, 1695–1888*, 1823–1888, 64–65.

16. "Michigan Marriages, 1822–1995," *Family Search*, database, https://familysearch.org, under Louis Cadette Jr. and Lucy St. Andre, 9 February 1874, citing reference Family History Library (FHL) microfilm 2,342,457.

17. "Baptismal Register," *Mackinac Register, 1695–1888*, 141.

18. "Baptismal Register," *Mackinac Register, 1695–1888*, 151.

19. "Baptismal Register," *Mackinac Register, 1695–1888*, 166.

20. *Liber Matrimonium, Mackinac Register, 1695–1888*, 68–69.

21. "Baptismal Register," *Mackinac Register, 1695–1888*, 183.

22. *Liber Defunctorum, Mackinac Register, 1695–1888*, 1823–1891, 104.

23. *Liber Defunctorum, Mackinac Register, 1695–1888*, 1823–1891, 114.

5. Mrs. Joseph Caron (Louise Vasseur)

1. Marthe Faribault-Beauregard, *La population des forts d'Amérique (XVIIIe siècle): Répertoire des baptêmes, mariages et sépultures célébrés dans les forts et les établissements français en Amérique du Nord au XVIIIe siècle* (Montreal: Editions Bergeron, 1983), 161. She was around six months old at the time of her baptism.

2. State Historical Society of Wisconsin (SHSW), *The Mackinac Register, 1695–1888,* vol. 18, *Marriages, 1725–1821* (Milwaukee: Wisconsin Historical Society Press, 1908), p. 507. See marriage record of Joseph Gautier dit Caron and Louise Vasseur. They were first married by Adhemar St. Martin, a justice of the peace on 30 December 1800. *The Mackinac Register, 1695–1888*, 18:504. Louise was thirteen years old at the time of her marriage.

3. For a comprehensive discussion of marriage *à la façon du pays*, see Sylvia Van Kirk, "The Custom of the Country," *Many Tender Ties* (Winnipeg, Manitoba: Watson and Dwyer, 1999).,

4. SHSW, "*The Mackinac Register, 1695–1888*, vol. 19 *Baptisms, 1695–1821*, (Milwaukee: Wisconsin Historical Society Press, 1910), p. 120. See baptism record of Joseph Gautier dit Caron.

5. *Liber Matrimonium, Mackinac Register, 1695–1888*, 11.

6. "Baptismal Register," *Mackinac Register, 1695–1888*, 65. Joseph Jr. was born at Bois Blanc Island.

7. Marriage record for Joseph Caron and Mary Ann "an Indian woman," "Port of Mackinac Records," Office of the Register of Deeds, St. Ignace, Mackinac County, MI, no. 203.

8. SHSW, *The Mackinac Register, 1695–1888*, 19:121. See baptism record of Marie Gautier dit Caron.

9. *Liber Matrimonium, Mackinac Register, 1695–1888*, 16.

10. *Liber Defunctorum, Mackinac Register, 1695–1888*, 88.

11. *Liber Matrimonium, Mackinac Register, 1695–1888*, 22.

12. *Liber Defunctorum, Mackinac Register, 1695–1888*, 91.

13. *Liber Matrimonium, Mackinac Register, 1695–1888*, 32.

14. "Find a Grave Index," *Family Search*, database, https://familysearch.org, under Angelique Caron Hudson, 1863, Burial: Calvary Cemetery Chapel of the Resurrection, Cheboygan, MI, *Find a Grave*, http://www.findagrave.com, record ID 76087692.

15. *Ste. Anne's Church Registers: 1704–1842*, microfilm, 3 rolls (Detroit, MI: St. Anne's of Detroit). See roll 3, *Chapelle du nordest: Baptisms, Marriages, Burials, 1810–1838*, arranged by date; see under Guillaume Carron, p. 50. (Hereafter, *Ste. Anne's* [Detroit] *Registers*.)

16. *Liber Matrimonium, Mackinac Register, 1695–1888*, 25.

17. *Ste. Anne's* [Detroit] *Registers*, see roll 3, p. 133.

18. *Liber Matrimonium, Mackinac Register, 1695–1888*, 29.

19. Joy Reisinger, ed., *Lost in Canada?* 16, no. 4 (Summer 1992): 184.

20. Theresa M. Schenck, *All Our Relations: Chippewa Mixed-Bloods and the Treaty of 1837* (Winnipeg, Manitoba: The Center for Rupert's Land Studies at the University of Winnipeg, 2010), 24.

21. Larry Wyckoff, trans., "Mixed-Blood Census Register, Ottawas and Chippewas of Michigan, Treaty of March 26, 1836," *Roots Web*, http://www.rootsweb.ancestry.com/~mimacki2/annuities/1836mb.pdf, n.d., no. 194–99.

34. Mrs. Moses Champagne (Sarah Martin)

1. "Baptismal Register," *Mackinac Register, 1695–1888*, 57. Her parents were listed as Antoine Martin and "Indiana."

2. Larry Wyckoff, trans., "Mixed-Blood Census Register, Ottawas and Chippewas of Michigan, Treaty of March 26, 1836," *Roots Web*, http://www.rootsweb.ancestry.com/~mimacki2/annuities/1836mb.pdf, n.d., no. 549.

3. Wyckoff, "Mixed-Blood Census Register, Ottawas and Chippewas of Michigan, Treaty of March 26, 1836." See "Remarks" column.

4. *Liber Matrimonium, Mackinac Register, 1695–1888*, 13.

5. *Liber Matrimonium, Mackinac Register, 1695–1888*, 13.

6. St. Ignatius Loyola (St. Ignace, MI), "Baptisms, 1838–1893," bk. 3, p. 6 (Letitia Plante, 1838), parish rectory.

7. *Liber Matrimonium, Mackinac Register, 1695–1888*, 23.

8. St. Ignatius Loyola (St. Ignace, MI), "Marriages, 1838–1893," bk. 1, p. 14 (Moyses Champagne and Sara Plante marriage, 1855), parish rectory.

9. St. Ignatius Loyola (St. Ignace, MI), "Baptisms, 1838–1893," bk. 3, p. 66 (Sarah Champagne, 1857), parish rectory.

10. "Michigan Marriages, 1822–1995," *Family Search*, database, https://familysearch.org,

under Patrick Holland and Sarah Champagne, 31 January 1876, citing Family History Library (FHL) microfilm 2,342,460.

11. St. Ignatius Loyola (St. Ignace, MI), "Baptisms, 1838–1893," bk. 3, p. 73 (Flavie Delima Champagne, 1858), parish rectory.

12. St. Ignatius Loyola (St. Ignace, MI), "Deaths, 1838–1893," bk. 1, p. 2 (Flavia Champagne, 1859), parish rectory.

13. St. Ignatius Loyola (St. Ignace, MI), "Baptisms, 1838–1893," bk. 3, p. 83 (Marie Elisabeth, 1861), parish rectory.

14. Michigan State Archives, "Death Records, 1897–1920," *Michiganology*, entry for John Champine, https://michiganology.org. Death record says he was buried in Naubinway, Michigan. Since a birth record for Jean Baptiste (John) was not found and one was found for the next sibling, Charles Augustin, John's birth date per his death certificate must be incorrect.

15. St. Ignatius Loyola (St. Ignace, MI), "Baptisms, 1838–1893," bk. 3, p. 102 (Charles Augustin Champagne, 1865), parish rectory.

16. *Liber Matrimonium, Mackinac Register, 1695–1888*, 23.

17. Michigan State Archives, "Death Records, 1921–1947," *Michiganology*, entry for Charles Shampine, 1928, https://michiganology.org.

18. St. Ignatius Loyola (St. Ignace, MI), "Baptisms, 1838–1893," bk. 3, p. 108 (Joseph Napolean Champagne, 1867), parish rectory.

19. "Michigan Marriages, 1868–1925," *Family Search*, database with images, https://familysearch.org, under Joseph Shompine and Maria Leveque, no. 147, 004207812, image 151 of 635, citing Department of Vital Records, Lansing.

20. "Michigan Marriages, 1822–1995," *Family Search*, database, https://familysearch.org, under William Champagn and Pearl Boutin, 29 November 1896, citing reference FHL microfilm 2,342,504.

21. Richard M. Dorson, *Bloodstoppers and Bearwalkers: Folk Traditions of the Upper Peninsula* (Cambridge, MA: Harvard University Press, 1972), 75.

22. "Michigan Deaths, 1867–1897," *Family Search*, database with images, https://familysearch.org, under Moses Shampim, 29 Mar 1895; citing p. 197, rn 3, Moran Twp., Mackinac, MI, Department of Vital Records, Lansing, FHL microfilm 2,363,834.

23. Death record for Sarah Champain, 1906, "Register of Deaths," Clerk's Office, City Hall, Mackinac Island, MI, p. 13.

30. Mrs. Bela Chapman (Marie Charette)

1. No baptism for Mary has been found, however, direct evidence that Mary is the daughter of Simon Charette and Marguerite La Grue comes from the 1826 Prairie de Chien Treaty

with the Chippewa. In the schedule listing land grants, referred to in Article 4, is the following: "To Mary Chapman, daughter of Equameeg, and wife of Bela Chapman, and to each of her children, one section." See "Treaty with the Chippewa Made at the Fond du Lac of Lake Superior, 1826," https://en.wikisource.org. Equameeg or Marguerite was the daughter of Keeshkemun and went by several names including Equameeg, Kinikinokwe, and *La Grue* (crane in French, her *ododem* or clan). See Theresa M. Schenck, *All Our Relations: Chippewa Mixed-Bloods and the Treaty of 1837* (Winnipeg, Manitoba: The Center for Rupert's Land Studies at the University of Winnipeg, 2010), 45.

2. François Victoire Malhiot, *American Fur Company Employees 1818 - 1819*, Wisconsin Historical Collections, 21 vols. (Madison: State Historical Society of Wisconsin, 1855–1915), vol. 12, 154–169 (1892): 156 – 157.

3. Larry Wyckoff, trans., "Mixed-Blood Census Register, Ottawas and Chippewas of Michigan, Treaty of March 26, 1836," *Roots Web*, http://www.rootsweb.ancestry.com/~mimacki2/annuities/1836mb.pdf, n.d., nos. 557–64: Mary Chapman, Eliza Chapman, Reuben Chapman, Amanda Chapman, Bela Chapman Jr., and James Chapman.

4. Bruce M. White, Grand Portage as a Trading Post: Patterns of Trade at "the Great Carrying Place" (Grand Maris, MN: National Park Service, 2005), p. 124.

5. Marriage record for Bela Chapman and Mary Charette, "Port of Mackinac Records," Office of the Register of Deeds, St. Ignace, Mackinac County, MI, no. 79.

6. Marriage record for Horatio N. Pease and Eliza Chapman, "Port of Mackinac Records," Office of the Register of Deeds, St. Ignace, Mackinac County, MI, no. 193.

7. "Find a Grave Index," *Family Search*, database, https://familysearch.org, under Reuben Chapman, 1860, record ID 131788296, Burial: Protestant Cemetery, Mackinac Island, Mackinac County, MI, *Find a Grave*, http://www.findagrave.com.

8. Marriage record for Reuben Champan and Marie Louise Desbrow [née Gravereat], "Port of Mackinac Records," Office of the Register of Deeds, St. Ignace, Mackinac County, MI, no. 437.

9. Marriage record for Edward Ashman and Amanda Chapman, "Port of Mackinac Records," Office of the Register of Deeds, St. Ignace, Mackinac County, MI, no. 337.

10. "Baptismal Register," *Mackinac Register, 1695–1888*, 122.

11. Marriage record for John Biddle and Lucy Chapman, "Port of Mackinac Records," Office of the Register of Deeds, St. Ignace, Mackinac County, MI, no. 314.

12. "Michigan Deaths, 1867–1897," *Family Search*, database with images, https://familysearch.org, under Lucy Biddle, 4 January 1879; citing p. 152, rn. 2, Mackinac, MI, Department of Vital Records, Lansing, FHL microfilm 2,363,667.

13. "Find a Grave Index," *Family Search*, database, https://familysearch.org, under John

Biddle, 1886, record ID 31541375, Burial: Protestant Cemetery, Mackinac Island, Mackinac, MI, *Find a Grave,* http://www.findagrave.com.

14. Marriage record for John Chapman and Sarah Ann Hudson, "Port of Mackinac Records," Office of the Register of Deeds, St. Ignace, Mackinac County, MI, no. 501.

15. "Baptismal Register," *Mackinac Register, 1695–1888,* 208.

16. "Michigan Marriages, 1868–1925," *Family Search,* database, https://familysearch.org, under John Shomin and Mary Chapman, 1868.

17. Chris Czopek, Who Was Who in Company K: Reliable Facts about the Native American Soldiers in Company K, 1st Michigan Sharpshooters, during the Civil War, 1861–1865 (Lansing, MI: Self-published, 2010), p. 118. For an excellent description of the battle at Petersburg and capture of Company K soldiers, read Ronald S. Coddington, "American Indians in Confederate Territory," *New York Times,* June 23, 2014, https://opinionator. blogs.nytimes.com/2014/06/23/american-indians-in-confederate-territory/.

18. "Michigan Death Certificates, 1921–1952," *Family Search,* database, https://familysearch. org, under Andrew Jackson Chapman, 27 November 1929; citing Mackinac Island, Mackinac, MI, Division for Vital Records and Health Statistics, Lansing, FHL microfilm 1,972,852.

19. George H. Turner, *Record of Service of Michigan Volunteers in the Civil War, 1861–1865,* vol. 37 (Kalamazoo, MI: Ihling Bros. & Everard, 1900), p. 30, https://catalog.hathitrust.org/ Record/003931700. See under Andrew J. Chapman.

20. *Liber Matrimonium, Mackinac Register, 1695–1888,* 70–71.

39. Mrs. Joseph Cheverow (Marie Charlotte Dejadon)

1. Larry Wyckoff, trans., "Mixed-Blood Census Register, Ottawas and Chippewas of Michigan, Treaty of March 26, 1836," *Roots Web,* http://www.rootsweb.ancestry. com/~mimacki2/annuities/1836mb.pdf, n.d., nos. 374 and 375.

2. Wyckoff, "Mixed-Blood Census Register, Ottawas and Chippewas of Michigan, Treaty of March 26, 1836," see column labeled "Remarks."

3. *Liber Matrimonium, Mackinac Register, 1695–1888,* 10.

4. "Baptismal Register," *Mackinac Register, 1695–1888,* 44. See under Chevreau. The parents listed for this child are Joseph Chevreau and Obitawegijigokwe. It is not known if the named Native woman is Marie Dejadon.

5. *Liber Matrimonium, Mackinac Register, 1695–1888,* 38.

6. *Liber Matrimonium, Mackinac Register, 1695–1888,* 34

7. *Liber Matrimonium, Mackinac Register, 1695–1888,* 54/55.

8. "Baptismal Register," *Mackinac Register, 1695–1888,* 73.

9. *Liber Matrimonium, Mackinac Register, 1695–1888,* 48/49.

10. "Baptismal Register," *Mackinac Register, 1695–1888*, 89.

11. *Liber Matrimonium, Mackinac Register, 1695–1888*, 38. The groom's last name is spelled Eslin, the bride is listed as Eliza Jane.

12. "Baptismal Register," *Mackinac Register, 1695–1888*, 98. Family name listed as Chevreau.

13. The only evidence that there was a marriage between Peter Aslin and Angelique Lessieur was the birth of Pauline Aslin on 4 January 1864. She was baptized 14 February 1864 at Ste. Anne's. Record indicates she was born on Bois Blanc Island; both parents are listed, and there is no indication she was illegitimate. It is possible that they were married on Bois Blanc by a justice of the peace.

14. *Liber Matrimonium, Mackinac Register, 1695–1888*, 56–57.

15. *Liber Matrimonium, Mackinac Register, 1695–1888*, 68–69.

16. "Baptismal Register," *Mackinac Register, 1695–1888*, 110. The family name is listed as Haslin.

17. "Baptismal Register," *Mackinac Register, 1695–1888*, 122. The family name is listed as Haslin.

18. *Liber Matrimonium, Mackinac Register, 1695–1888*, 54–55.

19. "Baptismal Register," *Mackinac Register, 1695–1888*, 130.

20. *Liber Matrimonium, Mackinac Register, 1695–1888*, 54–55. Son of Michel Bazinet.

21. "Baptismal Register," *Mackinac Register, 1695–1888*, 148. Surname is listed at Aslin dit Chevreaux.

22. "Baptismal Register," *Mackinac Register, 1695–1888*, 167.

23. *Liber Matrimonium, Mackinac Register, 1695–1888*, 62–63.

24. "Baptismal Register," *Mackinac Register, 1695–1888*, 182.

25. *Liber Defunctorum, Mackinac Register, 1695–1888*, 101.

26. "Find a Grave Index," *Family Search*, database, https://familysearch.org, under Joseph Louis Asselin/Aslin, 1887, Burial: Saint Anne's Cemetery, Mackinac Island, Mackinac, MI, *Find a Grave*, http://www.findagrave.com, record ID 136244413.

64. Mrs. Peter Closs (Julia Pond)

1. "Baptismal Register," *Mackinac Register, 1695–1888*, 40.

2. "United States Census, 1850," *FamilySearch*, database with images, https://familysearch.org, under Louis Claus, Michilimackinac, MI; citing family 250, NARA microfilm publication M432 (Washington, DC: National Archives and Records Administration, n.d.).

3. St. Ignatius Loyola (St. Ignace, MI), "Deaths, 1838–1893," bk. 1, p. 1 (Louis Claess [Closs], 1857), parish rectory.

4. St. Ignatius Loyola (St. Ignace, MI), "Deaths, 1838–1893," bk. 1, p. 9 (Catherine Classe

death, 1873), parish rectory.

5. St. Ignatius Loyola (St. Ignace, MI), "Marriages, 1838–1893," bk. 1, pp. 16–17 (Pierre Clauss and Julie Pound marriage, 1857), parish rectory.

6. St. Ignatius Loyola (St. Ignace, MI), "Baptisms, 1838–1893," bk. 3, p. 70 (Pierre Julien Claes baptisms, 1858), parish rectory. It appears that the other children were not baptized in a local Catholic Church (St. Ignatius or Ste. Anne's) although the family appeared on the Mackinac County, St. Ignace, censuses. The children whose marriages are listed below were married by a justice of the peace, except John Bouchard and Julia Closs.

7. "Michigan Marriages, 1868–1925," *FamilySearch*, database with images, https://familysearch.org, under Peter Closs in entry for John Bouchard and Julia Closs, 1892.

8. "Michigan Marriages, 1868–1925," *Family Search*, database with images, https://familysearch.org, under Peter Closs in entry for Stephen Riell and Annie Closs, 1888.

9. "Michigan Marriages, 1868–1925," *Family Search*, database with images, https://familysearch.org, under Peter Closs in entry for Amos R. Olmstead and Adeline Closs, 1888.

10. "Michigan Births, 1867–1902," *Family Search*, database with images, https://familysearch.org, under Mary A. Closs, 18 September 1885; citing item 2, p. 92, rn 82, St. Ignace Twp., Mackinac, MI, Department of Vital Records, Lansing, Family History Library (FHL) microfilm 2,320,840.

11. "Michigan Births, 1867–1902," *Family Search*, database with images, https://familysearch.org, under Oliver Close, 17 July 1876; citing item 2, p. 160, rn 179, St. Ignace, Mackinac, MI, Department of Vital Records, Lansing, FHL microfilm 2,320,449.

12. "Michigan Deaths, 1867–1897," *Family Search*, database with images, https://familysearch.org, under Peter Closs, 15 Nov 1890; citing p. 160, rn 31, Detour, Chippewa, Michigan, Department of Vital Records, Lansing, FHL microfilm 2,363,637.

13. St. Ignatius Loyola (St. Ignace, MI), "Index of Burials, 1894–1988," p. 16 (Mrs. Julia Clauss, 1912), parish rectory.

9. Mrs. Alice Cushway (Alice Graveraet Couchoise)

1. *Liber Matrimonium, Mackinac Register, 1695–1888*, 13.

2. Paul M. Wandrie, "Graveraet Sons Served in Civil War," *Town Crier*, 25 June 2011, http://www.mackinacislandnews.com.

3. Wandrie, "Graveraet Sons Served in Civil War."

4. Emmet County, *Vital Records Search*, searchable database, http://apps.emmetcounty.org/clerk/deathrecords.aspx, under Gravorat, Sophia G., liber 1, folio 94.

5. *Liber Matrimonium, Mackinac Register, 1695–1888*, 52–53.

6. "Baptismal Register," *Mackinac Register, 1695–1888*, 194B. Surname is spelled Cuchois.

7. "Find A Grave Index," database, *FamilySearch*, https://www.familysearch.org, under Rose S. Couchois, Burial: Saint Joseph Cemetery, River Grove, Cook County, Illinois, citing record ID 184093027, *Find a Grave*, http://www.findagrave.com.

8. "Baptismal Register," *Mackinac Register, 1695–1888*, 209. Surname is spelled Cochois.

9. *Liber Defunctorum, Mackinac Register, 1695–1888*, 104. Name is listed as Sophia Gravelotte.

10. "Find a Grave Index," *Family Search*, database, https://familysearch.org, under John B. Couchois, 1873, Burial: Sainte Anne's Cemetery, Mackinac Island, Mackinac, MI, record ID 40433133, *Find a Grave*, http://www.findagrave.com.

31. Mrs. Ambrose Davenport (Susan Descarreaux)

1. Marriage of Ambrose Davenport and Susan Descarreau, "Marriage Records, Chippewa County, Michigan," microfilm (Sault Ste. Marie, MI: Le Saut de Stainte Marie Chapter, Daughters of the American Revolution, [between 1900 and 1999?]), p. 11.

2. Theresa M. Schenck, *All Our Relations: Chippewa Mixed-Bloods and the Treaty of 1837* (Winnipeg, Manitoba: The Center for Rupert's Land Studies at the University of Winnipeg, 2010), 56.

3. Timothy Harrison, "The Davenport Lighthouse Legacy," *Lighthouse Digest Magazine*, August 2008.

4. Ambrose Davenport Jr., *Find a Grave*, www.findagrave.com, memorial no. 132960128.

5. Susan Des Carreaux Davenport, *Find a Grave*, www.findagrave.com, memorial no. 132960323.

6. Schenck, *All Our Relations,* 56.

7. *Liber Matrimonium, Mackinac Register, 1695–1888*, 33.

8. William Davenport, *Find a Grave*, www.findagrave.com, memorial no. 131789139.

9. Schenck, All Our Relations, 56.

10. *Liber Matrimonium, Mackinac Register, 1695–1888*, 39.

11. Henry L. Davenport, *Find a Grave*, www.findagrave.com, memorial no. 114147479, in Woodmere Cemetery, Detroit, Wayne County.

12. Schenck, All Our Relations, 56.

13. Marriage record for Charles James Lusignan and Mary Davenport, "Port of Mackinac Records," no. 366, p. 72.

14. Mary Davenport, *Find a Grave*, www.findagrave.com, memorial no. 131789250.

15. Schenck, All Our Relations, 56.

16. Joseph Davenport, *Find a Grave*, www.findagrave.com, memorial no. 131789154.

17. *Liber Matrimonium, Mackinac Register, 1695–1888*, 48–49.

18. www.findagrave.com, Memorial no. 8837870.

19. *Liber Matrimonium, Mackinac Register, 1695–1888,* 58–59.

20. *Liber Matrimonium, Mackinac Register, 1695–1888,* no. 119, p. 267.

21. "John Davenport," obituary, *St. Ignace Enterprise,* 11 December 1913, p. 3, col. 2.

22. Irene Vander Meulen Reidsma, *Tombstone Recordings of the Cemeteries on Mackinac Island, Michigan* (Holland, MI: I. V. M. Reidsma, 1982), p. 1. Calculation from inscription on tombstone. "Date of death 13 October 1873 at age 31 yr., 4 mo., 4 da. indicates a date of birth 9 June 1842."

23. *Liber Matrimonium, Mackinac Register, 1695–1888,* 56–57.

24. Reidsma, Tombstone Recordings, 1.

25. Julia Davenport Duclon, *Find a Grave,* www.findagrave.com, memorial no. 128089840.

26. Marriage record for William Dukeland and Julia Davenport, 2 May 1867, *Mackinac County Clerk Marriages Index, 1867–1887,* vol. 1, p. 3, no. 36, Michigan Family History Network (MFHN), http://www.mifamilyhistory.org/mackinac/marriages/record.aspx?id=475.

27. Julia Davenport Duclon, *Find a Grave,* www.findagrave.com, memorial no. 128089840.

28. William Henry Duclon, *Find a Grave,* www.findagrave.com, memorial no. 128089785.

29. Michigan State Archives, "Death Records, 1921–1947," *Michiganology,* entry for James Davenport, 1932, Cheboygan, MI, https://michiganology.org.

30. Marriage record for James Davenport and Madaline Lasley, 18 April 1870, *Mackinac County Clerk Marriages Index, 1867–1887,* vol. 1, p. 3, no. 36, MFHN, http://www.mifamilyhistory.org/mackinac/marriages/Default.aspx. Marriage record says he was born on Bois Blanc.

31. Michigan State Archives, "Death Records, 1921–1947," *Michiganology,* entry for James Davenport, 1932, Cheboygan, MI, https://michiganology.org.

32. Susan Davenport, *Find a Grave,* www.findagrave.com, memorial no. 131789168. The researcher listed her birth year as 1840, but from personal experience, the date on the monument is 1849.

33. Margaret Caroline Davenport Morris, *Find a Grave,* www.findagrave.com, memorial no. 29429446.

34. Marriage record for Samuel Morris and Margaret Caroline Davenport, 20 May 1874, *Mackinac County Clerk Marriages Index, 1867–1887,* vol. 1, p. 6, no. 81, MFHN, http://www.mifamilyhistory.org/mackinac/marriages/Default.aspx.

35. Margaret Caroline Davenport Morris, *Find a Grave,* www.findagrave.com, memorial no. 29429446.

36. "*Illinois, Deaths and Stillbirths Index, 1916–1947,*" *Ancestry,* database, (Provo, UT: Ancestry.com Operations Inc., 2011), https://www.ancestry.com, entry for Andrew Jackson Davenport, 25 April 1929, citing Cook County, IL, [Deaths] Family History Library (FHL) microfilm 1892365.

37. Marriage record for Andrew Davenport and Clara Hamman, 6 July 1874, *Mackinac County Clerk Marriages Index, 1867–1887*, vol. 1, p. 86, no. 36, MFHN, http://www.mifamilyhistory. org/mackinac/marriages/Default.aspx.

38. S.R., "The American Fur Company at Mackinaw," *Friends' Intelligencer* 39 (1882): 444, https://babel.hathitrust.org/cgi/pt?id=mdp.39015069396417&view=image&seq=456.

42. Mrs. William Davenport (Marie Dufault)

1. Theresa M. Schenck, *All Our Relations: Chippewa Mixed-Bloods and the Treaty of 1837* (Winnipeg, Manitoba: The Center for Rupert's Land Studies at the University of Winnipeg, 2010), 57.

2. Joy Reisinger, "Baptismal Records, 1835–1887, Kept at LaPointe & Bayfield, Indian Missions, by Iraneus Frederic Baraga," *Lost in Canada? Canadian-American Journal of History & Genealogy for Canadian, French & Métis Study* 1 (Winter 1992–1993): 26.

3. Gabriel Drouin, comp., *Drouin Collection* (Montreal: Institut Généalogique Drouin), p. 12–14, marriage of Louis Dufault and Marie Louise Mentosaky, 15 February 1779.

4. Schenck, All Our Relations, 57.

5. Schenck, All Our Relations, 57.

6. "Michigan Marriages, 1822–1995," *Family Search* database, https://familysearch.org, William Davenport and Theresa Dailey, 22 November 1863.

7. "Michigan Deaths and Burials, 1800–1995," *Family Search*, database, https://familysearch. org, Wm. Davenport in entry for Wm. Davenport, 9 August 1901; citing Cross Village, Emmet, MI, reference cn p. 59, Family History Library (FHL) microfilm 966,504.

8. *Liber Matrimonium, Mackinac Register, 1695–1888*, 58–59.

9. *General Index to Civil War and Later Pension Files, ca. 1949–ca. 1949*, National Archives at Washington, DC, NAI number 563268; "United States General Index to Pension Files, 1861–1934" (Washington, DC: National Archives and Records Administration, n.d.), microfilm T288, roll 112, Family Search, database with images, https://familysearch.org; Records of the Department of Veterans Affairs, 1773–2007, record group number 15.

10. "Michigan Deaths and Burials, 1800–1995," *Family Search*, database, https://familysearch. org, under Robert Davenport, 24 January 1885, citing Newton, Mackinac County, MI, reference yr. 1873–1899, p. 62, FHL microfilm 1,007,364.

11. Reidsma, *Tombstone*, 2. Also, author's notations and photos of many monuments in both Ste. Anne's and the Protestant cemeteries.

12. Schenck, All Our Relations, 57.

13. "United States Census, 1850," *Family Search*, database with images, https://familysearch. org, under William Davenport, Michilimackinac, MI, citing family 422, NARA microfilm publication M432 (Washington, DC: National Archives and Records Administration,

n.d.).

14. "Michigan Deaths, 1867–1897," *Family Search*, database with images, https://familysearch. org, under William Davenport, 1875, citing p. 156, rn 63, Holmes, Mackinac, MI, Department of Vital Records, Lansing, FHL microfilm 2,363,454. Note: There are no dates other than the year recorded for William Davenport in the Mackinac County records. In the probate records, William's death date as recorded in court papers was 6 April 1876.

60. Alexsie Dophena

1. *Liber Matrimonium, Mackinac Register, 1695–1888*, 35.
2. "Baptismal Register," *Mackinac Register, 1695–1888*, 153. See under Julia Dufine.
3. "Baptismal Register," *Mackinac Register, 1695–1888*, 163. See under François Dophina.
4. "Baptismal Register," *Mackinac Register, 1695–1888*, 173. See under Alexandre Dauphina.
5. *Liber Matrimonium, Mackinac Register, 1695–1888*, 54–55. See under Francis Dofina.
6. *Liber Matrimonium, Mackinac Register, 1695–1888*, 66–67. See under Alexander Dauphine and Marie Danis.
7. "United States Census, 1880," *Family Search*, database with images, https://familysearch. org, under Josephina Duffina, Holmes, Mackinac, MI, citing enumeration district ED 43, sheet 261D, NARA microfilm publication T9 (Washington DC: National Archives and Records Administration, n.d.), roll 0592, FHL microfilm 1,254,592.
8. "United States Census, 1900," *Family Search*, database with images, https://familysearch. org, under Alexander Duffine in household of Samuel Duffine, Hebron, Beaugrand, and Mackinaw townships (excluding Cheboygan city), Mackinaw City village (part), Cheboygan, Michigan, citing enumeration district (ED) 66, sheet 18A, family 9, NARA microfilm publication T623 (Washington, DC: National Archives and Records Administration, 1972.), FHL microfilm 1,240,706.
9. "Michigan Deaths and Burials, 1800–1995," *Family Search*, database, https://familysearch. org, under Elack Duffina, 1907.
10. Death certificate for Back Duffina, 1907, Cheboygan County, MI, *Michiganology*, https:// michiganology.org. The poor handwriting has been interpreted incorrectly to read "Back" instead of Aleck. As noted, he was buried in Mackinaw City, MI.

23. Mrs. Hyacinthe (François) Dophena (Josette Dejadon)

1. Marriage record for François Dufinais and Josette (Indian woman), "Port of Mackinac Records," Office of the Register of Deeds, St. Ignace, Mackinac County, MI, no. 55.
2. "Baptismal Register," *Mackinac Register, 1695–1888*, 22. See under François Douphine.
3. *Liber Matrimonium, Mackinac Register, 1695–1888*, 35. See under François Dauphina.
4. *Liber Matrimonium, Mackinac Register, 1695–1888*, 54–55. See under Francis Dofina.

5. "Michigan Deaths and Burials, 1800–1995," *Family Search*, database, https://familysearch. org, under Francis Duffina, 1898.

6. "Baptismal Register," *Mackinac Register, 1695–1888*, 34. See under Hyancintus Daufinet. No father is listed, only the mother, Josepha Daufinet.

7. Marriage record for Yassant Daufinnais and Josette Andress, "Port of Mackinac Records," Office of the Register of Deeds, St. Ignace, Mackinac County, MI, no. 508.

8. "Baptismal Register," *Mackinac Register, 1695–1888*, 42. See under Julie Daufinet.

9. "Baptismal Register," *Mackinac Register, 1695–1888*, 53. See under Alexandre Dauphine.

10. See her sister, no. 40 Mrs. Joseph Laslin.

11. *Liber Matrimonium, Mackinac Register, 1695–1888*, 52–53.

12. Alexander "Alex" Duffina, *Find a Grave*, www.findagrave.com, memorial no. 40024123. The monument includes the names of both Alexander and Ursula.

13. Ursula LaSeaur Duffina, www.findagrave.com, memorial no. 40024058.

14. "Baptismal Register," *Mackinac Register, 1695–1888*, 87. See under Guillaume Dauphine.

15. "Baptismal Register," *Mackinac Register, 1695–1888*, 92.

16. *Liber Matrimonium, Mackinac Register, 1695–1888*, 54–55. See under Jean Baptiste Besinet and Marie Dauphina.

17. *Liber Defunctorum, Mackinac Register, 1695–1888*, 112. See under John Besinant.

18. Michigan State Archives, "Death Records, 1897–1920," *Michiganology*, entry for Mrs. Mary Bezina, 1909, https://michiganology.org. The name given for Marie's mother is Josette Wine.

19. "Baptismal Register," *Mackinac Register, 1695–1888*, 106. See under Madorus Dophine.

20. "Michigan Marriages, 1822–1995," *Family Search* database, https://familysearch.org, Weddard Doffing and Christine Larvillio, 13 September 1868, citing FHL microfilm 1,007,362. The names have been recorded incorrectly. A review of the original document shows his name was recorded as Meddard Doffing and her name, Christine Levaillee.

21. *Liber Matrimonium, Mackinac Register, 1695–1888*, 27. See under Namenville.

22. *Liber Defunctorum, Mackinac Register, 1695–1888*, 91. See under Namenville.

23. "Record of Interments," Clerk's Office, City Hall, Mackinac Island, MI, p. 1, under Josephine Duffina, 1891.

14. Mrs. Joseph Fountain (Angelique Fagnant)

1. Gail Morin, *Métis Families: Deslauriers–Garand*, vol. 4, 3rd ed. (n.p.: CreateSpace Independent Publishing Platform, 2016), 128.

2. Morin, *Métis Families*, 128.

3. Library and Archives of Canada, "Kipling card index 1–1344," Canadiana Héritage, Parish Registers: Manitoba H-1344, microfilm publication, http://heritage.canadiana.ca/view/

oocihm.lac_reel_h1344. See entry for Mary Fontaine, born 27 October 1832, citing St. Boniface Church, image 1332.

4. *Liber Matrimonium, Mackinac Register, 1695–1888*, 52–53.
5. *Liber Matrimonium, Mackinac Register, 1695–1888*, 54–55.
6. Michigan State Archives, "Death Records 1921–1947," *Michiganology*, entry for Andrew Fountain, 1926, https://michiganology.org.
7. "Baptismal Register," *Mackinac Register, 1695–1888*, 95.
8. "Baptismal Register," *Mackinac Register, 1695–1888*, 109.
9. *Liber Matrimonium, Mackinac Register, 1695–1888*, 64–65.
10. "Baptismal Register," *Mackinac Register, 1695–1888*, 124.
11. "Baptismal Register," *Mackinac Register, 1695–1888*, 139.
12. "Baptismal Register," *Mackinac Register, 1695–1888*, 163.
13. *Liber Defunctorum, Mackinac Register, 1695–1888*, 176.
14. *Liber Defunctorum, Mackinac Register, 1695–1888*, 105
15. *Liber Defunctorum, Mackinac Register, 1695–1888*, 100.
16. *Liber Defunctorum, Mackinac Register, 1695–1888*, 105.

16. Mrs. Henry Hudson's Children (Angeline Caron)

1. *Liber Matrimonium, Mackinac Register, 1695–1888*, 22.
2. *Liber Defunctorum, Mackinac Register, 1695–1888*, 90–91.
3. *Liber Matrimonium, Mackinac Register, 1695–1888*, 32.
4. *Liber Defunctorum, Mackinac Register, 1695–1888*, 139.
5. Genealogical Death Indexing System, Michigan Department of Health and Human Services, Lansing, MI, http://www.mdch.state.mi.us. See entry for Emily Fisher, Cheboygan County, p. 155, no. 62.
6. "Baptismal Register," *Mackinac Register, 1695–1888*, 155. See under William Utsen.
7. "Baptismal Register," *Mackinac Register, 1695–1888*, 172.
8. *Applications for Headstones, Compiled 01/01/1925–06/30/1970, Documenting the Period ca. 1776–1970*, ARC: 596118, Records of the Office of the Quartermaster General, 1774–1985, RG 92, National Archives and Records Administration, Washington, DC. See James Hudson.
9. "Michigan Marriages, 1822–1995," *Family Search* database, https://familysearch.org, John Andrus and Alice Hudson, 16 June 1876.
10. *St. Mary's Parish Baptism Records, 1860–1892*, St. Mary Catholic Church (Cheboygan, MI) parish rectory office, under Angelique Hudson, 1862, p. 3.
11. Marriage of John McCarty and Angelin Hulson [*sic*], *Michigan, Marriage Records, 1867–1952*, Michigan Department of Community Health, Division for Vital Records and

Health Statistics.

12. Historical Data Systems, comp., *U.S., Civil War Soldier Records and Profiles, 1861–1865, Ancestry*, database, (Provo, UT: Ancestry.com Operations Inc., 2009), https://www.ancestry.com/search/collections/1555/. Record for Henry Hudson.

13. "United States Census of Union Veterans and Widows of the Civil War, 1890," *Family Search*, database with images, https://familysearch.org, under Henry Hudson, 1890, citing NARA microfilm publication M123 (Washington, DC: National Archives and Records Administration, n.d.), FHL microfilm 338,180.

14. "United States Veterans Administration Pension Payment Cards, 1907–1933," *Family Search*, database with images, https://familysearch.org, under Henry Hudson, 1907–1933, citing NARA microfilm publication M850 (Washington, DC: National Archives and Records Administration, n.d.), FHL microfilm 1,635,143.

15. "Find a Grave Index," *Family Search*, database, https://familysearch.org, under Henry Hudson, 1910, record ID 162437622, Burial: Calvary Cemetery, Cheboygan, Michigan, *Find a Grave*, http://www.findagrave.com.

22. Mrs. Peter Jacobear (Poline Martin)

1. While researching this family, I suspected Poline could be the child of Charles Martin and Marianne Ayabins. Marianne's family is from the Sugar Island, north shore area along Lake Huron. What little evidence was found suggests Poline traveled between the "Soo" and Mackinac. Perhaps, the person listed on the 1870 as Elizabeth Martin, sixteen, is no. 55 Lizette Martin? However, she was thirty-two when she married Antoine Truckey in 1874. Another thought, since many of these documents are grouped by family, she could be the daughter of Simon Martin and Marie Leveille. No. 22 is Mrs. Francis Martin. Francis was the son of Simon and Marie, but that search did not yield positive results. Until additional documents are found, Poline's heritage will remain a mystery. I suspect more research will need to be done in Canada.

2. "Baptismal Register," *Mackinac Register, 1695–1888*, 114.

3. St. Ignatius Loyola (St. Ignace, MI), "Marriages, 1838–1893," bk. 1, pp. 24–25 (Pierre Hebert and Pauline Martin, 1862), parish rectory.

4. Kathleen M. Hendricks, comp., *St. Mary's Catholic Church Baptisms: Sault Sainte Marie, Michigan, 1811–1900* (Sault Ste. Marie, MI: Holy Name of Mary Proto-Cathedral, 2005), entry 2062.

5. *Liber Defunctorum, Mackinac Register, 1695–1888*, 109. See under A'Bare.

6. "Michigan Marriages, 1822–1995," *Family Search* database, https://familysearch.org, under James Lefever and Nancy Abair, 30 September 1896, Family History Library (FHL) microfilm 1,007,362. Parents of the bride were listed at Peter Abair and Mary Martin.

7. "United States Census, 1910," *Family Search*, database with images, https://familysearch. org, under Thomas Valier, Garfield, Mackinac, MI, citing enumeration district (ED) ED 163, sheet 5B, family 101, NARA microfilm publication T624 (Washington, DC: National Archives and Records Administration, 1982), roll 658, FHL microfilm 1,374,671.

8. "Michigan Death Certificates, 1921–1952," *Family Search*, database, https://familysearch. org, under Nancy Vallier, 27 October 1932, citing Engadine, Mackinaw, MI, Division for Vital Records and Health Statistics, Lansing, FHL microfilm 1,972,852.

9. Hendricks, *St. Mary's Catholic Church Baptisms*, entry 2516.

10. *Liber Defunctorum, Mackinac Register, 1695–1888*, 104.

15. Mrs. Francis Johnston (Margaret Bennett-Beaubin)

1. Larry Wyckoff, trans., "Mixed-Blood Census Register, Ottawas and Chippewas of Michigan, Treaty of March 26, 1836," *Roots Web*, http://www.rootsweb.ancestry. com/~mimacki2/annuities/1836mb.pdf, n.d., no. 222. See under Margaret Beaubin.

2. "United States Census, 1900," *Family Search*, database with images, https://familysearch. org, under Frank Johnston, Hebron, Beaugrand, and Mackinaw townships (excluding Cheboygan city), Mackinaw City village (part), Cheboygan, Michigan, citing enumeration district (ED) 66, sheet 10B, family 207, NARA microfilm publication T623 (Washington, DC: National Archives and Records Administration, 1972.), FHL microfilm 1,240,706.

3. Marriage of Frank Johnson and Margarette Bennett, "Port of Mackinac Records," Office of the Register of Deeds, St. Ignace, Mackinac County, MI, no. 512.

4. "Mackinaw City," *Cheboygan Democrat*, 3 October 1913, p. 7, col. 7.

57. Edward Karrow

1. "Baptismal Register," *Mackinac Register, 1695–1888*, 195.

2. Marriage of Edward Karrow and Elizabeth Viedmer, *Michigan, Marriage Records, 1867–1952*, 1885 Alcona–1885 Lapeer, film 29, Michigan Department of Community Health, Division for Vital Records and Health Statistics.

3. Her last name and parents are speculation. Viedmer, or more likely Weidmer or Wiedemeyer, was possibly the name of a first husband, who was not found. Her death certificate lists John Pauls and Maggie Doulhier as her parents. Her children list her last name as Cole on marriage records.

4. "Policeman Hanson last night caught two men named Ed. Corrow and Wyler coming out of Mr. Barber's with seven chickens in their possession. He took them to the lock up. Owing to the absence of Prosecuting Attorney Roe, who was called to Indian River, they could not be tried today." *Cheboygan Democrat* (Cheboygan, MI), 16 October 1897, p. 2, col. 4.

Follow up: "Local Lore—Justice Partridge held court Saturday afternoon, and decided the fate of those caught in a fowl deed Friday night. Ed. Corrow was sent to jail for 90 days in default of a fine of $15 and costs. Jos. Wyler, 60 day or $10 fine and costs. J. Hudson, drunk, 90 days or $20 fine and costs." *Cheboygan Democrat* (Cheboygan, MI), 23 October 1897, p. 4, col. 6.

5. "Terse Tales of Town—Edward Corrow, Amos Lampman and Louis Belway were found sleeping in Pellenz's barn last night by the police and gathered in. This morning Judge Bouchard suspended sentence on them for 90 days and ordered them to get out of town before tomorrow morning and go to work and not show themselves in town inside of the 90 days. They have been loafing and drinking around town for some time." *Cheboygan Democrat* (Cheboygan, MI), 12 August 1904, p. 2, col. 2.

6. "Report of Superintendent of Poor for Month of September," *Cheboygan Democrat* (Cheboygan, MI), 6 November 1897, p. 8, col. 3. See Mrs. E. Carrow in Beaugrand Township.

7. "Report of Superintendent of Poor for Month of April," *Cheboygan Democrat* (Cheboygan, MI), 27 May 1899, p. 7, col. 5. See Ed Carrow in Beaugrand Township.

8. "HORRIBLE, Mrs. Corrow killed by cars at Bellant's Crossing. Another shocking accident occurred at Bellant's crossing, Monday morning before seven o'clock as she had an engagement to do the family washing for one of our citizens. One of her boys was driving her in on a dog sleigh. The air was frosty, the runners made some noise and the north bound passenger train was neither heard no seen by the mother or son. Perhaps as the train had been behind time so many mornings lately, Mrs. Corrow was not looking for it. The train was on time and as the dogs found it hard pulling over the tracks from which the snow had melted, they stopped just as the train was on them. The boy, Ed. Corrow, about twelve years old, jumped from the sleigh and escaped with a scalp wound and a blow on the back. Mrs. Corrow did not jump and the engine struck her. . . . She was brought to town by Chas. Bellant . . . the boy was also brought down. Reaching the city physician's office, Drs. Steffins and Moloney examined the poor woman, and found no possible hope for her, and Dr. Steffins ordered her sent to the Fountain House. Arriving at the latter place it was decided to take her home and she died on the way. The remains were taken to Undertaker St. Jean's morgue, where Dr. Maries, the coroner, took charge of the body. . . . Mrs. Corrow was an honest, hardworking woman and supported her family of three boys, the oldest of whom is about 16 years old. She did not live with her husband. The poor woman was buried from St. Charles church on Tuesday morning and taken to Calvary cemetery. The boy was not seriously hurt, Drs. Steffins and Moloney dressed the wound on his head, and Mrs. Steffins made him a cup of coffee, but he could not drink it. He was afterward taken to his uncle's house." *Cheboygan Democrat*, April 8, 1899, p. 4, col. 4.

9. "United States Census, 1900," *Family Search*, database with images, https://familysearch.org, under Edward Corrow in household of Louis Gerard, Hebron, Beaugrand, and Mackinaw townships (excluding Cheboygan city), Mackinaw City village (part), Cheboygan, Michigan, citing enumeration district (ED) 66, sheet 12B, family 234, NARA microfilm publication T623 (Washington, DC: National Archives and Records Administration, 1972.), FHL microfilm 1,240,706.

10. "United States Census, 1900," *Family Search*, database with images, https://familysearch.org, under Herbert Corrow in household of William Fullerton, Hebron, Beaugrand, and Mackinaw townships (excluding Cheboygan city), Mackinaw City village (part), Cheboygan, Michigan, citing enumeration district (ED) 66, sheet 15A, family 281, NARA microfilm publication T623 (Washington, DC: National Archives and Records Administration, 1972.), FHL microfilm 1,240,706.

11. "United States Census, 1900," *Family Search*, database with images, https://familysearch.org, under Rachel Corrow in household of Andrew Corrow, Cheboygan City Ward 3 and 5, Cheboygan, Michigan, citing enumeration district (ED) 71, sheet 1B, family 12, NARA microfilm publication T623 (Washington, DC: National Archives and Records Administration, 1972.), FHL microfilm 1,240,706.

12. *U.S., Social Security Death Index, 1935–2014* [database online] (Provo, UT: Ancestry.com Operations Inc, 2014).

13. "Michigan Marriages, 1822–1995," *Family Search*, database, https://familysearch.org, under Edward Carrow and Ethel McCash, 16 October 1912, p. 229, no. 2131, FHL microfilm 964,409.

14. "Michigan Death Index, 1971–1996," *Family Search*, database, https://familysearch.org, under Ethel I. Carrow, 17 November 1972, from *Ancestry*, http://www.ancestry.com, citing Cheboygan, MI, death certificate number 67668, Michigan Department of Vital and Health Records, Lansing.

15. "Michigan Death Index, 1971–1996," *Family Search*, database, https://familysearch.org, under Ethel I. Carrow, 17 November 1972, from *Ancestry*, http://www.ancestry.com, citing Cheboygan, MI, death certificate number 67668, Michigan Department of Vital and Health Records, Lansing.

16. "Michigan Births, 1867–1902," *Family Search*, database with images, https://familysearch.org, 004207551, image 428 of 1163; Department of Vital Records, Lansing.

17. "Michigan Marriages, 1822–1995," *Family Search*, database, https://familysearch.org, under Herbert A. Carrow and Lila Dettling, 1911.

18. "Ohio, County Marriages, 1789–2013," *Family Search*, database with images, https://familysearch.org, under Herbert Ash Carrow and Electa M, Swarthwood, 8 April 1944, citing Henry, OH, County Courthouses, FHL microfilm 1,575,511.

19. "Find a Grave Index," *Family Search*, database and images, https://familysearch.org, under Rachel E. *Carrow* Kingsley, 15 February 1892–11 June 1984, Burial: Oakwood Cemetery, Grand Ledge, Eaton County, MI, memorial no. 119495257, *Find a Grave*, http://www.findagrave.com.

20. "Indiana Marriages, 1811–2007," *Family Search*, database with images, https://familysearch.org, under Harvey Logan Millett and Rachel Eva Corrow, citing St. Joseph, IN, county clerk, FHL microfilm 1,503,531.

21. *Indiana, Death Certificates, 1899–2011* [database on-line] (Lehi, UT: Ancestry.com Operations, 2015), death certificates for 1912, roll 13.

22. "Michigan Marriages, 1822–1995," *Family Search*, database, https://familysearch.org, under Seth T. Kingsley and Racheal Carrow Millett, 1913.

23. "Find a Grave Index," *Family Search*, database and images, https://familysearch.org, under Rachel E. *Carrow* Kingsley, 15 February 1892–11 June 1984, Burial: Oakwood Cemetery, Grand Ledge, Eaton County, MI, memorial no. 119495257, *Find a Grave*, http://www.findagrave.com.

24. *Applications for Headstones, Compiled 01/01/1925–06/30/1970, Documenting the Period ca. 1776–1970*, ARC: 596118, Records of the Office of the Quartermaster General, 1774–1985, RG 92, National Archives and Records Administration, Washington, DC.

25. "United States Census, 1900," *Family Search*, database with images, https://familysearch.org, under Joseph Mallette in household of Alexander Mallette, Cheboygan City, Ward 2, Cheboygan, MI, citing enumeration district (ED) 70, sheet 8A, family 153, NARA microfilm publication T623 (Washington, DC: National Archives and Records Administration, 1972.), FHL microfilm 1,240,706.

26. US Army, *Lists of Incoming Passengers, 1917–1938; Lists of Outgoing Passengers, 1917–1938* (Washington, DC: National Archives and Records Administration, 1918), 26 April–12 March 1919, digital images, fold 3, *Ancestry*, https://ancestry.com, outgoing on the ship *Vestris*, entry number NM-81 2061, 10 December 1918.

27. US Army, *Lists of Incoming Passengers, 1917–1938; Lists of Outgoing Passengers, 1917–1938* (Washington, DC: National Archives and Records Administration), 22 August, 1919, incoming on the ship *Kaiserin Auguste Victoria*, entry number NM-81-2060.

28. She was first married to Frank Blay. She divorced him on 28 July 1922 in Wayne County, Michigan. *Michigan Divorce Records, 1897–1952* [database online] (Provo, UT: Ancestry. com Operations).

29. "Michigan Deaths and Burials, 1800–1995," *Family Search*, database, https://familysearch.org, under Emma Mollette, 10 March 1933, citing Beaugrand, Cheboygan, MI, reference vol. 3, p. 6, FHL microfilm 964,407. Note surname is Mollette instead of Mallette.

30. "Michigan, County Marriages, 1820–1940," *Family Search*, database with images, https://

familysearch.org, under Joseph Mallette and Margaret Bellant, 10 June 1935, Cheboygan, MI, FHL microfilm 1,837,911.

10. Mrs. Henry Karrow (Judithe Diotte)

1. Joy Reisinger, "Baptismal Records, 1835–1837, Kept at LaPointe & Bayfield, Indian Missions," *Lost in Canada? Canadian-American Journal of History & Genealogy for Canadian, French & Métis Study* 16, no. 4 (Summer 1992): 184. The baptism record lists the names of her parents.

2. Theresa M. Schenck, *All Our Relations: Chippewa Mixed-Bloods and the Treaty of 1837* (Winnipeg, Manitoba: The Center for Rupert's Land Studies at the University of Winnipeg, 2010), 24.

3. *Liber Matrimonium, Mackinac Register, 1695–1888*, 29. Spelling of witnesses' names per document.

4. *Ste. Anne's Church Registers: 1704–1842*, microfilm, 3 rolls (Detroit, MI: St. Anne's of Detroit). See roll 3, *Chapelle du nordest: Baptisms, Marriages, Burials, 1810–1838*, arranged by date, "Baptême de Henry Caron," p. 133. This record indicates he was born and baptized on Drummond Island, Michigan.

5. Larry Wyckoff, trans., "Mixed-Blood Census Register, Ottawas and Chippewas of Michigan, Treaty of March 26, 1836," *Roots Web*, http://www.rootsweb.ancestry. com/~mimacki2/annuities/1836mb.pdf, n.d., 199. See under Henry Carow.

6. "Baptismal Register," *Mackinac Register, 1695–1888*, 130.

7. "Baptismal Register," *Mackinac Register, 1695–1888*, 144. See under Corron.

8. "Baptismal Register," *Mackinac Register, 1695–1888*, 153. See under Charles Henri Karon.

9. "Baptismal Register," *Mackinac Register, 1695–1888*, 172.

10. "Baptismal Register," *Mackinac Register, 1695–1888*, 184.

11. "Baptismal Register," *Mackinac Register, 1695–1888*, 189A. There was a change of priest at p. 187. The new priest preferred the chart type of sacramental entry versus a long hand where everything is written out. Therefore, he needed a fresh page to make his columns. There is no page labeled 188. Between 189 and 191, there are four pages. The "extra" page has been labeled 189A (by the author) in my printed copy and falls directly after 189.

12. "Baptismal Register," *Mackinac Register, 1695–1888*, 195.

13. *Liber Defunctorum, Mackinac Register, 1695–1888*, 99. See under Henry Corron. The death record from Ste. Anne's states his birth place as Drummond Island.

14. *1870 US Census, Cheboygan County, MI, population schedule, Duncan, p. 16 (written), dwelling 123, family 123, Julie Caron, Ancestry*, https://www.ancestry.com, citing Family History Library (FHL) film 552168, roll M593_669.

15. "Deaths," *St. Mary's Parish Record, 1869–1962*, St. Mary Catholic Church (Cheboygan, MI)

parish rectory office, under Judice Gyot, 1885, p. 58.

29. Mary A. Karrow (Marianne Kedegekwanabe)

1. *Liber Matrimonium, Mackinac Register, 1695–1888*, 10.
2. St. Ignatius Loyola (St. Ignace, MI), "Marriages, 1838–1893," bk. 1, p. 2 (Josephus Caron and Marianna Ketakguane, 1839), parish rectory.
3. Programme de recherche en démographie historique (*PRDH*) (Université de Montréal, Canada), 1621–1849, certificate 304335, Joseph Louis Gautier, transcription, https://www.prdh-igd.com.
4. History of the Upper Peninsula of Michigan (Chicago, 1883), p. 372, https://babel.hathitrust.org.
5. "Registers of the Parish of Michilimackinac, Mackinac Baptism Records 1800–1809," AccessGenealogy, https://www.accessgenealogy.com/michigan/mackinac-baptism-records-1800-1809.htm, citing the baptism (13 June 1804) of Joseph Gauthier dit Caron.
6. *Liber Matrimonium, Mackinac Register, 1695–1888*, 11,
7. "Baptismal Register," *Mackinac Register, 1695–1888*, 65.
8. *Liber Matrimonium, Mackinac Register, 1695–1888*, 54–55.
9. "Baptismal Register," *Mackinac Register, 1695–1888*, 93.
10. "Michigan Deaths and Burials, 1800–1995," *Family Search*, database, https://familysearch.org, under John Carron, 15 December 1920, citing Cheboygan, Cheboygan, MI, reference vol. 3, p. 62, FHL microfilm 964,407.
11. "Baptismal Register," *Mackinac Register, 1695–1888*, 102.
12. "Baptismal Register," *Mackinac Register, 1695–1888*, 135.
13. "Deaths," *St. Mary's Parish Record, 1869–1962*, St. Mary Catholic Church (Cheboygan, MI) parish rectory office, under Marie Anne Caron, 1883, p. 51. *Liber Matrimonium, Mackinac Register, 1695–1888*.
14. "Baptismal Register," *Mackinac Register, 1695–1888*, 118. See under Angelique Carron.
15. "Baptismal Register," *Mackinac Register, 1695–1888*, 127. See under Joseph Carron.
16. "Baptismal Register," *Mackinac Register, 1695–1888*, 142. See under Marguerite Corron.
17. "Baptismal Register," *Mackinac Register, 1695–1888*, 155. See under Josephus, baptized 21 March at forty-five days old.
18. "Michigan Deaths, 1867–1897," *Family Search*, database with images, https://familysearch.org, under Joseph Corrow, 2 October 1869, citing p. 112 rn, Duncan Bay, Cheboygan, MI, Department of Vital Records, Lansing, FHL microfilm 2,363,448.
19. *Liber Defunctorum, Mackinac Register, 1695–1888*, 99.
20. "United States Census, 1900," *Family Search*, database with images, https://familysearch.org, under Agnes Carrow, Benton Township, Cheboygan, MI, ED 67, dwelling no. 185,

family no. 190, line no. 19, citing NARA microfilm publication T623 (Washington, DC: National Archives and Records Administration, n.d.), image 1 of 22. "United States Census, 1910," *Family Search*, database with images, https://familysearch.org, under Agnes Carrow, Benton, Cheboygan, MI Benton, ED 69, dwelling no. 46, family no. 46, line no. 65, citing NARA microfilm publication T624 (Washington, DC: National Archives and Records Administration, n.d.), image 6 of 22.

21. "Michigan Deaths and Burials, 1800–1995," *Family Search*, database, https://familysearch.org, under Mary Agnes Corrow, 12 September 1910, citing Benton Township, Cheboygan, MI, reference vol. 3, p. 3, FHL microfilm 964,407.

7. Mrs. William Karrow (Isabelle Morin)

1. Notre Dame de Montreal, P.Q., and Gabriel Drouin, comp., *Registres Photographies a la Paroisse* (Montreal: Institut Généalogique Drouin), Andre Morin baptism, 24 February 1797, *Ancestry* [database online], https://ancestry.com.

2. "Michigan Deaths, 1867–1897," *Family Search*, database with images, https://familysearch.org, under Andrew Morani, 22 Aug 1878, citing p. 127, rn 20, Benton, Cheboygan, Michigan, Department of Vital Records, Lansing, Family History Library (FHL) microfilm 2,363,666.

3. "Baptismal Register," *Mackinac Register, 1695–1888*, 51.

4. "1860 US Census," *Heritage Quest*, https://www.ancestryheritagequest.com, image, under Mary Moran, Holmes, Mackinac County, MI, p. 58, dwelling 699, family 347, citing NARA microfilm publication roll M653_542.

5. *Ste. Anne's Church Registers: 1704–1842*, microfilm, 3 rolls (Detroit, MI: St. Anne's of Detroit). See roll 3, *Chapelle du nordest: Baptisms, Marriages, Burials, 1810–1838*, arranged by date, Guillaume Caron on 15 September 1825, BHC no. 1252, reel 3.

6. *Liber Matrimonium, Mackinac Register, 1695–1888*, 25.

7. "Baptismal Register," *Mackinac Register, 1695–1888*, 119. Baptized Elizabeth.

8. *Liber Matrimonium, Mackinac Register, 1695–1888*, 54–55.

9. "Baptismal Register," *Mackinac Register, 1695–1888*, 115. Place of birth says *Grande terre*. Marriage record says Beaver Island.

10. "Michigan Marriages, 1822–1995," *Family Search*, database, https://familysearch.org, under George La Bell and Isabella Corrow, 30 December 1867.

11. "Baptismal Register," *Mackinac Register, 1695–1888*, 135.

12. "Baptismal Register," *Mackinac Register, 1695–1888*, 146. He was baptized André.

13. "Baptismal Register," *Mackinac Register, 1695–1888*, 158.

14. "Baptismal Register," *Mackinac Register, 1695–1888*, 194c.

15. "Baptismal Register," *Mackinac Register, 1695–1888*, 203–204.

16. *St. Mary's Parish Baptism Records, 1860–1892*, St. Mary Catholic Church (Cheboygan, MI) parish rectory office, under Mariane Caro, 1867, p. 9.

17. "Deaths," *St. Mary's Parish Record, 1860–1892*, St. Mary Catholic Church (Cheboygan, MI) parish rectory office, under Mariane Caro, 1870, p. 9.

18. "Michigan, Death Records, 1867–1952," *Ancestry*, database with images, https://www.ancestry.com, under Elizabeth Corrow, 19 August 1910, Cheboygan County.

19. "Michigan Deaths and Burials, 1800–1995," *Family Search*, database, https://familysearch.org, under Elizabeth Carrow, 1910.

19. Mrs. David Kniffen (Marie Bennet-Beaubin)

1. "Baptismal Register," *Mackinac Register, 1695–1888*, 34–35.

2. "United States Census, 1850," *Family Search*, database with images, https://familysearch.org, Michilimackinac, Michilimackinac County, MI, citing NARA microfilm publication M432 (Washington, DC: National Archives and Records Administration, n.d.), image 36 of 94.

3. *Liber Matrimonium, Mackinac Register, 1695–1888*, 41.

4. *Holy Cross Church Records* (Cross Village, MI), microfilm publication, 1 roll (Bentley Historical Library [BHL], University of Michigan), roll 1, arranged mostly alphabetically, see family 64, "Holles Kniffin."

5. "Michigan Marriages, 1822–1995," *Family Search*, database, https://familysearch.org, under Eustache Plant and Mary H. Kniffin, 7 June 1874, Family History Library (FHL) microfilm 964,409.

6. "Michigan Death Certificates, 1921–1952," *Family Search*, database, https://familysearch.org, under Mary Helen Plaunt, 30 May 1944, Cheboygan, MI, Division for Vital Records and Health Statistics, Lansing, FHL microfilm 1,973,215.

7. *Holy Cross Church Records*, roll 1, family 64, "Holles Kniffin."

8. "Michigan Deaths and Burials, 1800–1995," *Family Search*, database, https://familysearch.org, under Harriet C. Kniffin, 23 October 1884, Mackinaw, Cheboygan County, MI, reference vol. 1, p. 33, FHL microfilm 964,407.

9. *Holy Cross Church Records*, roll 1, family 64, "Holles Kniffin."

10. "Michigan Deaths and Burials, 1800–1995," *Family Search*, database, https://familysearch.org, under Hollis J. Kniffin in entry for David L. Kniffin, 23 January 1883, Mackinaw, Cheboygan County, MI, reference vol. 1, p. 31, FHL microfilm 964,407.

11. *Holy Cross Church Records*, roll 1, family 64, "Holles Kniffin."

12. *St. Mary's Parish Baptism Records, 1860–1892*, St. Mary Catholic Church (Cheboygan, MI) parish rectory office, under Miriam Kniffen, 1862, bk. 1, p. 1.

13. *Holy Cross Church Records*, roll 1, family 64, "Holles Kniffin."

14. "Baptismal Register," *Mackinac Register, 1695–1888*, 205.

15. "Michigan Death Certificates, 1921–1952," *Family Search*, database, https://familysearch. org, under Samuel H Kniffin, 10 May 1946, Mackinaw City, Cheboygan County, MI, Division for Vital Records and Health Statistics, Lansing, FHL microfilm 1,973,214.

16. *Holy Cross Church Records*, roll 1, family 64, "Holles Kniffin."

17. "Michigan Marriages, 1822–1995," *Family Search,* database, https://familysearch.org, under H. S. Kniffen in entry for Charles Kniffin and Maggie Andrus, 2 May 1904, citing reference p. 136, no. 742, FHL microfilm 964,409.

18. "Michigan Marriages, 1822–1995," *Family Search,* database, https://familysearch.org, under Charles Kniffin and Lizzie Richards, 18 September 1918, citing reference p. 283, no. 2933, FHL microfilm 964,409.

19. *Holy Cross Church Records*, roll 1, family 64, "Holles Kniffin."

20. "Michigan Marriages, 1822–1995," *Family Search*, database, https://familysearch.org, under James Kniffin and Ella Wing, 26 June 1920, FHL microfilm 1,007,362.

21. "Michigan Deaths and Burials, 1800–1995," *Family Search*, database, https://familysearch. org, under Mary Kniffin, 17 November 1911, citing Mackinaw, Cheboygan County, MI, reference vol. 3, p. 1, FHL microfilm 964,407.

25. Mrs. Michael Kuthron (Sophie Pogay)

1. "Michigan Deaths and Burials, 1800–1995," *Family Search*, database, https://familysearch. org, under Sophia Cadotte, 7 August 1921, citing Mackinac Island, Mackinac County, MI, reference yrs. 1899–1946, p. 102, Family History Library (FHL) microfilm 1,007,364.

2. John Read Bailey, *Mackinac, formerly Michilimackinac*, 4th ed. (Lansing, MI, 1899). Sophie's early history appears on page 14 of this book.

"There is now living on Mackinac Island a mixed blood Indian woman about 68 years old (who came here at the age of seventeen), of the Kilistinoux or Cree tribe. She was born in the Churchill river country, between Hudson's Bay and Great and Little Slave lakes. She says her people went to the north in summer by way of Great Slave lake to barter with the tribes on the 'Frozen Sea.'

"They started early in March and did not return until the next year. They met the people from the 'Sea' coming up the river, halfway. Some of her people returned and others went north and did not come back. Other parties went north by way of Red River (of the north) to trade and sell furs. They, too, would go one year, start in March, and not come back until the next season. Time then was no object. This woman, Madam Cadro (now Cadotte), is part French. Her people gave her in marriage to Cadro when she was only twelve years old. He was a 'Courier du Bois' and an 'Engagee' of the Hudson's Bay Company. Madam Cadro is an intelligent, industrious, hard working woman, and is generally respected."

3. "Québec, registres paroissiaux catholiques, 1621–1979," *Family Search*, database with images, https://familysearch.org, "Saint-Michel-d'Yamaska," image 339 of 710, *Baptêmes, mariages, sépultures, 1775–1809* (Montreal: Archives Nationales du Quebec [National Archives of Quebec]). See baptism of Michel Cadrin.

4. "United States, Veterans Administration Master Index, 1917–1940," *Family Search*, database, https://familysearch.org, under Michael Cadrow, 10 March 1866, citing Military Service, NARA microfilm publication 76193916 (St. Louis: National Archives and Records Administration, 1985), various roll numbers.

5. "United States, Veterans Administration Master Index, 1917–1940," *Family Search*, database, https://familysearch.org, under Michael Cadrow, 10 March 1866, citing Military Service, NARA microfilm publication 76193916 (St. Louis: National Archives and Records Administration, 1985), various roll numbers.

6. "Michigan Marriages, 1868–1925," *Family Search*, database with images, https://familysearch.org, under Michael Cadra and Mary Contin, 1869.

7. "United States, Veterans Administration Master Index, 1917–1940," *Family Search*, database, https://familysearch.org, under Michael Cadrow, 10 March 1866, citing Military Service, NARA microfilm publication 76193916 (St. Louis: National Archives and Records Administration, 1985), various roll numbers.

8. "Baptismal Register," *Mackinac Register, 1695–1888*, 138.

9. "Michigan Deaths and Burials, 1800–1995," *Family Search*, database, https://familysearch.org, Michael Cadran in entry for Joseph Cadran, 3 September 1910, citing Mackinac Island, Mackinac County, MI, reference yrs. 1899–1946, p. 48, FHL microfilm 1,007,364.

10. "Baptismal Register," *Mackinac Register, 1695–1888*, 154.

11. *Liber Matrimonium, Mackinac Register, 1695–1888*, 62–63.

12. "Baptismal Register," *Mackinac Register, 1695–1888*, 174.

13. "Baptismal Register," *Mackinac Register, 1695–1888*, 183

14. "Michigan Marriages, 1868–1925," *Family Search*, database with images, https://familysearch.org, under John Cadraw and Grace Decatur, 1898.

15. "Michigan Deaths and Burials, 1800–1995," *Family Search*, database, https://familysearch.org, John Codreau, 29 August 1930, citing Mackinac Island, Mackinac County, MI, reference yrs. 1899–1946, p. 143, FHL microfilm 1,007,364.

16. "Baptismal Register," *Mackinac Register, 1695–1888*, 194. See under Remi Joseph Cadreaux.

17. "Baptismal Register," *Mackinac Register, 1695–1888*, 203

18. "Michigan Marriages, 1868–1925," *Family Search*, database with images, https://familysearch.org, under Alfred Cadran and Theresa Bennett, 1889.

19. "Baptismal Register," *Mackinac Register, 1695–1888*, 211. See under Louis Edmund Cadron.

20. *Annual Report of the United States Life-Saving Service* (1883). See Joseph and Alfred Cardran under "Awards and Medals," p. 57–62. This the abbreviated story of the rescue:

"On the 15th of April 1883, the time being near at hand for the relighting of the lake coasts incident to the approaching opening of navigation, Mr. William Marshall, the keeper of the Spectacle Reef light-house, Lake Huron, undertook to go thither in a sail-boat from Mackinac Island, where he resides. . . . Mr. Marshall decided to take advantage of a favoring wind and set out in the sail-boat. The weather was cold; a gale from the southwest was blowing, with frequent puffs and squalls, and the lake was full of ice, both fixed and floating. . . . There were on board William Marshall, the keeper; Edward Chambers, first assistant keeper; James O. Marshall, the principal's son, second assistant keeper; and Edward Lasley, third assistant keeper. The boat also carried the men's clothing for the season and several weeks' supply of provisions. For seven or eight miles she followed the shores of Round Island and Bois Blanc Island, sailing through comparatively smooth water.

"When within about two miles of Bois Blanc light-house it became necessary to alter her course, and in order to do so shift the sail over from one side of the boat to the other. This was the moment of an unlooked for catastrophe. The fore-boom was longer than it should have been, and in coming over the end caught in the main halyards. Just then a short blast of wind from the west struck the detained canvas, and in a twinkling the horrified men found themselves in the water, with the capsized boat down on its beam ends and jumping about aimlessly on the waves. . . .

The mast and sail held the boat down sheer upon its side, so that the hold of the men, which was from the keel across the bottom to the gunwale, involved a long stretch over the hull, and was too difficult to be long maintained. . . . Young Marshall suffered the most, his place on the boat having chanced to be the worst, keeping him under water more than the others, and greatly exhausting him. His father in turn was greatly exhausted by the constant hold he kept upon him in the effort to help him maintain his position.

"Nothing could be more touching than the devotion and self-sacrifice of all these poor men, who from first to last seemed to forget themselves in the desire to encourage and sustain each other. . . . The evidence shows that they floated clinging to the boat for about three hours, or until they were within somewhat over a hundred yards from Bois Blanc Island. Here, as ill chance would have it, the chain which had run out of the boat formed a bight or loop, and dragging on the bottom caught some obstacle and stopped further progress toward the shore. The men then yelled with all their might for help and were heard by the keeper of Bois Blanc light-house, and three or four fishermen from Mackinac Island, who happened to be at the station and running out, saw and recognized in those holding on to the capsized boat the Spectacle Reef light-keeper and his associates.

"Among them was a gallant young fellow named Joseph Cardran, who at once undertook the task of rescue. The only boat available was a small skiff, with which his companions thought it impossible he could effect [sic] anything, inasmuch as a formidable array of breakers, thick with ice, was crashing upon the shore, and a rough sea rolling beyond. The essay was terribly perilous, but Cardran at length succeeded in forcing out the skiff to the unfortunate men upon the wreck.

"Young Marshall by this time was almost gone, and the first and third assistants, Chambers and Lasley—the latter half-crippled by an injury to one of his legs, incurred while trying to keep his hold upon the boat—nobly insisted that the keeper should take the first chance, and endeavor to reach shore with his failing son. . . . The boat under the management of young Cardran set out on the return, but as it neared the shore a sea filled it, and the next instant it was overthrown.   The three men got hold of it, but in a moment Cardran saw that it would not support them all, and shouting to the others to hold on, bravely let go and struck out for the land. It was but a few moments before the wretched father saw his son release his hold and go down. Unable through exhaustion to effectively help him, he himself became unconscious, and still clinging with a death grip to the skiff, was washed in among the dwarf icebergs in the surf. Cardran meanwhile battled valiantly with the sea, sank three or four times, and was finally dragged out of the bergs and breakers unconscious.

"Alfred Cardran, a youth of eighteen, brother to Joseph, rolled the inanimate body of the keeper up on shore. Then, with the spectacle of two apparently dead bodies before him, and one of them his brother, the brave boy, still alive to those in peril, quickly bailed out the skiff, launched it, and dauntlessly put out to the rescue. After much hardship and peril he reached Chambers and Lasley. . . . Joseph Cardran by this time had revived and helped to carry the insensible body of Mr. Marshall into the light house, where for five hours he was rubbed and otherwise ministered to, and was finally restored.

"It is evident that but for the heroic daring of the two Cardran boys everyone on board the light-house boat would have perished. In commemoration of their splendid gallantry the gold medal of the service was awarded to each of them, never in any instance more worthily."

21. "Mackinac," *Detroit Tribune and Advertiser* (Detroit, MI), 26 February 869, p. 1, col. 4. The other death was Minnie Frank.

22. "Michigan Marriages, 1868–1925," *Family Search*, database with images, https:// familysearch.org, under Francis Cadott and Sophia Bage, 1881.

23. "A Nonagenarian," *The Republican-News* (St. Ignace, MI), 6 August 1921, p. 8, col. 2.

24. "A Nonagenarian," *The Republican-News* (St. Ignace, MI), 6 August 1921, p. 8, col. 2.

25. Darlene Olson, "Boy do I remember how we were all afraid of 'ol lady bandana," Facebook, Mackinac Area Genealogy and Family History group, 4 June 2018, https://www.facebook.com/groups/106050736163832/.

26. Lois Cadotte Maki, "We had what we called a ghost in the old house on the island," Facebook, Mackinac Area Genealogy and Family History group, 4 June 2018, https://www.facebook.com/groups/106050736163832/.

27. John Cadotte, "Old burners is where she is," Facebook, Mackinac Area Genealogy and Family History group, 4 June 2018, https://www.facebook.com/groups/106050736163832/.

28. Dawn Clayton, "My mom (Phyllis Cassibo Schmidt) remembered seeing her," Facebook, Mackinac Area Genealogy and Family History group, 4 June 2018, https://www.facebook.com/groups/106050736163832/.

58. Mrs. Mary LaDuke (Mary Bruneau, Mrs. Jeremie LeDuc)

1. Theresa M. Schenck, *All Our Relations: Chippewa Mixed-Bloods and the Treaty of 1837* (Winnipeg, Manitoba: The Center for Rupert's Land Studies at the University of Winnipeg, 2010), 87. The testimony was taken for the 1837 Treaty of St. Peters Chippewa. Jeremie LeDuc and his family were there to apply for mixed-blood funds. Unfortunately, they were rejected. No record of application was found for the 1836 Half Breed Funds.

2. Archives of Manitoba, *North West Company Account Books (1795–1827)*, index. See Jeremie LeDuc, *North West Company Ledger*, 1812; *Servant Accounts*, 1819–1821; *English River equipment book*, 1820, https://www.gov.mb.ca/chc/archives/hbca/name_indexes/nwc_accounts.html. Used with permission.

3. Marriage of Jeremie LeDuc, 1823, "Red River Marriages, 1818–1831," Red River Collection, British Columbia Provincial Archives, Add. MSS 345, box 3, folder 135. The citation is from the original document. My document was a transcription copied from the old Sneakers website many years ago. It is no longer active.

4. St. Ignatius Loyola (St. Ignace, MI), "Marriages, 1838–1893," bk. 1, p. 5 (Louis Leduque and Josette Closs, 1844), parish rectory.

5. *Liber Matrimonium, Mackinac Register, 1695–1888*, 30.

6. *Liber Matrimonium, Mackinac Register, 1695–1888*, 23.

7. *Liber Matrimonium, Mackinac Register, 1695–1888*, 22.

8. *Liber Matrimonium, Mackinac Register, 1695–1888*, 39.

9. "Baptismal Register," *Mackinac Register, 1695–1888*, 29.

10. *Liber Matrimonium, Mackinac Register, 1695–1888*, 32.

11. "Find a Grave Index," *Family Search*, database and images, https://familysearch.org,

under Andrew Rapin, 1823–10 November 1899, Burial: Calvary Cemetery, Cheboygan, Cheboygan County, MI, memorial no. 162384744, *Find a Grave*, http://www.findagrave.com.

12. "Find a Grave Index," *Family Search*, database and images, https://familysearch.org, under Adelaide "Delia" *LeDuc* Rapin, 20 January 1820–21 November 1903, Burial: Calvary Cemetery, Cheboygan, Cheboygan County, MI, memorial no. 162384808, *Find a Grave*, http://www.findagrave.com.

13. "Baptismal Register," *Mackinac Register, 1695–1888*, 42.

14. "Baptismal Register," *Mackinac Register, 1695–1888*, 53.

15. St. Ignatius Loyola (St. Ignace, MI), "Baptisms, 1838–1893," bk. 3, p. 3 (Catharina Leduc, 1838), parish rectory.

16. *Liber Matrimonium, Mackinac Register, 1695–1888*, 48–49.

17. "United States Census, 1860," *Family Search*, database with images, https://familysearch.org, Octavius Toulous, Beaver Island, MI.

18. St. Ignatius Loyola (St. Ignace, MI), "Baptisms, 1838–1893," bk. 3, p. 14 (Isabella Leduc, 1841), parish rectory.

19. St. Ignatius Loyola (St. Ignace, MI), "Baptisms, 1838–1893," bk. 3, p. 22 (Chirstinan Leduc baptism, 1843), parish rectory.

20. Death certificate for Edward St. Antoine, 29 October 1916, Cheboygan County, MI, *Michiganology*, https://michiganology.org.

21. Death certificate for Christine St. Antoine, 1923, Cheboygan County, MI, *Michiganology*, https://michiganology.org.

22. "Baptismal Register," *Mackinac Register, 1695–1888*, 119.

23. *Liber Defunctorum, Mackinac Register, 1695–1888*, 96. See under Laduck.

24. *Liber Defunctorum, Mackinac Register, 1695–1888*, 102. Leduc died 1 February 1871.

25. "Deaths," *St. Mary's Parish Record, 1869–1962*, St. Mary Catholic Church (Cheboygan, MI) parish rectory office, under Jeremie Leduc, 1871, p. 6.

26. "Deaths," *St. Mary's Parish Record, 1869–1962*, St. Mary Catholic Church (Cheboygan, MI) parish rectory office, under Marie Leduc, 1880, p. 33.

32. Mrs. Joseph Lalotte (Lozon) (Marie Boyd)

1. "Baptismal Record," *Mackinac Register, 1695–1888*, 42.

2. "Find a Grave Index," *Family Search*, database and images, https://familysearch.org, under Joshua Johnson Boyd, 1805–21 October 1832, record ID 58328756, *Find a Grave*, http://www.findagrave.com.

3. "Find a Grave Index," *Family Search*, database and images, https://familysearch.org, under Joshua Johnson Boyd, 1805–21 October 1832, record ID 58328756, *Find a Grave*, http://

www.findagrave.com.

4. *Liber Matrimonium, Mackinac Register, 1695–1888*. See the next note.

5. *Liber Matrimonium, Mackinac Register, 1695–1888*, 4. Ste. Anne's marriage record indicates that the couple was married earlier in a civil ceremony on 15 July 1819. Four children were born before their marriage in the church. They were: Joseph, born 10 June 1816; Pierre, born 9 May 1822; Alexis, born 2 February 1822; and Magdelaine, born 12 February 1826. Locations were not noted.

6. Marriage Record, *Mackinac Register, 1695–1888*, 29.

7. Baptismal Record, *Mackinac Register, 1695–1888*, 134.

8. Marriage Record, *Mackinac Register, 1695–1888*, 64–65.

9. "Michigan Deaths and Burials, 1800–1995," *Family Search*, database, https://familysearch. org/, under Joseph Lozon, 5 March 1900, Holmes Township, Mackinac, MI, reference yrs. 1899–1946, p. 6, FHL microfilm 1,007,364.

12A, B & C. Sarah, Louisa, and Charles Lalotte (Lozon)

1. *Liber Matrimonium, Mackinac Register, 1695–1888*, 4. When Joseph and Elisabeth Nancy Pelotte were married by the priest on 9 October 1824, they also declared several children who were recorded and recognized as their legitimate children. As with most remote settlements, a permanent priest was uncommon. Several years may pass before a minister or priest would be seen that could marry a couple. This practice was accepted by the community, and no stigma was attached to the couple or the children.

2. "United States Census, 1850," *Ancestry*, https://www.ancestry.com, under Alexander Lozon, Mary Lozon, Isaac Stockman, Michilimackinac, Mackinac County, MI, dwelling 408, family 416, p. 460 (stamped), citing National Archives Microfilm Publication M432, roll M432_357, p. 231B, image 453.

3. St. Ignatius Loyola (St. Ignace, MI), "Baptisms, 1838–1893," bk. 3, p. 62 (Maria Achidowan, 1855), parish rectory.

4. *Mackinac Island Miscellanea* (1), Alicia. S. Poole Papers, Bentley Historical Library, University of Michigan–Ann Arbor, 1925, file no. 5408.

5. St. Ignatius Loyola (St. Ignace, MI), "Marriages, 1838–1893," bk. 1, p. 14 (Alexius Lauzon and Maria D'Ashidowan, 1855), parish rectory.

6. St. Ignatius Loyola (St. Ignace, MI), "Baptisms, 1838–1893," bk. 3 (Sarah Bridgett Lauzon, 1851), parish rectory.

7. "Baptismal Register," *Mackinac Register, 1695–1888*, 146.

8. St. Ignatius Loyola (St. Ignace, MI), "Baptisms, 1838–1893," bk. 3, p. 63 (Guillaume Lauzon, 1855), parish rectory.

9. Burial Register, *Mackinac Register, 1695–1888*, 96.

10. *Liber Matrimonium, Mackinac Register, 1695–1888*, 54–55.

12A. Sarah Lalotte (Mrs. Paul Lancour)

1. Sally Ann Cummings, *Correspondence, Field Notes, and the Census Roll of All Members or Descendants of Members Who Were on the Roll of the Ottawa and the Chippewa Tribes of Michigan in 1870, and Living on March 4, 1907 (Durant Roll)* (Washington, DC: National Archives and Records Administration, 1996), p. 13. See Miss Sarah Lalotte, no. 12.

2. *Liber Matrimonium, Mackinac Register, 1695–1888*, 62–63. Marriage record lists the groom's name as Lincort.

3. St. Ignatius Loyola (St. Ignace, MI), "Baptisms, 1838–1893," bk. 3, p. 40 (Paulus Lincourt, 1849), parish rectory.

4. "Baptismal Register," *Mackinac Register, 1695–1888*, 222.

5. *St. Mary's Parish Baptism Records, 1860–1892*, St. Mary Catholic Church (Cheboygan, MI) parish rectory office, under Caroline Lincour, 1870, p. 48.

6. "Baptismal Register," *Mackinac Register, 1695–1888*, 230.

7. "Michigan Deaths and Burials, 1800–1995," *Family Search*, database, https://familysearch.org, under Sarah Mcgivon, 6 May 1915, citing Mackinac Island, Mackinac, MI, reference yrs. 1899–1946, p. 74, FHL microfilm 1,007,364.

8. "Michigan Marriages, 1868–1925," *FamilySearch*, database with images, https://familysearch.org, under Ferguson E. Mcguire and Addie Lancour, 1901.

9. *St. Mary's Parish Baptism Records, 1860–1892*, St. Mary Catholic Church (Cheboygan, MI) parish rectory office, under Phibianum Anna Lincourt, 1876, p. 113.

10. *St. Mary's Parish Baptism Records, 1860–1892*, St. Mary Catholic Church (Cheboygan, MI) parish rectory office, under Olivier Lincour, 1878, p. 127. "Deaths," *St. Mary's Parish Record, 1860–1892*, St. Mary Catholic Church (Cheboygan, MI) parish rectory office, under Olivier Lincourt, 1880, p. 32.

11. "Deaths," *St. Mary's Parish Record, 1860–1892*, St. Mary Catholic Church (Cheboygan, MI) parish rectory office, under Marie Josephine Lincourt, 1881, p. 38.

12. "Michigan Marriages, 1868–1925," *FamilySearch*, database with images, https://familysearch.org, under Chester Maguire and Gertrude Lancour, 1904.

13. "Michigan Births and Christenings, 1775–1995," *FamilySearch*, database, https://familysearch.org, under Charles Lancour, 18 October 1883, citing Duncan, Cheboygan, MI, reference, FHL microfilm 2,320,695.

14. "Michigan Marriages, 1868–1925," *FamilySearch*, database with images, https://familysearch.org, under Chas. Lancons and Rose Bray, 17 February 1909, p. 191, n. 1559, FHL microfilm 964,409.

15. "Michigan Death Certificates, 1921–1952," *FamilySearch*, database, https://familysearch.

org, under Charles Lancour, 30 January 1939, citing Detroit, Wayne, MI, Division for Vital Records and Health Statistics, Lansing, FHL microfilm 1,972,888.

16. *St. Mary's Parish Baptism Records, 1860–1892*, St. Mary Catholic Church (Cheboygan, MI) parish rectory office, under Felizem Arthurum Lincourt, 1888, bk. 1, p. 305.

17. "Deaths," *St. Mary's Parish Record, 1860–1892*, St. Mary Catholic Church (Cheboygan, MI) parish rectory office, under Arthur Lincourt, 1889, p. 87.

18. "United States World War I Draft Registration Cards, 1917–1918," *FamilySearch*, database with images, https://familysearch.org, under Alfred Roy Lancour, 1917–1918, citing Mackinac County, MI, NARA microfilm publication M1509 (Washington, DC: National Archives and Records Administration, n.d.), FHL microfilm 1,675,810. "Michigan Deaths and Burials, 1800–1995," *Family Search*, database, https://familysearch.org, under Alfred R. Lancour, 7 November 1920, citing Cheboygan, Cheboygan County, MI, reference vol. 3, p 64, FHL microfilm 964,407.

19. *St. Mary's Parish Baptism Records, 1860–1892*, St. Mary Catholic Church (Cheboygan, MI) parish rectory office, under Virginia Elizabetha Lincourt, 1892, bk. 2, p. 4.

20. "Michigan Marriages, 1868–1925," *FamilySearch*, database with images, https://familysearch.org, under Frank E. Beachett and Elizabeth V. Lancour, 1914.

21. *St. Mary's Parish Baptism Records, 1860–1892*, St. Mary Catholic Church (Cheboygan, MI) parish rectory office, under Hevam Lincourt,1894, bk. 2, p. 127.

22. *Find a Grave*, Sarah Lozon Lancour, https://www.findagrave.com, memorial no. 176174216.

12B. Marie Louise Lozon (Mrs. John Poupard)

1. "Michigan Death Certificates, 1921–1952," *Family Search*, database, https://familysearch.org, under Mary Louise Pupor, 16 January 1929, citing Flint, Genesee, MI, Division for Vital Records and Health Statistics, Lansing, FHL microfilm 1,972,702. Birth date taken from her death certificate.

2. *St. Mary's Parish Baptism Records, 1860–1892*, St. Mary Catholic Church (Cheboygan, MI) parish rectory office, under Joannem Roy Poupart, 1885, bk. 1, p. 236.

3. "Deaths," *St. Mary's Parish Record, 1860–1892*, St. Mary Catholic Church (Cheboygan, MI) parish rectory office, under Jean Baptiste Poupard, 1885, p. 60.

4. *St. Mary's Parish Baptism Records, 1860–1892*, St. Mary Catholic Church (Cheboygan, MI) parish rectory office, under Petrum Alexandrum Lincourt, 1886, bk. 1, p. 262.

5. *St. Mary's Parish Baptism Records, 1860–1892*, St. Mary Catholic Church (Cheboygan, MI) parish rectory office, under Marium Olevinam Lincourt, 1888, bk. 1, p. 304.

6. *St. Mary's Parish Baptism Records, 1860–1892*, St. Mary Catholic Church (Cheboygan, MI) parish rectory office, under Joannim Elmour Lincourt, 1890, bk. 1, p. 356.

7. *St. Mary's Parish Baptism Records, 1860–1892*, St. Mary Catholic Church (Cheboygan, MI)

parish rectory office, under Marium Josephinum Lincourt, 1892, bk. 2, p. 6.

8. *St. Mary's Parish Baptism Records, 1860–1892*, St. Mary Catholic Church (Cheboygan, MI) parish rectory office, under Ludivicum Carolum Lincourt, 1894, bk. 2, p. 127.

9. Michigan State Archives, "Death Records, 1897–1920," *Michiganology*, https://michiganology.org, entry for John Puper. Flint, MI.

10. Michigan State Archives, "Death Records, 1897–1920," *Michiganology*, https://michiganology.org, entry for Mary Louise Pupor. Flint, MI.

12c. Charles Lozon

1. "Baptismal Register," *Mackinac Register, 1695–1888*, 146.

2. *Liber Matrimonium, Mackinac Register, 1695–1888*, 70–71.

3. *Liber Defunctorum, Mackinac Register, 1695–1888*, 107. See under Helena Hamlin.

4. "Michigan Marriages, 1822–1995," *Family Search*, database, https://familysearch.org, under Charles Lozon and Mary C. Mesatigoe, 9 February 1880, Family History Library (FHL) microfilm 2,342,466.

5. St. Ignatius Loyola (St. Ignace, MI), "Baptisms, 1838–1893," bk. 3, p 55 (Marie Satagon), parish rectory.

6. "United States Census, 1930," *Family Search*, database with images, https://familysearch.org, St. Ignace, Mackinac, MI, ED 14, citing NARA microfilm publication T626 (Washington, DC: National Archives and Records Administration, 2002), image 4 of 14.

7. Emerson E. Smith, *Before the Bridge* (St. Ignace, MI: Kiwanis Club of St. Ignace, 1957), 78.

8. St. Ignatius Loyola (St. Ignace, MI), "Deaths, 1894–1988," p. 34 (Charles Lozon, 1928), parish rectory.

9. St. Ignatius Loyola (St. Ignace, MI), "Deaths, 1894–1988," p. 38 (Mrs. Mary Lozon, 1931), parish rectory.

51. Mrs. Jane Lancour (Genevieve Pond)

1. Theresa M. Schenck, *All Our Relations: Chippewa Mixed-Bloods and the Treaty of 1837* (Winnipeg, Manitoba: The Center for Rupert's Land Studies at the University of Winnipeg, 2010), 83.

2. *Liber Matrimonium, Mackinac Register, 1695–1888*, 10. See under Joseph William Lincourt and Genevieve Robescar.

3. St. Ignatius Loyola (St. Ignace, MI), "Pond Family Deaths," prepared by the church secretary, not published, 2010.

4. St. Ignatius Loyola (St. Ignace, MI), "Deaths, 1838–1893," bk. 1, p. 8 (Ludovica Pont vulg. Robisco, 1871), parish rectory.

5. Schenck, *All Our Relations*, 105.

6. Bill McDonald, *The Peter Pond Society*, newsletter 28 (April 2007), http://www.peterpondsociety.com/news28.

7. McDonald, *The Peter Pond Society*, newsletter 28.

8. McDonald, *The Peter Pond Society*, newsletter 28.

9. St. Ignatius Loyola (St. Ignace, MI), "Deaths, 1838–1893," bk. 1, p. 258 (Augustin Pound vulgo Rabasco, 1844), parish rectory.

10. "United States Census, 1850," *Family Search*, database with images, https://familysearch.org, under Louisa Pond, Michilimackinac, Michilimackinac County, MI, citing dwelling 278, family 284, NARA microfilm publication M432 (Washington, DC: National Archives and Records Administration, n.d.).

11. St. Ignatius Loyola (St. Ignace, MI), "Deaths, 1838–1893," bk. 1, p. 8 (Ludovica Pont vulg. Robisco, 1871), parish rectory.

12. Société historique de Saint-Boniface (St. Boniface, Manitoba, Canada), Centre du patrimonie, *Voyageur Contracts Database* (https://archivesshsb.mb.ca), under Francois Boucher.

13. Schenck, *All Our Relations*, 29–30.

14. *Liber Matrimonium, Mackinac Register, 1695–1888,* 10. See under Joseph William Lincourt and Genevieve Robescar.

15. *Liber Matrimonium, Mackinac Register, 1695–1888,* 16. See under Carolus Bodequin and Rachel Pond.

16. Julien Hamelin and Hubert A. Houle, *Moyen-Nord Ontarien*, vol. 11, *Sault Ste. Marie, Wawa* (Ottawa, Ontario: Centre De Genealogie SC, 1985), Achille Cadot and Louise Pont, p. 32. The four Cadotte girls living with Marie Louise in the 1850 census are Louise and Achille's daughters. Louise (the younger) died and Achille went to Marquette. During the Civil War, he enlisted (1 February 1862) in Company C, 4th Minnesota Volunteer Infantry, and was later discharged for disability (Vicksburg, 3 July 1863). Ancestry.com. *Minnesota, Civil War Records, 1861–1865* [database online] (Provo, UT: Ancestry.com Operations, 2011). The next year (8 August 1864), he enlisted in Company G, 17th Wisconsin Infantry, and mustered out on 2 June 1865. Historical Data Systems, comp., *U.S., Civil War Soldier Records and Profiles, 1861–1865, Ancestry*, database, (Provo, UT: Ancestry.com Operations Inc., 2009), https://www.ancestry.com/search/collections/1555/. Possibly, due to his disability, he may have returned to the Mackinac area. A person named Achille Cadotte died 30 January 1867 and was buried on Mackinac Island (*Deaths, Mackinac Register, 1695–1888*, 100).

17. St. Ignatius Loyola (St. Ignace, MI), "Deaths,1838–1893," bk. 2, p. 260 (Ludovica Ponte Robescar, 1847), parish rectory.

18. St. Ignatius Loyola (St. Ignace, MI), "Marriages, 1838–1893," bk. 1, p. 8 (Carolus Minsier

and Marie Anna Pont, 1849), parish rectory.

19. *Ste. Anne's Church Registers: 1704–1842*, microfilm, 3 rolls (Detroit, MI: St. Anne's of Detroit). See roll 3, *Chapelle du nordest: Baptisms, Marriages, Burials, 1810–1838*, arranged by date, baptism of Augustin Pond, p. 78. This record indicates he was born and baptized on Drummond Island, MI.

20. St. Ignatius Loyola (St. Ignace, MI), "Marriages, 1838–1893," bk. 1, p. 5 (August Pond and Maria Boudwin, 1845), parish rectory. Augustin Pond was at the center of the most famous court case in Mackinac County. The following website contains the history of the case (and a very good description of a nineteenth century fishing village). However, local lore says Blanchard was drunk and wanted Pond's wife. See *Pond v. People*, 8 Mich. 150 (1860), *Gun Control* [website], http://www.guncite.com/court/state/8mi150.html.

21. "Baptismal Register," *Mackinac Register, 1695–1888*, 20.

22. St. Ignatius Loyola (St. Ignace, MI), "Marriages, 1838–1893," bk. 1, p. 11 (Cyrillus Pond and Susanna Grondin, 1853), parish rectory.

23. St. Ignatius Loyola (St. Ignace, MI), "Marriages, 1838–1893," bk. 1, p. 9 (Ludovicus Pant and Catharina Mincier, 1850), parish rectory.

24. St. Ignatius Loyola (St. Ignace, MI), "Deaths, 1838–1893," bk. 2, p. 3 (Catherine Minsier, 1860), parish rectory.

25. St. Ignatius Loyola (St. Ignace, MI), "Marriages, 1838–1893," bk. 1, pp. 26–27 (Louis Pond and Marie Anne Lessort, 1864), parish rectory.

26. "Baptismal Register," *Mackinac Register, 1695–1888*, 49.

27. St. Ignatius Loyola (St. Ignace, MI), "Marriages, 1838–1893," bk. 1, p. 16–17 (Pierre Pont and Josette Perrault, 1857), parish rectory.

28. "Baptismal Register," *Mackinac Register, 1695–1888*, 62.

29. St. Ignatius Loyola (St. Ignace, MI), "Marriages, 1838–1893," bk. 1, p. 16 (Pierre Clauss and Julie Pound, 1857), parish rectory.

30. St. Ignatius Loyola (St. Ignace, MI), "Births, 1838–1893," bk. 3, p. 3 (Elizabetha Pond, 1838), parish rectory.

31. St. Ignatius Loyola (St. Ignace, MI), "Births, 1838–1893," bk. 3, p. 12 (Simon Pound, 1840), parish rectory.

32. *Liber Matrimonium, Mackinac Register, 1695–1888*, 10.

33. St. Ignatius Loyola (St. Ignace, MI), "Deaths, 1838–1893," p. 262 (William Lencour, 1852), parish rectory.

34. "United States Census, 1850," *Family Search*, database with images, https://familysearch.org, Michilimackinac, Michilimackinac County, MI, image 48 of 94, citing NARA microfilm publication M432 (Washington, DC: National Archives and Records Administration, n.d.).

35. "Baptismal Register," *Mackinac Register, 1695–1888*, 49.

36. St. Ignatius Loyola (St. Ignace, MI), "Marriages, 1838–1893," bk. 1, p. 10 (Theophilus Fontaine and Genoveva Lincourt, 1851), parish rectory.

37. "Baptismal Register," *Mackinac Register, 1695–1888*, 57.

38. Marriage of George Bourassa and Egot Lancour, "Port of Mackinac Records," Office of the Register of Deeds, St. Ignace, Mackinac County, MI, no. 431.

39. *St. Ignace News*, 9 January 1897, p. 5, col. 4.

    "Mrs. Therrien's Death, Died: In this city, Thursday, Jan. 7th of consumption. Mrs. Joseph Therrien aged 69 years and 6 months. [Her age was actually 57 years, 6 months using the information printed in this obituary.] The funeral services took place at the R.C. church today at 9 a.m. and were largely attended. Justine Lancour the deceased was born in St. Ignace June 25, 1839, and was married to Eli Bouchard in 1857. Her husband was killed in the battle of Fontelroy in 1863. Five sons were born from this union, three of whom are living. Oliver, William and Henry. In 1875 she married Mr. Joseph Therrien, late deputy Sheriff of this county, from which union two sons were born, Eugene and Alfred aged respectively 20 and 18 years. The sympathy of all is extended to the bereaved husband and sons, who are left to mourn her loss. Mrs. Therrien was beloved and esteemed by all who knew her, and her death is generally regretted."

40. George H. Turner, *Record of Service of Michigan Volunteers in the Civil War, 1861–1865*, vol. 37 (Kalamazoo, MI: Ihling Bros. & Everard, 1900), p. 18, https://catalog.hathitrust.org/Record/003931700. See under Eli Bouchard.

41. "United States General Index to Pension Files, 1861–1934" (Washington, DC: National Archives and Records Administration, n.d.), microfilm T288, roll 43, under Boreman, Thomas I.–Boulson, Kenneth C.; *Family Search*, database with images, https://familysearch.org, image 3498 of 4120.

42. "Michigan Marriages, 1822–1995," *Family Search*, database, https://familysearch.org, under Joseph Terrien and Justine Lincour, 8 October 1875.

43. "Michigan Deaths, 1867–1897," database with images, *FamilySearch*, https://familysearch.org, image 94 of 1188, citing Department of Vital Records, Lansing.

44. St. Ignatius Loyola (St. Ignace, MI), "Marriages, 1838–1893," bk. 1, p. 16–17 (Alexandre Charbonneau and Flavie Lincourt, 1857), parish rectory.

45. St. Ignatius Loyola (St. Ignace, MI), "Deaths, 1838–1893," bk. 2, p. 16 (Flavia Lincourt [Charbonneau], 1846), parish rectory.

46. St. Ignatius Loyola (St. Ignace, MI), "Births, 1838–1893," bk. 3, p. 30 (Maria Lincourt, 1845), parish rectory.

47. St. Ignatius Loyola (St. Ignace, MI), "Deaths, 1838–1893," bk. 1, p. 259 (Marie Lincourt, 1846), parish rectory.

48. St. Ignatius Loyola (St. Ignace, MI), "Births, 1838–1893," bk. 3, p. 36 (Cecelia Lincourt, 1847), parish rectory.

49. St. Ignatius Loyola (St. Ignace, MI), "Births, 1838–1893," bk. 3, p. 40 (Paulus Lincourt, 1849), parish rectory.

50. *Liber Matrimonium, Mackinac Register, 1695–1888*, 62–63.

51. St. Ignatius Loyola (St. Ignace, MI), "Births, 1838–1893," bk. 3, p. 47 (Adeline Lincourt, 1851), parish rectory.

52. "United States Census, 1880," *Family Search*, database with images, https://familysearch. org, under Joseph Terrien, 1880, citing enumeration district ED 43, sheet 250A, NARA microfilm publication T9 (Washington, DC: National Archives and Records Administration, n.d.), roll 0592, Family History Library microfilm 1,254,592.

4. Mrs. Edward Lasley (Therese Bennett)

1. *Liber Matrimonium, Mackinac Register, 1695–1888*, 6. See under Louis Benet-Beaubin.

2. Larry M. Wyckoff, trans. and compiler, "Mixed-Blood Census Register, Ottawas and Chippewas of Michigan Treaty of March 28, 1836," *Roots Web*, http://www.rootsweb. ancestry.com/~mimacki2/annuities/1836mb.pdf, nos. 220–227.

3. "Baptismal Register," *Mackinac Register, 1695–1888*, 134. *Liber Matrimonium, Mackinac Register, 1695–1888*, 31.

4. "Baptismal Register," *Mackinac Register, 1695–1888*, 133.

5. "Baptismal Register," *Mackinac Register, 1695–1888*, 144. Mother's name listed as Benette.

6. "Michigan Marriages, 1822–1995," *Family Search*, database, https://familysearch.org, under Louis Lasley and Louise Robinson, 18 April 1871. Emmet County, *Vital Records Search*, searchable database, http://apps.emmetcounty.org/clerk/deathrecords.aspx, under Louis Lasley, liber 3, folio 353.

7. "Baptismal Register," *Mackinac Register, 1695–1888*, 154.

8. "Baptismal Register," *Mackinac Register, 1695–1888*, 179.

9. "Baptismal Register," *Mackinac Register, 1695–1888*, 188. See under Lassly

10. "Baptismal Register," *Mackinac Register, 1695–1888*, 198. Mother's name listed as Beaubin.

11. "Baptismal Register," *Mackinac Register, 1695–1888*, 202. Mother's name listed as Benette.

12. Corey Lasley, *The Lasley Family of Old Mackinac: Samuel C. Lasley, His Descendants, and Their Connections*, 1775 to 2015, 2nd. ed. (self-pub.), 247.

13. Lasley, *The Lasley Family of Old Mackinac*, 247.

14. *Holy Cross Church Records* (Cross Village, MI), microfilm publication, one roll, Bentley Historical Library, University of Michigan, roll 1, arranged mostly alphabetically; see family 66, "Edward Lasley."

15. George H. Turner, *Record of Service of Michigan Volunteers in the Civil War, 1861–1865*, vol.

37 (Kalamazoo, MI: Ihling Bros. & Everard, 1900), p. 82, https://catalog.hathitrust.org/
Record/003931700. See under "Edward Leslie."

16. "United States General Index to Pension Files, 1861–1934" (Washington, DC: National
Archives and Records Administration, n.d.), microfilm T288, roll 274, under Edward
Lasley; *Ancestry* (Provo, UT: Ancestry.com Operations, 2000).

17. "Find a Grave Index," *Family Search*, database and images, https://familysearch.org,
under Edward Edmond Lasley, 1896, Burial: Saint James Township Cemetery, St. James,
Charlevoix County, MI, record ID 13204330, *Find a Grave*, http://www.findagrave.com.

18. Central Michigan University, *Beaver Island History, Helen Collar Papers*. https://www.
cmich.edu/library/clarke/ResearchResources/Michigan_Material_Local/Beaver_Island_
Helen_Collar_Papers/Pages/default.aspx (Mt. Pleasant: Central Michigan University),
under Mrs. Lasley.

19. Joyce B., "Last summer (2004) Edward Norman Lasley Jr. and his wife Eunice," Beaver
Island Forum: Lasley & Bishop Families 1800's, Monday 14 February 2005, http://www.
beaverislandforum.com/viewtopic.php?t=292&highlight=lasley.

40. Mrs. Joseph Laslin (Julia Lesieur Aslin)

1. "Baptismal Register," *Mackinac Register, 1695–1888*, 62. The middle name Victoria was
written on her tombstone in Ste. Anne's cemetery.

2. *Programme de recherche en démographie historique (PRDH)* (Université de Montréal,
Canada), 1621–1849, certificate 433723, Edouard Lesieur, transcription, https://www.
prdh-igd.com. This baptism accompanied by the family certificate no. 86481 shows that
the family was in Yamachiche at the time the three-year voyageur contract with the
Hudson's Bay Company was made (27 April 1825 at the Lac Huron [La Cloche, Ontario]
location). The baptism provides the identity of his parents and the family certificate
indicates their son Edouard did not marry or die in Quebec up to 1849.

3. Société historique de Saint-Boniface (St. Boniface, Manitoba, Canada), Centre du
patrimonie, *Voyageur Contracts Database* (voyageurs.shsb.mb.ca/fr), under Edouard
Lesieur.

4. Marriage of Edward Lesieur and Angelique Peltier, "Port of Mackinac Records," Office of
the Register of Deeds, St. Ignace, Mackinac County, MI, no. 67.

5. "Baptismal Register," *Mackinac Register, 1695–1888*, 44. His mother was recorded as
Obitawegijogokwe.

6. *Liber Matrimonium, Mackinac Register, 1695–1888*, 38.

7. "Baptismal Register," *Mackinac Register, 1695–1888*, 179. Listed under Asselin.

8. "Baptismal Register," *Mackinac Register, 1695–1888*, 184. Listed under Asslin.

9. "Michigan Marriages, 1822–1995," *FamilySearch*, database, https://familysearch.org, under

Charles Johnson and Elizabeth Aslin, 29 November 1883; Family History Library (FHL) microfilm 1,007,362.

10. Michigan State Archives, "Death Records, 1897–1920," *Michiganology*, https://michiganology.org, entry for Elizabeth Johnson, St. Ignace, Mackinac County.

11. *Holy Cross Church records* (Cross Village, MI), microfilm publication, one roll, Bentley Historical Library, University of Michigan, roll 1, arranged mostly alphabetically; see family 6, "Aslin, Joseph (Shövler)."

12. *Holy Cross Church Records*, roll 1, family 6, "Aslin, Joseph (Shövler)."

13. "Michigan Marriages, 1822–1995," *Family Search*, database, https://familysearch.org, under Peter J Aslin and Agathy Peck, 20 May 1882; citing FHL microfilm 1,007,362.

14. St. Ignatius Loyola (St. Ignace, MI), "Record of Interments: 1894–1988" (Peter Aslin burial, 1927), parish rectory, p. 33.

15. St. Ignatius Loyola (St. Ignace, MI), "Record of Interments: 1894–1988" (Agatha Aslin burial, 1934), parish rectory, p. 41.

16. *Holy Cross Church Records*, roll 1, family 6, "Aslin, Joseph (Shövler)."

17. "Baptismal Register," *Mackinac Register, 1695–1888*, 199. Listed under Asselin.

18. "Michigan Marriages, 1868–1925," *Family Search*, database with images, https://familysearch.org, under Edward Landre and Mary Jane Aslin, 1885.

19. "Michigan Death Certificates, 1921–1952," *Family Search*, database, https://familysearch.org, under Napoleon Landry in entry for Edward Landry, 24 Jun 1932, Moran, Mackinac County, MI, Division for Vital Records and Health Statistics, Lansing, FHL microfilm 1,972,852.

20. St. Ignatius Loyola (St. Ignace, MI), "Record of Interments: 1894–1988" (Mrs. Mary Jane Landry burial, 1934), parish rectory, p. 43.

21. "Baptismal Register," *Mackinac Register, 1695–1888*, 210.

22. *Holy Cross Church Records*, roll 1, family 6, "Aslin, Joseph (Shövler)."

23. *Holy Cross Church Records*, roll 1, family 6, "Aslin, Joseph (Shövler)."

24. St. Ignatius Loyola (St. Ignace, MI), "Marriages, 1838–1893," bk. 1, p. 47 (Antoine Martin and Harriette Asselin marriage, 1883), parish rectory.

25. "Find a Grave Index," *Family Search*, database and images, https://familysearch.org, under Harriet Martin, 2 October 1866–29 October 1916, Burial: Lakeview Cemetery, Manistique, Schoolcraft County, MI, record ID 5939951, *Find a Grave*, http://www.findagrave.com.

26. Michigan State Archives, "Death Records, 1897–1920," *Michiganology*, https://michiganology.org, entry for Antoine Martin, Manistique, Schoolcraft County, MI.

27. *Holy Cross Church Records*, roll 1, family 6, "Aslin, Joseph (Shövler)."

28. "Michigan Marriages, 1822–1995," *Family Search*, database, https://familysearch.org, under William Aslin and Myrtle Bush, 5 June 1894, FHL microfilm 1,007,362.

29. "Michigan Death Certificates, 1921–1952," *Family Search*, database, https://familysearch. org, under William Aslin, 8 September 1942, Detroit, Wayne, MI, Division for Vital Records and Health Statistics, Lansing, FHL microfilm 1,972,902.

30. *Holy Cross Church Records*, roll 1, family 6, "Aslin, Joseph (Shövler)."

31. St. Ignatius Loyola (St. Ignace, MI), "Record of Interments: 1894–1988," p. 6 (Reuben Aslin burial, 1903), parish rectory.

32. "Michigan Marriages, 1822–1995," *Family Search*, database, https://familysearch.org, Edmund Aslin and Josephine Lavalley, 2 September 1911, FHL microfilm 1,007,362.

33. "Find a Grave Index," *Family Search*, database, https://familysearch.org, under Josephine Valley Aslin, 1917, Burial: Edgewood Cemetery, Cedarville, Mackinac County, MI, record ID 92406847, *Find a Grave*, http://www.findagrave.com.

34. "Michigan Marriages, 1822–1995," *Family Search*, database, https://familysearch.org, under Joseph Aslin in entry for Edmund Aslin and Roseann Bobley, 5 June 1919; citing FHL microfilm 1,007,362.

35. "United States Census, 1920," *Family Search*, database with images, https://familysearch. org, citing enumeration district 24, Drummond, Chippewa, MI, NARA microfilm publication T625 (Washington, DC: National Archives and Records Administration, n.d.), image 2 of 16.

36. Michigan State Archives, "Death Records, 1921–1947," *Michiganology*, https:// michiganology.org, entry for Edward Aslin, 1922. Note: the death certificate and 1920 census listed Edmund as Edward; however, Rose Ann married Edmund.

37. *Holy Cross Church Records*, roll 1, family 6, "Aslin, Joseph (Shövler)."

38. "Baptismal Register," *Mackinac Register, 1695–1888*, 244. Listed under Assler. His birth date was listed as 23 March 1878, then crossed out and written as 1881. He was probably born 23 March 1879. His mother died 25 March 1879.

39. *Liber Defunctorum, Mackinac Register, 1695–1888*, 108.

45. Mrs. Samuel LeBlanc (Elizabeth Belonga)

1. "Baptismal Register," *Mackinac Register, 1695–1888*, 61.

2. *Programme de recherche en démographie historique (PRDH)* (Université de Montréal, Canada), 1621–1849, certificate 3373498, Anslem LeBlanc, transcription, https://www. prdh-igd.com.

3. "United States Census, 1850," *Family Search*, database with images, https://familysearch. org, under Paul Lablon, Michilimackinac, Michilimackinac County, MI, citing family 600, NARA microfilm publication M432 (Washington, DC: National Archives and Records Administration, n.d.).

4. *Liber Matrimonium, Mackinac Register, 1695–1888*, 38.

5. "Baptismal Register," *Mackinac Register, 1695–1888*, 168.

6. "Baptismal Register," *Mackinac Register, 1695–1888*, 180.

7. "Baptismal Register," *Mackinac Register, 1695–1888*, 189. See under Samuel Laubley and Elizabeth Boulangia.

8. "Baptismal Register," *Mackinac Register, 1695–1888*, 194. See under 9 May 1860, Samuel Leblanc and Isabel Belangia. Born on Bois Blanc Island, Mackinac County, MI.

9. "Michigan Marriages, 1868–1925," *Family Search*, database with images, https://familysearch.org, under Alexander Leblanc and Mary Ann Fontain, 1882.

10. "Baptismal Register," *Mackinac Register, 1695–1888*, 204. The priest wrote this child was born on *Ile à la Trinité*. This location is unknown.

11. "Baptismal Register," *Mackinac Register, 1695–1888*, 210.

12. "Michigan Death Certificates, 1921–1952," *Family Search*, database, https://familysearch.org, under William White, 5 March 1931, citing Marquette, Marquette, MI, Division for Vital Records and Health Statistics, Lansing, Family History Library (FHL) microfilm 1,972,867.

13. "Michigan Marriages, 1868–1925," *Family Search*, database with images, https://familysearch.org, under William White and Hattie Lapier, 1895.

14. "Michigan Death Certificates, 1921–1952," *Family Search*, database, https://familysearch.org, under Eugene White, 5 August 1926, citing Marquette, Marquette County, MI, Division for Vital Records and Health Statistics, Lansing, FHL microfilm 1,972,867. The death certificate states that he was born in St. James, MI, the main city on Beaver Island.

15. John L. Hagen and Georgia M. Rhoades, comps., *Moran Township: When the Moon Is High.* (St. Ignace, MI: Moran Township Board of Trustees, 1997), C140, Moran Township.

16. "Michigan Births and Christenings, 1775–1995," *FamilySearch*, database, https://familysearch.org, under Joseph Lablanc, 10 December 1874, citing Chandler, Manitou (Charlevoix), MI, reference P5 RN 64, FHL microfilm 965,391.

17. "Michigan Marriages, 1868–1925," *Family Search*, database with images, https://familysearch.org, under Joseph Leblance and Minnie Davenport, 1897.

18. "Michigan Deaths and Burials, 1800–1995," *Family Search*, database, https://familysearch.org, under Elizabeth Lablanc, 7 August 1898, citing Newton, Mackinac County, MI, reference yrs. 1873–1899, p. 94, FHL microfilm 1,007,364.

19. "Michigan Deaths and Burials, 1800–1995," *Family Search*, database, https://familysearch.org, under Sam Lablanc, 24 April 1908, citing Cheboygan, Cheboygan County, MI, reference v. 3, p. 8, FHL microfilm 964,407.

35. Mrs. Alixse Lelone (Marie Louise Cadotte)

1. "Baptismal Register," *Mackinac Register, 1695–1888*, 105.

2. "Baptismal Register," *Mackinac Register, 1695–1888*, 108.

3. *Liber Matrimonium, Mackinac Register, 1695–1888*, 14.

4. Marriage of Alexander Lelonde and Mary Cadotte, "Port of Mackinac Records," Office of the Register of Deeds, St. Ignace, Mackinac County, MI, no. 542.

5. "Baptismal Register," *Mackinac Register, 1695–1888*, 198.

6. George H. Turner, *Record of Service of Michigan Volunteers in the Civil War, 1861–1865*, vol. 27 (Kalamazoo, MI: Ihling Bros. & Everard, 1900), p. 75, https://catalog.hathitrust.org/Record/003931700. See under Alexander Lalonde.

7. *Liber Matrimonium, Mackinac Register, 1695–1888*, 66–67.

8. Michigan State Archives, Death Records, *Michiganology*, https://michiganology.org, entry for Mary Deloria, 1914, Mackinac County.

54. Mrs. Angeline Louisignon (Angelique Aslin)

1. "Michigan Deaths and Burials, 1800–1995," *Family Search*, database, https://familysearch.org, under Angeline Louisiguaw, 17 Nov 1906, citing Mackinac Island, Mackinac, MI, reference yrs. 1899–1946, p, 31, FHL microfilm 1,007,364. Birth date on death certificate says 10 December 1834.

2. Larry M. Wyckoff, trans. and compiler, "Mixed-Blood Census Register, Ottawas and Chippewas of Michigan Treaty of March 28, 1836," *Roots Web*, http://www.rootsweb.ancestry.com/~mimacki2/annuities/1836mb.pdf, no. 376.

3. Theresa M. Schenck, *All Our Relations: Chippewa Mixed-Bloods and the Treaty of 1837* (Winnipeg, Manitoba: The Center for Rupert's Land Studies at the University of Winnipeg, 2010), 16.

4. Schenck, *All Our Relations*, 16–17.

5. *Liber Defunctorum, Mackinac Register, 1695–1888*, 101.

6. "Find a Grave Index," *Family Search*, database and images, https://familysearch.org, under Joseph Louis Asselin/Aslin, 1887, Burial: Saint Anne's Cemetery, Mackinac Island, Mackinac, MI, record ID 136244413, *Find a Grave*, http://www.findagrave.com.

7. *Liber Matrimonium, Mackinac Register, 1695–1888*, 34.

8. "United States Census, 1860," *Family Search*, database with images, https://familysearch.org, under Angelic Therrian, 1860.

9. *Liber Matrimonium, Mackinac Register, 1695–1888*, 54–55.

10. "Baptismal Register," *Mackinac Register, 1695–1888*, 20.

11. Wyckoff, "Mixed-Blood Census Register," no. 266.

12. Marriage of Charles Louesyneau and Mary Davenport, "Port of Mackinac Records," Office of the Register of Deeds, St. Ignace, Mackinac County, MI, no. 366.

13. "Find a Grave Index," *Family Search*, database and images, https://familysearch.org, under

Mary Davenport, 1855, Burial: Protestant Cemetery, Mackinac Island, Mackinac, MI, record ID 131789250, *Find a Grave*, http://www.findagrave.com. She was buried under the name "Davenport" not Louisignan.

14. "Baptismal Register," *Mackinac Register, 1695–1888*, 201.

15. *Liber Defunctorum, Mackinac Register, 1695–1888*, 101.

16. "Baptismal Register," *Mackinac Register, 1695–1888*, 216.

17. "Michigan Marriages, 1822–1995," *Family Search*, database, https://familysearch.org, under Charles Lousignan in entry for William Chapman and Mary E. Lousignan, 29 November 1889, Family History Library (FHL) microfilm 1,007,362.

18. "Baptismal Register," *Mackinac Register, 1695–1888*, 221.

19. *Liber Defunctorum, Mackinac Register, 1695–1888*, 103.

20. "Michigan Births, 1867–1902," *Family Search*, database with images, https://familysearch.org, under Charles Louisignau in entry for Ida Louisignau, 1873. *Liber Defunctorum, Mackinac Register, 1695–1888*, 103.

21. *Liber Defunctorum, Mackinac Register, 1695–1888*, 112.

22. "Michigan Death Certificates, 1921–1952," *Family Search*, database, https://familysearch.org, under Lucy Bailey, 5 June 1936, Wayne, MI, Division for Vital Records and Health Statistics, Lansing, FHL microfilm 1,972,878. According to her death certificate, she was born on St. Helena Island, Michigan, on 16 March 1875 and died in Detroit on 5 June 1936.

23. "Michigan Marriages, 1822–1995," *Family Search*, database, https://familysearch.org, under Fred L Bailey and Lucy Lousegnau, 14 November 1894, FHL microfilm 2,342,499.

24. "Keepers of McGulpin Point Light," http://www.terrypepper.com/lights/michigan/mcgulpin/keepers.html.

25. "Keepers of McGulpin Point Light."

26. "United States Census, 1900," *Family Search*, database with images, https://familysearch.org, under Chas Louisignaw, Holmes Township, Mackinac Island City, Mackinac County, MI, citing enumeration district (ED) 99, sheet 1A, family 9, NARA microfilm publication T623 (Washington, DC: National Archives and Records Administration, 1972), FHL microfilm 1,240,726.

27. "Michigan Deaths and Burials, 1800–1995," *Family Search*, database, https://familysearch.org, under Chas. J. Louisignaw, 8 April 1903, Mackinac Island, Mackinac County, MI, reference yrs. 1899–1946, p. 17, FHL microfilm 1,007,364.

28. Michigan State Archives, Death Records, *Michiganology*, https://michiganology.org, entry for Angeline Louisignan, 1906, Mackinac County.

47. Miss Rosalie Louisignan (Lusignan)

1. *Liber Matrimonium, Mackinac Register, 1695–1888*, 4.

2. Les and Jeanne Rentmeester, *The Wisconsin Creoles* (Melbourne, FL: self-published, 1987), 290.

3. This excerpt was taken from Ontario Historical Society, *Papers and Records*, vol. 3, *Migration of Voyageurs from Drummond Island* (Toronto: Ontario Historical Society, 1901), 147–148, http://www.woolverton.ca/Sources/papersrecordsontv3onta.pdf. Angelique Langlade was the sister of Agathe Langlade Lusignan. Their father was Charles Langlade Jr. It is doubtful they shared the same mother. Estimates indicate Angelique Langlade was born around 1820, while Agathe was born circa 1782. The following excerpt mentions that Angelique had a sister that stayed and married at Mackinac.

"Angelique Langlade. The concluding narrative of these personal recollections is that of Angelique Langlade, still living in Penetanguishene at an advanced age, and the last survivor but one of a somewhat noted family. Her command of English is very limited, but her mixed dialect so picturesque and pointed, that I am constrained to present it almost verbatim, in her own simple but expressive style, with apologies to several writers of dialect literature.

"Her Narrative. Ma name, Angelique Langlade; born Drummon Islan; me Chippawa half-breed; ma mudder, Josephine Ah-quah-dah, Chippawa squaw, Yankee tribe; ma fadder, Charles Langlade, French half-breed, hees born Mackinaw, an move Drummon Islan wid Breeteesh. I no spik good Eengleesh ver well. I not know how old I be—ha-a—I no chicken—me. I tink bout seven, ten, mebbe tirteen year ole when we come Pentang. Mebbe some day God tell me how ole I be when I die. Ma fadder, mudder, Charlie, Louie, Pierre, two Marguerites, Angelique, dats me, an Delede, all come in big bateau from Nort shore. Priess mak mistak an baptize two Marguerites. Katrine born Pentang. All dead but two, Delede (Mrs. Precourt) an me—dat's Angelique. We come Gordon's pinte; mak Wigwam cedar bark, stay dare leetle tam; wait for land, den come ware McAvela's place on de hill, an leeve dare lang, lang tam. Soldiers come nex year after we come Gordon's pinte. Ma granfadder Capn. Charles Langlade—Good French, come Montreal; work for Hudson Bay Co., marry Chippawa squaw—big, big soldier in Breeteesh army—he fight fer Mackinaw 1812—much good, loyal to Eengleesh—had ver fine sword—after war went to Green Bay, where he die—had tousan acre lan—built ver big fine stone house, where he lef hees sword, piano an lots money—var, ver rich. Had tree sons an tree daughters—Alixe, Indians mak him big chief way, way off in Unat Stat; Charlie, dats ma fadder, he come Drummond Islan wid Breeteesh soldiers and den he come Pentang; Napoleon, he go way an nevare come back no more—nevare hear from him every years—speks lak hees dead long tam. One daughter kep Mackinaw, where she married an leeve; two go to school, Montreal, get married an go to Lac Montaigne to leeve. Lots ma friens anglades leeve Montreal—fine peoples—ver rich. Ma granmudder, Angelique Langlade, she come on visit from Green Bay an die in Pentang. She ver, ver ole when she die. Father Point, missionary Prices, on veesit from Wek-wam-i-kon, he bury her. He say she more as hunner year ole. Ma sister, Marguerite, she marry George Gordon, hees secon wife. She die in Toronto. Odder Marguerite, she die in Pentang."

4. Donna Valley Russell, ed., *Michigan Censuses, 1710–1830: Under the French, British, and Americans* (Detroit: Detroit Society for Genealogical Research, 1982), 123. See under François Louisenois.

5. American Board of Commissioners for Foreign Missions Papers, *Children at Mackinaw, 1833,* Houghton Library, Harvard University, 18.5.7.I:36.

6. Wyckoff, "Mixed-Blood Census Register," no. 258–267.

7. *Liber Defunctorum, Mackinac Register, 1695–1888,* 92.

8. *Liber Defunctorum, Mackinac Register, 1695–1888,* 99.

9. "United States Census, 1860," *Family Search,* database with images, https://familysearch.org, under Rosella Louisignon in entry for Francis Louisignon.

10. "United States Census, 1870," *Family Search,* database with images, https://familysearch.org, under Frank J. Louisymean in household of Joseph L., Michigan, citing family 89, NARA microfilm publication M593 (Washington, DC: National Archives and Records Administration, n.d.), p. 13, FHL microfilm 552,186.

11. "United States Census, 1880," *Family Search,* database with images, https://familysearch.org, under Joseph Louisingnaw, Holmes, Mackinac County, MI, citing enumeration district ED 43, sheet 259C, NARA microfilm publication T9 (Washington, DC: National Archives and Records Administration, n.d.), roll 0592, FHL microfilm 1,254,592.

12. City of Mackinac Island, MI, "Register of Interments" (1891), p. 1; citing Rose Louisignon, City Clerk's Office, Mackinac Island Courthouse. Record gives her birth place as Green Bay, WI.

53. Mrs. Moses Maillet (Angelique McClure)

1. Larry M. Wyckoff, trans. and compiler, "Mixed-Blood Census Register, Ottawas and Chippewas of Michigan Treaty of March 28, 1836," *Roots Web,* http://www.rootsweb.ancestry.com/~mimacki2/annuities/1836mb.pdf, no. 421.

2. *Liber Matrimonium, Mackinac Register, 1695–1888,* 25. (Some Catholic priests used abbreviations when recording sacraments. The months September through December are sometimes 7bris = September, 8bris = October, 9bris = November and Xbris [Roman numeral ten] = December.)

3. Marriage of John McClure and an Indian woman, April 1828, "Port of Mackinac Records," Office of the Register of Deeds, St. Ignace, Mackinac County, MI, no. 58.

4. *Programme de recherche en démographie historique* (*PRDH*) (Université de Montréal,

Canada), 1621–1849, certificate 2691097, François Moses Maillet, transcription, https://www.prdh-igd.com.

5. *PRDH*, certificate no. 2693731.
6. "Baptismal Register," *Mackinac Register, 1695–1888*, 116.
7. "Baptismal Register," *Mackinac Register, 1695–1888*, 180.
8. "Baptismal Register," *Mackinac Register, 1695–1888*, 189.
9. "Baptismal Register," *Mackinac Register, 1695–1888*, 197.

2. Mrs. Louis Maishtaw (Marie Bennett-Beaubin)

1. "Baptismal Register," *Mackinac Register, 1695–1888*, 32.
2. Marriage of Louis Maston and Mary Pockrow, "Port of Mackinac Records," Office of the Register of Deeds, St. Ignace, Mackinac County, MI, no. 210.
3. "Baptismal Register," *Mackinac Register, 1695–1888*, 102. See under Louis Mastore. Born at Old Fort Mackinac, now Mackinaw City.
4. "Baptismal Register," *Mackinac Register, 1695–1888*, 130.
5. "Baptismal Register," *Mackinac Register, 1695–1888*, 32.
6. Emmet County, *Vital Records Search*, searchable database, http://apps.emmetcounty.org/clerk/ marriagerecords.aspx, under Amab LaQuea and Mary Mastaw, liber 1, folio 4.
7. "Michigan Deaths and Burials, 1800–1995," *Family Search*, database, https://familysearch.org, under Louis Mastow in entry for Mary Laquer, 18 December 1915, citing Mackinaw City, Cheboygan County, MI, reference v. 3, p. 3, Family History Library (FHL) microfilm 964,407.
8. "Baptismal Register," *Mackinac Register, 1695–1888*, 130.
9. Emmet County, *Vital Records Search*, searchable database, http://apps.emmetcounty.org/clerk/ marriagerecords.aspx, under Laverin Kegedjiewan and Christine Masta, liber 1862, folio 37.
10. "Michigan Marriages, 1822–1995," *Family Search*, database, https://familysearch.org, under Joseph St. Peter and Christina Maslaw or Zepharon, 1 January 1880. He was first married to Julianna Caroline Metivier and was apparently divorced. In the La Croix church records it says (spelling best guess) "*Conjust Julianae Carolinae Metivier sea seperatus secundum legerri civilem et iterum conjunctus in Matrimonio clandestino corum Magistrato civile AD 1880 cum vidua Christina Mastow.*" [Joseph was separated civilly (divorced) from Julianna Caroline Metivier and entered into a clandestine marriage with the widow Christina Mastow.]
11. "Baptismal Register," *Mackinac Register, 1695–1888*, 141.
12. "Baptismal Register," *Mackinac Register, 1695–1888*, 156.
13. "Baptismal Register," *Mackinac Register, 1695–1888*, 156.

14. "Michigan Marriages, 1868–1925," *Family Search*, database, https://familysearch.org, under Charles Cadotte and Matilda Masters, 1873.

15. "Michigan Marriages, 1868–1925," *Family Search*, database, https://familysearch.org, under John Masters and Harriette Cadotte, 1873. This branch of the family still uses the Masters name.

16. "Michigan Marriages, 1822–1995," *Family Search*, database, https://familysearch.org, under Louis Cadotte and Matilda Cadotte, 3 October 1880, FHL microfilm 2,342,466.

17. "Ontario Marriages, 1869–1927," *Family Search*, database, https://familysearch.org, under Alfred Knitel and Matilda Cadotte, 13 June 1882, citing registration, Sault Sainte Marie, Algoma, Ontario, Archives of Ontario, Toronto, FHL microfilm 1,869,758.

18. "Michigan Death Certificates, 1921–1952," *Family Search*, database, https://familysearch.org, under Matilda Kensil, 17 April 1922, citing Mackinaw City, Cheboygan County, MI, Division for Vital Records and Health Statistics, Lansing, FHL microfilm 1,973,214.

19. "Baptismal Register," *Mackinac Register, 1695–1888*, 173.

20. "Michigan Marriages, 1822–1995," *Family Search*, database, https://familysearch.org, under Joseph Masta and Rosalia Kosekwad, 8 June 1880.

21. "Michigan Death Certificates, 1921–1952," *Family Search*, database, https://familysearch.org, under Joseph Mastaw, 11 July 1931, citing Mackinaw City, Cheboygan County, MI, Division for Vital Records and Health Statistics, Lansing, FHL microfilm 1,973,214.

22. "Baptismal Register," *Mackinac Register, 1695–1888*, 184.

23. "Baptismal Register," *Mackinac Register, 1695–1888*, 190.

24. "Baptismal Register," *Mackinac Register, 1695–1888*, 32.

25. "Baptismal Register," *Mackinac Register, 1695–1888*, 207.

21. Mrs. Francis Martin (Agatha Fountain)

1. "Baptismal Register," *Mackinac Register, 1695–1888*, 95.

2. Kathleen M. Hendricks, comp., *St. Mary's Catholic Church Baptisms: Sault Sainte Marie, Michigan, 1811–1900* (Sault Ste. Marie, MI: Holy Name of Mary Proto-Cathedral, 2005), entry 365.

3. "United States Census, 1850," *Family Search*, database with images, https://familysearch.org, image 36 of 94, Michilimackinac, Michilimackinac County, MI, citing NARA microfilm publication M432 (Washington, DC: National Archives and Records Administration, n.d.).

4. *Liber Matrimonium, Mackinac Register, 1695–1888*, 52–53. The bride was listed as Nancy Fountain, born at Fort William.

5. "Baptismal Register," *Mackinac Register, 1695–1888*, 194c.

6. "Baptismal Register," *Mackinac Register, 1695–1888*, 201. There is another *Franciscus*

Martin baptized at Cross Village, born 4 March 1864. It is not known if this is a duplicate entry or another Francis. See note 8.

7. "Michigan Marriages, 1822–1995," *Family Search*, database, https://familysearch.org, under Frank Martin and Mary Lozon, 9 June 1897, citing Family History Library (FHL) microfilm 1,007,362.

8. *Holy Cross Church Records* (Cross Village, MI), microfilm publication, one roll, Bentley Historical Library, University of Michigan, roll 1, arranged mostly alphabetically; see family 70, "Franciscus Martin."

9. "Michigan Marriages, 1822–1995," *Family Search*, database, https://familysearch.org, under Joseph A Martin and Helen Delona, 17 March 1891, FHL microfilm 1,007,362.

10. "Michigan Deaths and Burials, 1800–1995," *Family Search*, database, https://familysearch.org, under Ellen Martin, 21 April 1920, citing Mackinac Island, Mackinac, Michigan, reference yrs. 1899–1946, p. 94, FHL microfilm 1,007,364.

11. "Michigan Deaths and Burials, 1800–1995," *Family Search*, database, https://familysearch.org, under Joseph Antoine Martin, 2 September 1941, citing Mackinac Island, Mackinac, MI, reference yrs. 1899–1946, p. 184, FHL microfilm 1,007,364.

12. *Holy Cross Church Records*, roll 1, family 70, "Franciscus Martin."

13. "Michigan Marriages, 1822–1995," *Family Search*, database, https://familysearch.org, under Antoine N. Perault and Agatha Martin, 1 September 1885, FHL microfilm 2,342,477.

14. "Michigan Deaths and Burials, 1800–1995," *Family Search*, database, https://familysearch.org, under Agatha Perault, 28 September 1927, citing Mackinac Island, Mackinac, MI, reference yrs. 1899–1946, p. 128, FHL microfilm 1,007,364.

15. "Michigan Death Certificates, 1921–1952," *Family Search*, database, https://familysearch.org, under Nickolas A Perault, 18 December 1931, citing Mackinac Island, Mackinac, MI, Division for Vital Records and Health Statistics, Lansing, FHL microfilm 1,972,852.

16. *Holy Cross Church Records*, roll 1, family 70, "Franciscus Martin."

17. "Michigan Marriages, 1868–1925," *Family Search*, database, https://familysearch.org, under Thomas Bazinaw and Mary Martin, 1889.

18. "Michigan Marriages, 1868–1925," *Family Search*, database, https://familysearch.org, under Julius Andress and Mary Bazinaw, 1897.

19. "Michigan Deaths and Burials, 1800–1995," *Family Search*, database, https://familysearch.org, under Julius Andress, 24 May 1932, citing Mackinac Island, Mackinac, MI, reference yrs. 1899–1946, p. 149, FHL microfilm 1,007,364.

20. "Michigan Deaths and Burials, 1800–1995," *Family Search*, database, https://familysearch.org, under Mary Andres, 3 May 1934, citing Mackinac Island, Mackinac, MI, reference yrs. 1899–1946, p. 158, FHL microfilm 1,007,364.

21. "Baptismal Register," *Mackinac Register, 1695–1888*, 231.

22. The other men who drowned were John Newton, 19; Paul Pelky, 55; William Mulchrone, 20; and Vital Bourassa Jr., 17. "Michigan Deaths, 1867–1897," *Family Search*, database, https://familysearch.org, 004207944, image 724 of 1418, citing Department of Vital Records, Lansing. See line 74, Francis Martin.

The *Cheboygan Free Press* reported the following:

> "Five Men Scalded to Death on the Tug "Bennett." Full particulars of the Sad Affair
> Cheboygan Free Press, November 16, 1876. Original Article. Our village was suddenly startled with the report yesterday morning that five men on the tug *Bennett* had been scalded to death on Tuesday morning, while that boat was aground on Epoufette's Reef. Mr. W. Newton of St. Helena, one of the owners of the tug, brought the sad intelligence to the village and from him we learned the following particulars. The Bennett got aground at Epoufette's on Monday while having in tow a schooner. On the tug is a small room directly over the boiler with a sliding door on either side opening on to the deck. In the after end of this room there is also an opening looking into the engine room. The Capt., Paul Pelke[y], the mate, Francis Martin, the fireman, William Mulcrone, John Newton, linesman, the son of Obediah Newton, and Vetal Burasaw, the cook, had all gone into the little room over the boiler for the purpose of warming and drying themselves as they had become thoroughly chilled and wet while at work and the sliding doors were closed. The engineer, James Aines, together with Obediah Newton were down in the engine room. About half past five o'clock in the morning the government valve attached to the boiler, suddenly blew open and in some manner got caught and was held in that position. The escaping steam and hot water poured directly into the room where the Capt. and his hands were asleep, with such force and rapidity as to bewilder the occupants and render escape impossible. The engineer closed the valve as soon as it could be done, but it was too late, Death had got its victims. In all probability it was almost instantaneous. One of the five, Martin the mate, was rescued before life was extinct, but at last reports, he was not expected to live. The sight presented by the dead bodies made the stoutest hearts quail. They were all black as coal, and the hair on the heads of the unfortunate victims pulled off at the slightest touch, the poor creatures being litterally [*sic*] scalded to death.
>
> "The Captain was a resident of Mackinaw and leaves a wife. John Newton was about 16 years old and was a nephew of A. P. Newton of this place and lived at St. Helena. Mulcrone was also a resident of Mackinaw where his parents and brothers now live. Burasaw, the cook was about 16 years of age and also lived in Mackinaw. His father was one of the victims of the "Dormer" when she was burned a few years ago at Beaver Harbor. Martin the mate, leaves quite a large family in Mackinaw.   "There is no blame whatever attached to the engineer. He closed the valve just as soon as it was possible to do it. The fact of the valve getting caught so as to be held open is said to be owing to the

slanting position in which the tug was lying while aground. The tug was pulled off and taken to St. Helena in a somewhat leaky condition."

55. Miss Lizzette Martin (later Mrs. Antoine Truckey)

1. St. Ignatius Loyola (St. Ignace, MI), "Baptisms 1838–1893," bk. 3, p. 17 (Elizabeth Martin, 1842), parish rectory.
2. *Liber Matrimonium, Mackinac Register, 1695–1888*, 1. Antoine Martin and Suzanne Kinokwe were married 11 August 1823 at Ste. Anne's. Her name is fully spelled out.
3. *Liber Matrimonium, Mackinac Register, 1695–1888*, 10. Marriage record for Charles Martin and Marianne Ayabins. Marianne's father is listed as Yabins, and mother was recorded as *Indiana* (Indian woman).
4. St. Ignatius Loyola (St. Ignace, MI), "Baptisms 1838–1893," bk. 3, p. 51.
5. *Liber Matrimonium, Mackinac Register, 1695–1888*, 66–67.
6. "Michigan Births, 1867–1902," *Family Search*, database with images, https://familysearch.org, under Peter Truckey, 30 September 1876, citing item 2, p. 159, rn 163, Moran, Mackinac County, MI, Department of Vital Records, Lansing, FHL microfilm 2,320,449.
7. St. Ignatius Loyola (St. Ignace, MI), "Baptisms 1838–1893," bk. 3, p. 138.
8. "Michigan Deaths and Burials, 1800–1995," *Family Search*, database with images, https://familysearch.org, under Augustus Truckey, 19 August 1902, citing Marquette, Marquette County, MI, reference v. 3, p. 82, FHL microfilm 1,007,539. He died single.
9. St. Ignatius Loyola (St. Ignace, MI), "Baptisms, 1838–1893," bk. 3, p. 150.
10. St. Ignatius Loyola (St. Ignace, MI), "Record of Interments, 1894–1988" (1934), p. 41.
11. St. Ignatius Loyola (St. Ignace, MI), "Baptisms, 1838–1893," bk. 3, p. 154.
12. St. Ignatius Loyola (St. Ignace, MI), "Baptisms, 1838–1893," bk. 3, p. 165.
13. "United States Census, 1900," *Family Search*, database with images, https://familysearch.org, under Angus Truckey, St. Ignace, Ward 1–4, Mackinac County, MI, ED 102, citing NARA microfilm publication T623 (Washington, DC: National Archives and Records Administration, n.d.), image 1 of 46.
14. "Michigan Marriages, 1822–1995," *Family Search*, database, https://familysearch.org, under Samuel Guerney and Agnes Truckey, 10 July 1907, FHL microfilm 1,007,362.
15. St. Ignatius Loyola (St. Ignace, MI), "Record of Interments, 1894–1988" (as Mary McGarney, 1910), p. 14.
16. St. Ignatius Loyola (St. Ignace, MI), "Record of Interments, 1894–1988" (1917), p. 22. The register says he died of exposure and was buried in Gros Cap Cemetery.
17. "Michigan Death Certificates, 1921–1952," *Family Search*, database, https://familysearch.org, under Isabel Truckey, 26 March 1924, citing St Ignace, Mackinac County, MI, Division for Vital Records and Health Statistics, Lansing, FHL microfilm 1,972,852.

49. Mrs. Benjamin McGulpin (Elizabeth Boyd)

1. "Baptismal Register," *Mackinac Register, 1695–1888*, 44–45.

2. The baptismal record above has a notation "illeg." or illegitimate after the parents' name.

3. Larry Wyckoff, trans., "Mixed-Blood Census Register, Ottawas and Chippewas of Michigan, Treaty of March 26, 1836," *Roots Web*, http://www.rootsweb.ancestry.com/~mimacki2/annuities/1836mb.pdf, n.d., no. 172 Alexander Boyd. Remarks section says his mother is a "half-breed Chippewa."

4. Wyckoff, "Mixed-Blood Census Register," see under no. 173 Eliza Boyd.

5. Wyckoff, "Mixed-Blood Census Register," no. 172 and no. 173.

6. Les Rentmeester and Jeanne Rentmeester, *The Wisconsin Creoles* (Melbourne, FL: self-published, 1987), 216.

7. François Victoire Malhiot, *A Wisconsin Fur Trader's Journal: 1804–1805*, vol. 19 (Madison, WI: State Historical Society of Wisconsin, 1910), p. 202.

8. Wyckoff, "Mixed-Blood Census Register," no. 172 and no. 173; see "To Whom Payable" column. Yarns appears in the 1830 census for Michilimackinac County. "There is one boy under 5, one girl under 5, one adult male between 50–60 and one adult female between 20–30."

9. Wyckoff, "Mixed-Blood Census Register," no. 174. The 1826 Treaty of with the Chippewa (Fond du Lac), granted Susan Yarns, daughter of Odanbitogeezhigoqua, one section in Sault Ste. Marie. Debi Hanes, transcriber, "Chippewa County History," http://genealogytrails.com/mich/chippewa/upperpen.html.

10. Register of Deeds, Mackinac County, Deed Book B, p. 110–111.

11. "Baptismal Register," *Mackinac Register, 1695–1888*, 18.

12. "A Well Known Character Dies at Mackinac," *Cheboygan Democrat*, Friday, 22 July 1910, p. 8, col. 4.

13. "Deeds, Book B," p. 116, City Clerk's Office, Mackinac Island Courthouse, City of Mackinac Island, MI.

14. "Michigan Marriages, 1822–1995," *Family Search*, database, https://familysearch.org, under Benjamin Mcgulpin in entry for Gill Sellew Mcgulpin and Lenora E. Chapman, 29 October 1900, FHL microfilm 1,007,362.

15. "Michigan. Divorce Records, 1897–1852," *Ancestry*, database, https://search.ancestry.com, divorce of Jane McGulpin and Benjamin McGulpin, no. 792, granted 23 January 1911. The original marriage record could not be located but is documented on the divorce petition.

16. "Michigan Deaths and Burials, 1800–1995," *Family Search*, database, https://familysearch.org, under Ben Mcgulpin in entry for Ben Mcgulphin, 12 August 1914, citing Cross Village, Emmet, MI, reference cn 115, FHL microfilm 966,504.

17. "Michigan Marriages, 1822–1995," *Family Search*, database, https://familysearch.org,

under Louis Belonger and Mollie M. Mcgulpin, 22 September 1878, FHL microfilm
1,007,362.

18. "Michigan Deaths and Burials, 1800–1995," *Family Search*, database, https://familysearch.
org, under Maria Belonrgea, 13 February 1943, citing Cross Village, Emmet County, MI,
reference cn 46, FHL microfilm 966,505.

19. "Baptismal Register," *Mackinac Register, 1695–1888*, 189A.

20. "Michigan Deaths and Burials, 1800–1995," *Family Search*, database, https://familysearch.
org, under William J. Mcgulpin, 11 February 1926, citing Cross Village, MI, reference cn 39,
FHL microfilm 966,505.

21. "Baptismal Register," *Mackinac Register, 1695–1888*, 194A.

22. "Michigan Marriages, 1822–1995," *Family Search*, database, https://familysearch.org,
under Patrick Tobin and Annie Mcgulpin, 19 May 1878, FHL microfilm 2,342,463.

23. "Michigan Marriages, 1822–1995," *Family Search*, database, https://familysearch.org,
under Henry Perault and Annie Toban, 11 January 1893, FHL microfilm 1,007,362.

24. "Michigan Deaths and Burials, 1800–1995," *Family Search*, database, https://familysearch.
org, under Benjamin Mcgulpin in entry for Anna Perault, 13 October 1940, citing
Wyandotte, Wayne County, MI, reference v. 15, cn 270, FHL microfilm 2,115,276.

25. "Baptismal Register," *Mackinac Register, 1695–1888*, 197.

26. "Michigan Death Certificates, 1921–1952," *Family Search*, database, https://familysearch.
org, under Elizabeth Ursula Wehner, 3 November 1933, citing Kingsley, Grand Traverse,
MI, Division for Vital Records and Health Statistics, Lansing, FHL microfilm 1,972,716.

27. *Liber Matrimonium, Mackinac Register, 1695–1888*, 70–71.

28. "Baptismal Register," *Mackinac Register, 1695–1888*, 203.

29. "Michigan Deaths and Burials, 1800–1995," *Family Search*, database, https://familysearch.
org, under Benjamin Mcgulpin in entry for James George Mcgulpin, 30 March 1945,
citing Mackinac Island, Mackinac, MI, reference yrs. 1899–1946, p. 196, FHL microfilm
1,007,364.

30. "Baptismal Register," *Mackinac Register, 1695–1888*, 208.

31. "Baptismal Register," *Mackinac Register, 1695–1888*, 216.

32. "Baptismal Register," *Mackinac Register, 1695–1888*, 224. Mother listed as Aloysia (Louise)
Bois.

33. "Baptismal Register," *Mackinac Register, 1695–1888*, 235. Baptized under the name
Gulielmus (William).

34. "Michigan Marriages, 1822–1995," *Family Search*, database, https://familysearch.org,
under Benjamin Mcgulpin in entry for Gill Sellew Mcgulpin and Lenora E. Chapman, 29
October 1900, citing FHL microfilm 1,007,362.

35. "Michigan Deaths and Burials, 1800–1995," *Family Search*, database, https://familysearch.

org, under Benjamin Mcgulpin, 12 July 1910, citing Mackinac Island, Mackinac County, MI, reference yrs. 1899–1946, p. 48, FHL microfilm 1,007,364.

36. "Find a Grave Index," *Family Search*, database and images, https://familysearch.org, under Elizabeth Ann Boyd McGulpin, 1916, Burial: Sainte Anne's Cemetery, Mackinac Island, Mackinac County, MI, record ID 113261691, *Find a Grave*, http://www.findagrave.com.

52. Miss Mary McGulphin (later Mrs. Mary Garrison)

1. "Baptismal Register," *Mackinac Register, 1695–1888*, 183.

2. *Liber Matrimonium, Mackinac Register, 1695–1888*, 68–69.

3. Lois Hines, comp., *Michigan Western, 1884 Directory* [database online] (Provo, UT: Ancestry.com Operations Inc, 2001), https://www.ancestry.com/search/collections/6072/.

4. "Baptismal Register," *Mackinac Register, 1695–1888*, 234.

5. "Baptismal Register," *Mackinac Register, 1695–1888*, 239.

6. "Michigan Marriages, 1868–1925," *Family Search*, database, https://familysearch.org, under W. M. Newton and Mary Garrison, 1904.

7. "Baptismal Register," *Mackinac Register, 1695–1888*, 241.

8. "Michigan Marriages, 1868–1925," *Family Search*, database, https://familysearch.org, under John O. Garrison in entry for John P. Garrison and Rose M. Francis, 1904.

9. "Michigan Marriages, 1868–1925," *Family Search*, database, https://familysearch.org, under John P. Garrison and Dena Demmink, 1913.

10. Michigan State Archives, Death Records, *Michiganology*, https://www.michiganology.org, entry for John Peter Garrison, 1916, Kent County.

11. "Baptismal Register," *Mackinac Register, 1695–1888*, 245.

12. "Michigan Marriages, 1868–1925," *Family Search*, database, https://familysearch.org, under Delos K. Sayles and Katherine Garrison, 1905.

13. "Florida Death Index, 1877–1998," *Family Search*, database, https://familysearch.org, Katherine E. Sayles, April 1966, *Ancestry*, database, www.ancestry.com, 2004, citing vol. 2820, certificate number 22228, Florida Department of Health, Office of Vital Records, Jacksonville.

14. "Baptismal Register," *Mackinac Register, 1695–1888*, 249.

15. "Illinois, Cook County Marriages, 1871–1920," *Family Search*, database, https://familysearch.org, under Fred L. Garrison and Josephine Nelson, 16 September 1905, citing Cook County Courthouse, Chicago, IL, 417434, Family History Library (FHL) microfilm 1,030,391.

16. "Michigan Death Certificates, 1921–1952," *Family Search*, database, https://familysearch.org, under John P. Garrison in entry for Fred L. Garrison, 20 November 1948, citing Cascade, Kent, MI, Division for Vital Records and Health Statistics, Lansing, FHL

microfilm 1,972,815.

17. R. L. Polk's Grand Rapids directories for the years 1890–1905. See under https://babel. hathitrust.org/cgi/mb?a=listis;c=1648165062;sort=title_a;pn=1.

18. Michigan State Archives, Death Records, *Michiganology*, https://www.michiganology.org, entry for John O. Garrison, 1910, Kent County.

19. "Michigan Death Certificates, 1921–1952," *Family Search*, database, https://familysearch. org, under Mary Jane Garrison, 30 March 1932, citing Grand Rapids, Kent, MI, Division for Vital Records and Health Statistics, Lansing, FHL microfilm 1,972,821.

41. Miss Nancy McGulpin

1. "Baptismal Register," *Mackinac Register, 1695–1888*, 34. The person in this baptism was named Anna.

2. *Liber Matrimonium, Mackinac Register, 1695–1888*, 13.

3. "Baptismal Register," *Mackinac Register, 1695–1888*, 61.

4. Larry Wyckoff, trans., "Mixed-Blood Census Register, Ottawas and Chippewas of Michigan, Treaty of March 26, 1836," *Roots Web*, http://www.rootsweb.ancestry. com/~mimacki2/annuities/1836mb.pdf, n.d., nos. 228–235. Father George McGulpin is no. 231. Nancy McGulpin is no. 230. It says she is twenty-six years old, indicating a birth date of around 1809.

5. "United States Census, 1870," *Family Search*, database with images, https://familysearch. org, under Nancy Magulpin, Inverness, Cheboygan County, MI, family 181, p. 26, citing NARA microfilm publication M593 (Washington, DC: National Archives and Records Administration, n.d.), FHL microfilm 552,168.

6. Emmet County, *Vital Records Search*, searchable database, http://apps.emmetcounty.org/ clerk/deathrecords.aspx, under Nancy McGulpin, liber 1, folio 13.

44. Mrs. Joseph Menasaw (Mary Belanger)

1. "Baptismal Register," *Mackinac Register, 1695–1888*, 52.

2. *Programme de recherche en démographie historique (PRDH)* (Université de Montréal, Canada), 1621–1849, certificate 4376461, Joseph Hercule Menançon, transcription, https://www.prdh-igd.com.

3. *Liber Matrimonium, Mackinac Register, 1695–1888*, 40.

4. "Baptismal Register," *Mackinac Register, 1695–1888*, 178.

5. "Wisconsin, County Marriages, 1836–1911," *Family Search*, database, https://familysearch. org, under Lewis Menasso and Mary Sanville, 28 December 1876, citing Sturgeon Bay, Door, WI, Wisconsin Historical Society, Madison, Family History Library (FHL) microfilm 1,275,987.

6. "Find a Grave Index," *Family Search*, database, https://familysearch.org, under Louis William Monosso, 1925, Burial: Bayside Cemetery, Sturgeon Bay, Door County, WI, record ID 130382646, *Find a Grave*, http://www.findagrave.com.

7. *Liber Matrimonium, Mackinac Register, 1695–1888*, 66–67.

8. "Michigan Deaths and Burials, 1800–1995," *Family Search*, database, https://familysearch.org, under Michael Gorman, 6 November 1898, citing St. Ignace Township, Mackinac County, MI, reference yrs. 1899–1946, p. 2, FHL microfilm 1,007,364.

9. "Washington Death Certificates, 1907–1960," *Family Search*, database, https://familysearch.org, under Rose Gorman, 11 March 1923, citing Everett, Snohomish County, Washington, ref. 57, Bureau of Vital Statistics, Olympia, FHL microfilm 1,992,974.

10. St. Ignatius Loyola (St. Ignace, MI), "Baptisms, 1838–1893," bk. 3, p. 71 (Genevieve Menancon, 1858), parish rectory.

11. "Find a Grave Index," *Family Search*, database, https://familysearch.org, under Jennie Vertz, 1917, Burial: Clay Banks Cemetery, Door County, WI, record ID 59428059, *Find a Grave*, http://www.findagrave.com.

12. "Wisconsin Marriages, 1836–1930," *Family Search*, database, https://familysearch.org, under John Monoso and Anna Stanitz, 15 August 1887, FHL microfilm 1,292,262.

13. "Joseph Monosso, formerly of Clay Banks," *The Independent* (Sturgeon Bay, WI), Friday, 11 October 1889, p. 2, col. 1.

14. "Wisconsin Marriages, 1836–1911," *Family Search*, database, https://familysearch.org, under Joseph Monosso in entry for Burton Whaples and Mary Monosso, 24 February 1878, citing Clay Banks, Door County, WI, Wisconsin Historical Society, Madison, FHL microfilm 1,275,987.

15. "Circuit Court, Door County, Wisconsin," *Weekly Expositor Independent* (Sturgeon Bay, WI), 5 February 1886, p. 2, col. 4.

16. "Michigan Marriages, 1822–1995," *Family Search*, database, https://familysearch.org, under Joseph Manosco and Annie Elizabeth Stamnitz, 11 April 1891, FHL microfilm 2,342,490.

17. Marriage of Joseph Monosso and Marie Peterson, *Michigan, Marriage Records, 1867–1952* [database online], 21 June 1933, county file number 25, state file number 75 518, Michigan Department of Community Health, Division for Vital Records and Health Statistics, Lansing (Provo, UT: Ancestry.com Operations, 2015.)

18. *Special Schedules of the Eleventh Census (1890) Enumerating Union Veterans and Widows of Union Veterans of the Civil War*, National Archives at Washington, DC, *Records of the Department of Veterans Affairs*, record group number 15 (1773–1985), microfilm M123, "Clay Banks, Door County, WI," roll 114, *Ancestry* [database online] (Provo, UT: Ancestry.com Operations Inc, 2005).

19. *General Index to Civil War and Later Pension Files, ca. 1949–ca. 1949*, National Archives at Washington, DC, Records of the Department of Veterans Affairs (1773–2007), record group number 15, NAI number 563268, "United States General Index to Pension Files, 1861–1934" (Washington, DC: National Archives and Records Administration, n.d.), microfilm T288, roll 311, under Joseph Manasso, application no. 613.623, certificate no. 622.303. *Ancestry*, (Provo, UT: Ancestry.com Operations Inc, 2000).

20. "Joseph Monosso Dies Suddenly," *Sturgeon Bay* (WI) *Advocate*, 29 April 1915, p. 5, cols. 3–4.

18. Mrs. Daniel Moore (Louise Charbonneau)

1. "Québec, registres paroissiaux catholiques, 1621–1979," *Family Search*, database with images, https://familysearch.org, "Immaculée-Conception, Saint-Ours," image 361 of 1007, *Baptêmes, mariages, sépultures, 1775–1809* (Montreal: Archives Nationales du Quebec [National Archives of Quebec]).

2. *Ste. Anne's Church Registers: 1704–1842*, microfilm, 3 rolls (Detroit, MI: St. Anne's of Detroit). See roll 3, *Chapelle du nordest: Baptisms, Marriages, Burials, 1810–1838*, arranged by date, marriage record of Louis Charbonneau and Susanne Godin, University of Michigan, Bentley Historical Library (BHL) no. 1252, reel 3, p. 128.

3. "Mackinac Baptism Records 1810–1821," AccessGenealogy, https://www.accessgenealogy.com/michigan/mackinac-baptism-records-1810-1821.htm, citing the baptisms of Therese, Archange, Jean Baptiste, and Basil Carbonneau dit Provençal, children of Louis Carbonneau dit Provençal and "a woman savage of the Sioux nation." Spelling per document. Translation from a copy of the original in possession of the parish church of Ste. Anne at Mackinac.

4. Marriage record of Louis Charbonneau and Susanne Godin, *Ste. Anne's Church Registers*, reel 3, p. 127–128.

5. Marriage record of Louis Charbonneau and Susanne Godin, *Ste. Anne's Church Registers*, reel 3, p. 127–128.

6. Marriage of Joseph Biron (dit LaPine) and Loise [*sic*] Charbonneau, "Port of Mackinac Records," Office of the Register of Deeds, St. Ignace, Mackinac County, MI, no. 50, p. 77.

7. "Baptismal Register," *Mackinac Register, 1695–1888*, 34.

8. *Liber Matrimonium, Mackinac Register, 1695–1888*, 35.

9. *Liber Matrimonium, Mackinac Register, 1695–1888*, 48–49.

10. "Baptismal Register," *Mackinac Register, 1695–1888*.

11. *Liber Matrimonium, Mackinac Register, 1695–1888*, 50–51. May was the daughter of his mother's half-sister Archange who married Peter Brunette 13 August 1836 in Brown County, WI.

12. "Baptismal Register," *Mackinac Register, 1695–1888*, 49. See under L'apine.

13. *Liber Matrimonium, Mackinac Register, 1695–1888*, 35.

14. St. Ignatius Loyola (St. Ignace, MI), "Baptisms, 1838–1893," bk. 3, p.1 (Victor Lapine, 1837), parish rectory.

15. Marriage of Victor Lapine and Ermine Archambau, "Port of Mackinac Records," Office of the Register of Deeds, St. Ignace, Mackinac County, MI, no. 507, p. 86.

16. St. Ignatius Loyola (St. Ignace, MI), "Baptisms, 1838–1893," bk. 3, p. 12 (Isaac Lapine, 1840), parish rectory.

17. George H. Turner, *Record of Service of Michigan Volunteers in the Civil War, 1861–1865*, vol. 37 (Kalamazoo, MI: Ihling Bros. & Everard, 1900), p. 81, https://catalog.hathitrust.org/Record/003931700. See under Isaac Lapine.

18. *Liber Matrimonium, Mackinac Register, 1695–1888*, 56–57.

19. *Liber Defunctorum, Mackinac Register, 1695–1888*, 113.

20. *Liber Defunctorum, Mackinac Register, 1695–1888*, 113.

21. There is a possible death record for Joseph. In the St. Ignatius (St. Ignace, MI) *Liber Defunctorum*, the first page (p. 258) has a notation for the death of a Joseph L'Epine during the month of April 1841. There is no additional information to determine who this individual was.

22. *Liber Defunctorum, Mackinac Register, 1695–1888*, 111. Her death record states she was born at Fort William.

3. Mrs. Andrew Moran (Mary Kekematiwain)

1. "Baptismal Register," *Mackinac Register, 1695–1888*, 60. See under Marie Kenkenime.

2. *Liber Matrimonium, Mackinac Register, 1695–1888*, 10.

3. *Programme de recherche en démographie historique* (*PRDH*) (Université de Montréal, Canada), 1621–1849, certificate 3373498, Anslem LeBlanc, transcription, https://www.prdh-igd.com.

4. *St. Mary's Parish Marriage Records, 1860–1865* [*sic*], St. Mary Catholic Church (Cheboygan, MI) parish rectory office, under marriage of Francis Morin and Marie Carow, 1867. This register contains old original records in the front that are a mixture of baptisms and marriages. Some pages are numbered with Roman numerals, and other pages were not. The label of 1865 is incorrect. It is also labeled *St. Mary's Parish Baptisms Records, 1860–1892*.

5. "Baptismal Register," *Mackinac Register, 1695–1888*, 207. Mother listed as Alexie Corron.

6. "Michigan Marriages, 1822–1995," *Family Search*, database, https://familysearch.org, under Oliver Morrow and Elizabeth Clark, 30 June 1891, Family History Library (FHL) microfilm 1,007,362.

7. *St. Mary's Parish Baptism Records, 1860–1892*, St. Mary Catholic Church (Cheboygan, MI) parish rectory office, under Margaret Caron, 1868), ix.

8. "Michigan Marriages, 1822–1995," *Family Search*, database, https://familysearch.org, under Andrew Morrow in entry for Ned Davis and Maggie Morrow, 3 August 1907, citing reference p. 174, no. 1305, FHL microfilm 964,409. Mother's name listed as Mary Smith.

9. "Michigan Death Certificates, 1921–1952," *Family Search*, database, https://familysearch.org, under Angeline Shampine, 12 October 1931, citing Pellston, Emmet, MI, Division for Vital Records and Health Statistics, Lansing, FHL microfilm 1,973,233. Her birth date was taken from the Death Certificate.

10. "Michigan Marriages, 1822–1995," *Family Search*, database, https://familysearch.org, under Henry Demar and Angeline Morrow, 22 November 1902, citing reference p. 123, no. 542, FHL microfilm 964,409.

11. "Michigan Marriages, 1822–1995," *Family Search*, database, https://familysearch.org, under Charles Champine and Angeline Morrow, 19 June 1911, citing reference p. 215, no. 1924, FHL microfilm 964,409.

12. "Michigan Deaths, 1867–1897," *Family Search*, database with images, https://familysearch.org, under Andrew Morani, 22 August 1878, citing p. 127, rn. 20, Benton, Cheboygan, MI, Department of Vital Records, Lansing, FHL microfilm 2,363,666.

13. "United States Census, 1880," *Family Search*, database with images, https://familysearch.org, under Mary Morrow, Cheboygan, Cheboygan County, MI, citing enumeration district (ED) 32, sheet 88C, NARA microfilm publication T9 (Washington, DC: National Archives and Records Administration, n.d.), roll 0576, FHL microfilm 1,254,576.

14. "Deaths," *St. Mary's Parish Record, 1869–1962*, St. Mary Catholic Church (Cheboygan, MI) parish rectory office, under Marie Caron *viduae* Andre Morin, 1886, p. 63.

11. Mrs. Ignace Pelotte (Rosalie Boucher)

1. Mackinac State Historic Parks, "1938 Survey of Ste. Anne's Cemetery," S. Alicia Poole Papers, Petersen Library (Mackinaw City, MI), Alice Poole Vertical File.

2. Larry Wyckoff, trans., "Mixed-Blood Census Register, Ottawas and Chippewas of Michigan, Treaty of March 26, 1836," *Roots Web*, http://www.rootsweb.ancestry.com/~mimacki2/annuities/1836mb.pdf, n.d., no. 214. See under the "Remarks" column.

3. *Mackinac Island Miscellanea* (1), Alicia. S. Poole Papers, Bentley Historical Library, University of Michigan–Ann Arbor, 1925, file no. 5408.

4. "Baptismal Register," *Mackinac Register, 1695–1888*, 15.

5. "Marriages, 1805–1820," *Circuit Court Records*, Clerk's Office, St. Ignace, Mackinac County, MI, ID 205, Ignace Pelotte–Lisette La Sauteuse, 3 January 1807, transcript p. 2.

6. *Liber Matrimonium, Mackinac Register, 1695–1888*, 6.

7. *Sauteuse* is the feminine version of Saulteur, plural Saulteaux. This name was used by French speaking people when referring to the Ojibwe, yet Lisette was Ottawa.

8. Father Dejean labeled this page (written in French) *Registre des Sepultures*, beginning 19 August 1828. However, it looks like Ignace was the only entry. It is listed in the Ste. Anne's CD-ROM index under "Miscellaneous." Translation of the document follows: "Ignace Pilate died the 17 August 1828 and was buried by me, undersigned curate, in the Mackinac cemetery, the next day, aged around fifty years. In the presence of Jeremie Le Duc and of Simon Champagne and others who could not sign. Dejean, pretre."

9. Letter from Mary Anne Fisher to Elizabeth Baird, 6 December 1841, Henry and Elizabeth Baird Papers, 1798–1937, Wisconsin Historical Society, Wis. Mss. V, box 1, folder 6, http:// content.wisconsinhistory.org/cdm/compoundobject/collection/baird/id/882/rec/6.

10. Marriage of Ignace Pilotte and Rosalia Pushelog, "Port of Mackinac Records," Office of the Register of Deeds, St. Ignace, Mackinac County, MI, no. 176 and no. 508.

11. *Liber Matrimonium, Mackinac Register, 1695–1888*, 15.

12. *Liber Matrimonium, Mackinac Register, 1695–1888*, 56–57.

13. "Baptismal Register," *Mackinac Register, 1695–1888*, 15.

14. *Liber Matrimonium, Mackinac Register, 1695–1888*, 48–49.

15. "Baptismal Register," *Mackinac Register, 1695–1888*, 97.

16. *Liber Matrimonium, Mackinac Register, 1695–1888*, 54–55.

17. "Baptismal Register," *Mackinac Register, 1695–1888*, 107. See under Pilote.

18. "United States Civil War Soldiers Index, 1861–1865," *Family Search*, database, https:// familysearch.org, under Gabriel P. Pelotte, Private, Company K, 7th Regiment, Michigan Cavalry, Union, citing NARA microfilm publication M545 (Washington, DC: National Archives and Records Administration, n.d.), roll 32, FHL microfilm 881,945.

19. Theresa Weller, "Mackinac County Men Participate in Company K, 7th Cavalry of the Civil War," *Saint Ignace News*, 3 April 2014, https://www.stignacenews.com/articles/ mackinac-county-men-participate-in-company-k-7th-cavalry-of-the-civil-war.

20. *Liber Defunctorum, Mackinac Register, 1695–1888*, 105.

21. "Baptismal Register," *Mackinac Register, 1695–1888*, 126.

22. "Michigan Marriages, 1822–1995," *Family Search*, database, https://familysearch.org, under John Gallagher and Catherine R. Pelotte, 17 January 1878, FHL microfilm 1,007,362.

23. "Baptismal Register," *Mackinac Register, 1695–1888*, 134.

24. "Baptismal Register," *Mackinac Register, 1695–1888*, 151. See under Guillaume Pilote.

25. "Baptismal Register," *Mackinac Register, 1695–1888*, 168.

26. "Baptismal Register," *Mackinac Register, 1695–1888*, 178.

27. "Michigan Marriages, 1822–1995," *Family Search*, database, https://familysearch.org, under Samuel O. Decator and Christine Pelotte, 3 May 1874, FHL microfilm 1,007,362.

28. Mackinac State Historic Parks, "1938 Survey of Ste. Anne's Cemetery."
29. "Souvenir Edition of the Enterprise," *St. Ignace Enterprise*, July 1897, pp. 13–14.
30. "Ignace Pelott, better known as Grandpere Pelott . . ." (there is no title), *St. Ignace* (MI) *News*, p. 5, col. 3.

65. Victoire Peltier (Mrs. David Bellaire)

1. Theresa M. Schenck, *All Our Relations: Chippewa Mixed-Bloods and the Treaty of 1837* (Winnipeg, Manitoba: The Center for Rupert's Land Studies at the University of Winnipeg, 2010), 103.
2. Larry Wyckoff, trans., "Mixed-Blood Census Register, Ottawas and Chippewas of Michigan, Treaty of March 26, 1836," *Roots Web*, http://www.rootsweb.ancestry. com/~mimacki2/annuities/1836mb.pdf, n.d., no. 512.
3. Wyckoff, "Mixed-Blood Census Register," no. 512.
4. Wyckoff, "Mixed-Blood Census Register," nos. 518–521. See under Angelique LeSieur
5. Wyckoff, "Mixed-Blood Census Register," no. 522.
6. *Liber Matrimonium, Mackinac Register, 1695–1888*, 22. See under David Bellere.
7. Lyman Granger was the lighthouse keeper at Bois Blanc Island, Mackinac County, from 2 September 1845 to 27 July 1854, locally called "Bob-lo" Island. "Bois Blanc Island," http://www.terrypepper.com/lights/huron/boisblanc/boisblanc.htm.
8. "Baptismal Register," *Mackinac Register, 1695–1888*, 153. See under Theodore Louis Belleir.
9. Michigan State Archives, Death Records, *Michiganology*, https://www.michiganology.org, entry for Theodore Blair, 1932, Mackinac County.
10. "Michigan Deaths and Burials, 1800–1995," *Family Search*, database, https://familysearch.org, under Victorine Bellare, 10 March 1874, citing Mackinaw, Mackinac County, MI, reference yrs. 1873–1899, p. 3, FHL microfilm 1,007,364.

13. Mrs. Francis Rastoul (Christine Bennet-Beaubin)

1. "Baptismal Register," *Mackinac Register, 1695–1888*, 52.
2. St. Ann Catholic Church (Penetanguishene, Ontario), *Registre des baptêmes, des mariages et des sépultures de l'année 1835 [à 1846]*, parish records, entry of 28 June 1838, baptism of François Rostoll, 3 microfilm reels, not paginated, Family History Library (FHL) 1305885.
3. "Michigan Marriages, 1822–1995," *Family Search*, database, https://familysearch.org, under Nils Anderson and Isabella Postool, 8 February 1882, citing reference p. 34, no. 14, FHL microfilm 964,409.
4. "United States Census, 1880," *Family Search*, database with images, https://familysearch.org, Beaugrand, Cheboygan County, MI, citing enumeration district (ED) 31, NARA microfilm publication T9 (Washington, DC: National Archives and Records

Administration, n.d.), image 12 of 12.

5. "United States Census, 1870," *Family Search*, database with images, https://familysearch.
org, Inverness, Cheboygan County, MI, citing NARA microfilm publication M593
(Washington, DC: National Archives and Records Administration, n.d.), image 26 of 36.

6. "Baptismal Register," *Mackinac Register, 1695–1888*, 198. Mother listed as Isabell.

7. "Michigan Deaths, 1867–1897," *Family Search*, database with images, https://familysearch.
org, under Charles Rastool, 25 September 1884, citing p. 168, rn. 23, Hebron, Cheboygan
County, MI, Department of Vital Records, Lansing, FHL microfilm 2,363,673.

8. "Baptismal Register," *Mackinac Register, 1695–1888*, 208.

9. "Michigan Deaths, 1867–1897," *Family Search*, database with images, https://familysearch.
org, under Matilda Rostel, 10 April 1882, citing p. 145, rn. 48, Beaugrand Township,
Cheboygan County, MI, Department of Vital Records, Lansing, FHL microfilm 2,363,670.

10. "Michigan Births and Christenings, 1775–1995," *FamilySearch*, database, https://
familysearch.org, under Mary Rustoul, 28 December 1875, citing Cheboygan, MI.

11. "Michigan Death Certificates, 1921–1952," *Family Search*, database, https://familysearch.
org, under Eliza Restool, 9 November 1945, citing Saginaw, Saginaw County, MI, Division
for Vital Records and Health Statistics, Lansing, FHL microfilm 1,973,089.

12. "Find a Grave Index," *Family Search*, database, https://familysearch.org, under Jennie
V. Restool Morse, Burial: Oakwood Cemetery, Saginaw, Saginaw County, MI, record ID
134244227, *Find a Grave*, http://www.findagrave.com. Jennie's birth date was taken from
her death certificate. If this is correct, Christine had two babies in one year.

13. "Michigan Marriages, 1822–1995," *Family Search*, database, https://familysearch.org,
under Milton A. Morse and Jennie Restole, 7 December 1895, citing reference p. 61, no.
344, FHL microfilm 964,409.

14. "Michigan Death Certificates, 1921–1952," *Family Search*, database, https://familysearch.
org, under Milton A Morse, 22 December 1951, citing Thomas, Saginaw County, MI,
Division for Vital Records and Health Statistics, Lansing, FHL microfilm 1,973,080.

15. "Find a Grave Index," *Family Search*, database, https://familysearch.org, under Jennie
V. Restool Morse, Burial: Oakwood Cemetery, Saginaw, Saginaw County, MI, record ID
134244227, *Find a Grave*, http://www.findagrave.com.

16. "Michigan, County Births, 1867–1917," *Family Search*, database with images, https://
familysearch.org, under Rastool, 25 December 1877.

17. "United States Registers of Enlistments in the U.S. Army, 1798–1914," *Family Search*,
database with images, https://familysearch.org, under Frank L Restool, 30 October
1901, citing p. 38, vol. 108, Mackinaw City, MI, NARA microfilm publication M233
(Washington, DC: National Archives and Records Administration, n.d.), roll 56, FHL
microfilm 1,465,942.

18. "United States Registers of Enlistments in the U.S. Army, 1798–1914," *Family Search*, database with images, https://familysearch.org, May 1901–1902, L–Z, pp. 108–109, image 353 of 700, citing NARA microfilm publication M233 (Washington, DC: National Archives and Records Administration, n.d.).

19. *Returns from Regular Army Infantry Regiments, June 1821–1916*, (Washington, DC: National Archives and Records Administration, n.d.), microfilm serial M665, roll 273, citing Frank L. Restool, 28th Infantry, 1901–1902.

20. *Returns from Regular Army Infantry Regiments, June 1821–1916*, (Washington, DC: National Archives and Records Administration, n.d.), microfilm serial M665, roll 89, citing Frank L. Restool, 7th Infantry, 1911–1916.

21. "Michigan, County Marriages, 1820–1940," *Family Search*, database with images, https://familysearch.org, under Frank L. Restool and Anna Reck, 10 November 1913, FHL microfilm 966,507.

22. "United States Census, 1920," *Family Search*, database with images, https://familysearch.org, under Frank Restool in household of Frank L. Restool, Lansing, Ward 1, Ingham County, MI, ED 88, sheet 1A, line 35, family 10, NARA microfilm publication T625 (Washington, DC: National Archives and Records Administration, 1992), roll 771, FHL microfilm 1,820,771.

23. "United States Census, 1900," *Family Search*, database with images, https://familysearch.org, Bliss and Carp Lake Township, Mackinaw City Village, Emmet County, MI, ED 84, image 16 of 27, NARA microfilm publication T623 (Washington, DC: National Archives and Records Administration, n.d.).

24. Michigan State Archives, Death Records, *Michiganology*, https://www.michiganology.org, entry for Frank Restool, 1920, Ingham County.

48. Mrs. Benjamin A. Rice (Ursula Lusignan)

1. "Baptismal Register," *Mackinac Register, 1695–1888*, 42.

2. Marriage of Benjamin Rice and Ursula Louisigneaw, 1851, "Port of Mackinac Records," Office of the Register of Deeds, St. Ignace, Mackinac County, MI, no. 309.

3. "Baptismal Register," *Mackinac Register, 1695–1888*, 155.

4. *Liber Matrimonium, Mackinac Register, 1695–1888*, 66–67. Post returns from Fort Mackinac indicate First Lieutenant Thomas Sharp was granted leave from 6–12 January 1874 for his wedding.

5. *United States Military Registers, 1902–1985* (Salem, OR: Oregon State Library), under Thomas Sharp, 508, https://www.ancestry.com/search/collections/2345/.

6. *Liber Defunctorum, Mackinac Register, 1695–1888*, 111.

7. "Baptismal Register," *Mackinac Register, 1695–1888*, 171.

8. *Liber Matrimonium, Mackinac Register, 1695–1888*, 66–67.

9. *Liber Defunctorum, Mackinac Register, 1695–1888*, 115.

10. *Liber Defunctorum, Mackinac Register, 1695–1888*, 51.

11. "Baptismal Register," *Mackinac Register, 1695–1888*, 189.

12. "Michigan Marriages, 1868–1925," *Family Search*, database, https://familysearch.org, under Alexis Lozon and Ursula Louisignan Rice, 1879, Mackinac County.

13. "Michigan, Death Records, 1867–1950," *Ancestry*, database with images, https://www. ancestry.com, under Urusla Lozon, 1901, Mackinac County.

14. His parents are listed on his marriage to Sarah E. Dunlap. See note 15.

15. "Minnesota, Grand Army of the Republic Membership Records, 1869–1940," *Family Search*, database with images, https://familysearch.org, under Benj. A. Rice, 1869–1940, citing Military Service, Minneapolis, MN, Minnesota Historical Society, St. Paul, Family History Library (FHL) microfilm 2,321,171. He served a total of three years, ten months, and seven days.

16. Roster, residents' records, Minnesota Soldiers Home, *List Board of Trustees, Officers, Consulting Surgeons and Resident Members* (Minneapolis, MN, 1898), Minnesota Historical Society, http://www2.mnhs.org/library, p. 3.

17. "United States Veterans Administration Pension Payment Cards, 1907–1933," *Family Search*, database with images, https://familysearch.org, under Benjamin A Rice, 1907–1933, citing NARA microfilm publication M850 (Washington, DC: National Archives and Records Administration, n.d.), FHL microfilm 1,635,913.

18. At the author's request, *Find a Grave* confirmed with Lakewood Cemetery (1 November 2016) that there is no marker on Benjamin A. Rice's grave; however, it has been confirmed that he is buried there.

19. "Illinois, Cook County Deaths, 1878–1994," *Family Search*, database, https://familysearch.org, under Sarah E. Rice, 18 July 1929, Chicago, IL.

59. Angel Robinson (Mrs. George Lamyott)

1. St. Ignatius Loyola (St. Ignace, MI), "Births, 1838–1893," bk. 3, p. 14 (Angela Robeson, 1840), parish rectory.

2. St. Ann Catholic Church (Penetanguishene, Ontario), *Registre des baptêmes, des mariages et des sépultures de l'année 1835 [à 1846]*, parish records, entry of 28 July 1837, baptism of Georges Amiot, 3 microfilm reels, not paginated, Family History Library (FHL) 1305885.

3. St. Ignatius Loyola (St. Ignace, MI), "Marriages, 1838–1893," bk. 1, pp. 22–23 (Georges Amiotte and Angile Robinson, 1861), parish rectory.

4. St. Ignatius Loyola (St. Ignace, MI), "Baptisms, 1838–1893," bk. 3, p. 101 (Anne Amiotte, 1865), parish rectory.

5. St. Ignatius Loyola (St. Ignace, MI), "Baptisms, 1838–1893," bk. 3, p. 107 (Georges Edmond Amiotte, 1867), parish rectory.

6. "Michigan Marriages, 1822–1995," *Family Search*, database, https://familysearch.org, under George Lamiotte and Elizabeth Paquin, 7 July 1890, FHL microfilm 1,007,362.

7. "Pedigree Resource File," *Family Search*, database, https://familysearch.org, under George Lamiotte, file 2:2:2:MM4X-Y7Y, submitted 31 March 2012.

8. "Michigan Death Certificates, 1921–1952," *Family Search*, database, https://familysearch. org, under Mary P. Therrien, 14 April 1937, citing Port Huron, St Clair, MI, Division for Vital Records and Health Statistics, Lansing, FHL microfilm 1,973,105. Her death certificate lists her birth date as 8 June 1868.

9. "Michigan Marriages, 1868–1925," *Family Search*, database with images, https:// familysearch.org, under Mary Lamyotte in entry for Joseph Lajoie and Joan Deboer, 1924.

10. "Michigan Marriages, 1822–1995," *Family Search*, database, https://familysearch.org, under Angele Robinson in entry for Joseph Therrien and Mary P. Lajoie, 12 October 1899, citing FHL microfilm 2,342,512.

11. "Michigan Death Certificates, 1921–1952," *Family Search*, database, https://familysearch. org, under George Laymott in entry for Mary P. Therrien, 14 April 1937, citing Port Huron, St Clair, MI, Division for Vital Records and Health Statistics, Lansing, FHL microfilm 1,973,105.

12. "Michigan Marriages, 1868–1925," *Family Search*, database with images, https:// familysearch.org, under Oliver Femen and Agnes Anicott, 1896.

13. "Michigan Deaths and Burials, 1800–1995," *Family Search*, database, https://familysearch. org, under Agnes Themen, 27 January 1898, citing St. Ignace, Mackinac, MI, reference yrs. 1873–1899, p. 93, FHL microfilm 1,007,364.

14. "Michigan Marriages, 1868–1925," *Family Search*, database with images, https:// familysearch.org, under John Arnicott and Teressa Ance, 1894.

15. "Find a Grave Index," *Family Search*, database, https://familysearch.org, under John R. Lamyotte, Burial: Saint Ignace, Mackinac County, MI, Saint Ignatius Catholic Cemetery, record ID 109385409, *Find a Grave*, http://www.findagrave.com.

16. "Michigan Births, 1867–1902," *Family Search*, database with images, https://familysearch. org, under Octavia Amcot, 1873.

17. "Michigan Marriages, 1822–1995," *Family Search*, database, https://familysearch.org, under Joseph B Lavake and Octavia Lamiott, 18 February 1901, FHL microfilm 1,007,362.

18. "Michigan Deaths and Burials, 1800–1995," *Family Search*, database, https://familysearch. org, under Octavia La Vake, 4 August 1937, citing St. Ignace, Mackinac County, MI, reference yrs. 1899–1946, p. 171, FHL microfilm 1,007,364.

19. "Michigan Marriages, 1822–1995," *Family Search*, database, https://familysearch.org,

under Angeline Robinson in entry for Henry Valier and Anna Lauriette, 11 June 1896, FHL microfilm 1,007,362.

20. "Michigan Marriages, 1822–1995," *Family Search*, database, https://familysearch.org, under George Amiott in entry for Antone Founier and Anna Valier, 14 Oct 1919, FHL microfilm 1,007,362.

21. "Michigan Death Certificates, 1921–1952," *Family Search*, database, https://familysearch.org, under George L'Amiotte in entry for Anna A. Fournier, 1 June 1951, citing Saint Ignace, Mackinac County, MI, Division for Vital Records and Health Statistics, Lansing, FHL microfilm 1,972,853.

22. "United States World War I Draft Registration Cards, 1917–1918," *Family Search*, database with images, https://familysearch.org, under Frank Lamyott, 1917–1918, citing Mackinac County, MI, NARA microfilm publication M1509 (Washington, DC: National Archives and Records Administration, n.d.), FHL microfilm 1,675,810.

23. "Michigan Deaths and Burials, 1800–1995," *Family Search*, database, https://familysearch.org, under George Lamyott in entry for Frank P. Lamyott, 3 October 1918, citing St. Ignace, Mackinac, MI, reference yrs. 1899–1946, p. 87, FHL microfilm 1,007,364. The family name in Quebec and Ontario was Amiot. It is not known when the "L" was added.

24. "Michigan Deaths and Burials, 1800–1995," *Family Search*, database, https://familysearch.org, under Angeline Amiott, 25 September 1900, citing St. Ignace, Mackinac, MI, reference yrs. 1899–1946, p. 8, FHL microfilm 1,007,364.

25. "Michigan Deaths and Burials, 1800–1995," *Family Search*, database, https://familysearch.org, under George L'Amiotte, 6 May 1920, citing St. Ignace, Mackinac, MI, reference yrs. 1899–1946, p. 94, FHL microfilm 1,007,364.

33. David Robinson

1. Gabriel Drouin, comp., *Drouin Collection* (Montreal: Institut Généalogique Drouin), p. 27, baptism of François Robisson, 1797, Ste. Genevieve, Berthierville; *Quebec, Canada, Vital and Church Records (Drouin Collection), 1621–1968* [database online], *Ancestry* (Provo, UT: Ancestry.com Operations, 2008). This family was pro-British and emigrated to Canada after the Revolutionary War. In the United States, the name was Robertson.

2. "United States Census, 1860," *Family Search*, database with images, https://familysearch.org, under Francis Robinson, 1860.

3. Charles Joseph Kappler, ed. and compiler, "Treaty with the Ottawa, etc., 1836," in *Indian Affairs: Laws and Treaties*, vol. 2, *Treaties* (Washington, DC: Government Printing Office, 1904), p. 455, https://dc.library.okstate.edu/digital/collection/kapplers/id/26296/rec/1.

4. "Michigan, County Marriages, 1820–1940," *Family Search*, database with images, https://familysearch.org, under Francis Robinson and Josette, 11 September 1826, Mackinac

County, MI, FHL microfilm 926,733.

5. St. Ignatius Loyola (St. Ignace, MI), "Baptisms, 1838–1893," bk. 3, p. 30 (David Robeson baptism, 1846), parish rectory.

6. "Michigan Deaths and Burials, 1800–1995," *Family Search*, database, https://familysearch. org, under David Robinson, 4 September 1927, citing Mackinac Island, Mackinac County, MI, reference yrs. 1899–1946, p. 128, FHL microfilm 1,007,364.

27. Mrs. Charles Roussain (Rousseau) (Charlotte Martin)

1. Marriage of Solomon Martin and Lisette Du Perrais, "Port of Mackinac Records," Office of the Register of Deeds, St. Ignace, Mackinac County, MI, no. 103.

2. The priest used "Lake Superior" as a birth place. Possible locations could be Fort William or LaPointe, WI.

3. When Father Mazzuchelli uses the symbol *N*, he indicated the individual was Native or First Nations. The spelling "Duperrais" is Mazzuchelli's. One individual was found in the voyageur contract from St. Boniface (see bibliography) named Thomas Duperet from Montreal dated 1787. A more common spelling for the name appears to be Dupéré. Since Charlotte and her sister were recorded as half-Chippewa and Salomon had no Indian blood, along with the *N* notation from Mazzuchelli, it is likely that Lisette Duperrais was a full-blood Ojibwe.

4. Gabriel Drouin, comp., *Drouin Collection* (Montreal: Institut Généalogique Drouin), p. 27, baptism of Solomon Martin, 13 March 1797, St. Jacques de L'Achigan; *Quebec, Canada, Vital and Church Records (Drouin Collection), 1621–1968* [database online], *Ancestry* (Provo, UT: Ancestry.com Operations, 2008).

5. Société historique de Saint-Boniface (St. Boniface, Manitoba, Canada), Centre du patrimonie, *Voyageur Contracts Database* (voyageurs.shsb.mb.ca/fr), under Salomon Martin.

6. "Michigan Mortality Schedules, 1850–1880," *Family Search*, database, https:// familysearch.org, under Solomon Martin, 1869.

7. St. Ignatius Loyola (St. Ignace, MI), "Deaths, 1838–1893," bk. 1, p. 258 (Lisette Martin, 1870), parish rectory.

8. "Baptismal Register," *Mackinac Register, 1695–1888*, 46. Mother listed as Louise Dupéré.

9. "Baptismal Register," *Mackinac Register, 1695–1888*, 54. Mother listed as Lisette Dupris.

10. St. Ignatius Loyola (St. Ignace, MI), "Births, 1838–1893," bk. 3, p. 10 (Joseph Michael Martin, 1939), parish rectory.

11. Larry Wyckoff, trans., "Mixed-Blood Census Register, Ottawas and Chippewas of Michigan, Treaty of March 26, 1836," *Roots Web*, http://www.rootsweb.ancestry. com/~mimacki2/annuities/1836mb.pdf, n.d., nos. 304 and 305.

12. *Liber Matrimonium, Mackinac Register, 1695–1888*, 34. The marriage record said Charlotte was from Île St. Hélène.

13. St. Ignatius Loyola (St. Ignace, MI), "Births, 1838–1893," bk. 3, p. 47 (Antoine Babinaux dit Delaurier, 1851), parish rectory.

14. "Baptismal Register," *Mackinac Register, 1695–1888*, 177.

15. St. Ignatius Loyola (St. Ignace, MI), "Births, 1838–1893," bk. 3, p. 67 (Charles Rousseau, 1857), parish rectory.

16. St. Ignatius Loyola (St. Ignace, MI), "Births, 1838–1893," bk. 3, p. 76 (Macale Isidore Rousseau, 1859), parish rectory.

17. St. Ignatius Loyola (St. Ignace, MI), "Deaths, 1838–1893," bk. 1, p. 3 (1860), parish rectory.

18. St. Ignatius Loyola (St. Ignace, MI), "Births, 1838–1893," bk. 3, p. 107 (Joseph Michel Rousseau, 1867), parish rectory.

19. St. Ignatius Loyola (St. Ignace, MI), "Deaths, 1838–1893," bk. 1, p. 20 (1882), parish rectory.

20. St. Ignatius Loyola (St. Ignace, MI), "Births, 1838–1893," bk. 3, p. 112 (Charlotte Josephine Rousseau, 1868), parish rectory.

21. St. Ignatius Loyola (St. Ignace, MI), "Deaths, 1838–1893," bk. 1, p. 8 (1871), parish rectory.

22. "Michigan Births and Christenings, 1775–1995," *Family Search*, database, https://familysearch.org, under John Russow, 30 May 1875, citing Chandler, Manitou, MI, reference v. 1, p. 6, FHL microfilm 965,391.

23. No marriage record was located outside of their children's birth records. "Minnesota Deaths and Burials, 1835–1990," *Family Search*, database, https://familysearch.org, under John Jonas Rousseau, 25 January 1950, citing Duluth, St. Louis County, MN, reference 28399, FHL microfilm 2,139,358.

24. Michigan Veterans Home Residents Resident Listing, Western Michigan Genealogical Society, under Charles Rosseau, registration no. M-2483, film no. 26, p. 1 of 9, http://data.wmgs.org.

25. Michigan Veterans Home Residents Resident Listing, under Charles Rosseau, registration no. M-2483, film no. 26, p. 1 of 9.

26. Michigan Veterans Home Residents Resident Listing, under Charles Rosseau, registration no. M-2483, film no. 26, p. 1 of 9.

27. James Blanchard, private register, Bentley Historical Library, University of Michigan, Ann Arbor.

46. Mrs. Louis St. Onge (Catharine Peltier)

1. *Ste. Anne's Church Registers: 1704–1842*, microfilm, 3 rolls (Detroit, MI: St. Anne's of Detroit). See roll 3, *Chapelle du nordest: Baptisms, Marriages, Burials, 1810–1838*, arranged by date, baptism record of Catherine Peltier, University of Michigan, Bentley Historical

Library (BHL) no. 1252. The record says she was born in the month of January 1809 and was baptized 3 September 1825. It also says her parents were living together without being married. They were probably married "according to the custom of the country."

2. *Programme de recherche en démographie historique (PRDH)* (Université de Montréal, Canada), 1621–1849, certificate 693816, Louis Marie Stonge, transcription, https://www. prdh-igd.com.

3. Société historique de Saint-Boniface (St. Boniface, Manitoba, Canada), Centre du patrimonie, *Voyageur Contracts Database* (voyageurs.shsb.mb.ca/fr), under Louis St. Onge.

4. Marriage of Louis St. Onge and Catharine Peltier, and of Edward Lessieur and Angelique Peltier, "Port of Mackinac Records," Office of the Register of Deeds, St. Ignace, Mackinac County, MI, nos. 66–67.

5. Larry Wyckoff, trans., "Mixed-Blood Census Register, Ottawas and Chippewas of Michigan, Treaty of March 26, 1836," *Roots Web*, http://www.rootsweb.ancestry. com/~mimacki2/annuities/1836mb.pdf, n.d., nos. 512–516, Catharine St. Onge, Angelique St. Onge, Louis (Lewis) St. Onge, Theophile (Zaophile) St. Onge, and Catherine St. Onge. Under Remarks column, it reads "Relation to St. Marie Indians."

6. *Liber Matrimonium, Mackinac Register, 1695–1888*, 29.

7. "Baptismal Register," *Mackinac Register, 1695–1888*, 46.

8. St. Ignatius Loyola (St. Ignace, MI), "Marriages, 1838–1893," bk. 1, p. 18–19 (Theophile St. Onge and Elise Plant, 1859), parish rectory.

9. St. Ignatius Loyola (St. Ignace, MI), "Marriages, 1838–1893," bk. 1, p. 20–21 (Joseph St. Onge and Marie Misweninimi, 1859), parish rectory.

10. "Baptismal Register," *Mackinac Register, 1695–1888*, 60.

11. "Baptismal Register," *Mackinac Register, 1695–1888*, 61.

12. Marriage of Wellington Force and Catharine Saintoge, "Port of Mackinac Records," Office of the Register of Deeds, St. Ignace, Mackinac County, MI, no. 469. The marriage was officiated by Father Edward Jacker.

13. "Baptismal Register," *Mackinac Register, 1695–1888*, 40. See under Louis St. Ange.

14. Marriage of Louis Saintange and Margareth Derochier, 1857, "Port of Mackinac Records," Office of the Register of Deeds, St. Ignace, Mackinac County, MI, no. 477.

15. "Michigan Marriages, 1822–1995," *Family Search*, database, https://familysearch.org, under Louis St Onge and Elenore Archambeaw, 12 May 1884, Family History Library (FHL) microfilm 1,007,362.

16. "Baptismal Register," *Mackinac Register, 1695–1888*, 93.

17. "Baptismal Register," *Mackinac Register, 1695–1888*, 106.

18. St. Ignatius Loyola (St. Ignace, MI), "Marriages, 1838–1893," bk. 1, p. 22–23 (Edward St.

Onge and Sophie Derocher, 1861), parish rectory.

19. "Baptismal Register," *Mackinac Register, 1695–1888*, 115.

20. "Michigan Marriages, 1822–1995," *Family Search*, database, https://familysearch.org, under John St. Onge and Josephine Gingwan, 1 September 1906, FHL microfilm 2,342,674.

21. "Find a Grave Index," *Family Search*, database, https://familysearch.org, under John B. St. Onge, 1920, Burial: Saint Ignatius Catholic Cemetery, Saint Ignace, Mackinac County, MI, record ID 109387270, *Find a Grave*, http://www.findagrave.com.

22. "Baptismal Register," *Mackinac Register, 1695–1888*, 129.

23. "Michigan Marriages, 1822–1995," *Family Search*, database, https://familysearch.org, under Alexander Panquin and Rose Sarutong, 10 January 1875, FHL microfilm 1,007,362.

24. "Baptismal Register," *Mackinac Register, 1695–1888*, 142.

25. St. Ignatius Loyola (St. Ignace, MI), "Marriages, 1838–1893," bk. 1, p. 32–33 (Olivier Labutte and Marie Louise St. Onge, 1873), parish rectory.

26. "Michigan Deaths, 1867–1897," *Family Search*, database, https://familysearch.org, under Oliver Labute, 19 December 1885, citing p. 162, rn. 39, Moran Township, Mackinac, MI, Department of Vital Records, Lansing, FHL microfilm 2,363,630. "Michigan Marriages, 1822–1995," *Family Search*, database, https://familysearch.org, under Alphonse Cody and Mary St. Ange, 25 September 1892, FHL microfilm 2,342,493.

37. Miss Martha Tanner

1. Edwin James, ed., A Narrative of the Captivity and Adventures of John Tanner during Thirty Years Residence among the Indians in the Interior of North America (Minneapolis, MN: Ross and Haines, 1956), https://www.gutenberg.org/files/61291/61291-h/61291-h.htm.

2. "Baptismal Register," *Mackinac Register, 1695–1888*, 34. Her parents were listed as *Joannes* and *Theresia* Tanner. The godparents were Samuel and Mary Bridget Abbott. Samuel Abbott was a prominent businessman on the island.

3. Letter from Florimond Bonduel to Martha Tanner, 7 June 1836, Burton Historical Collection, Detroit Public Library. This date seems unlikely. A few years later, Martha was enumerated on the 1836 Half Breed Census where she was listed as twenty-three years old. A birth year of 1813 seems consistent in many records including her tombstone.

4. John E. McDowell, "Therese Schindler of Mackinac: Upward Mobility in the Great Lakes Fur Trade," *Wisconsin Magazine of History* 61, no. 2 (1977): 138.

5. *Liber Defunctorum, Mackinac Register, 1695–1888*, 92.

6. Mackinac State Historic Parks, "1938 Survey of Ste. Anne's Cemetery," S. Alicia Poole Papers, Petersen Library (Mackinaw City, MI), Alice Poole Vertical File.

7. American Board of Commissioners for Foreign Missions Papers, *Children at Mackinaw, 1833*, Houghton Library, Harvard University, 18.5.7.I:36. Alicia Poole writes, "Mayme

Holden 1935 says that John Tanner is buried by Martha."

8. John Fierst, "Return to 'Civilization' John Tanner's Troubled Years at Sault Ste. Marie," *Minnesota History* (Spring 1986): 30.

9. Malcolm Rosholt and John Britten Gehl, *Florimond J. Bonduel: Missionary to Wisconsin Territory* (Amherst, WI: Palmer, 1976), 26.

10. Larry Wyckoff, trans., "Mixed-Blood Census Register, Ottawas and Chippewas of Michigan, Treaty of March 26, 1836," *Roots Web*, http://www.rootsweb.ancestry. com/~mimacki2/annuities/1836mb.pdf, n.d., no. 171. She was listed as twenty-three years old and half-Ottawa.

11. Rosholt and Gehl, *Florimond J. Bonduel*, 26.

12. Email from Katie Santa Ana, archivist, Loretto Heritage Center, to Theresa Weller, 2 July 2018. Ms. Santa Ana informed me "Martha Anne Tanner is not coming up in any of our lists of vowed members and I am not aware of any of our Sisters serving in Michigan in that timeframe. So, I suspect she did not end up becoming a vowed Sister of Loretto." Since we only have their responses, it is apparent Martha wrote letters to Father Mazzuchelli and Father Bonduel asking their advice about joining the convent. She apparently decided against it.

13. Tanner to Fitch, 10 November 1858.

14. Tanner to Fitch, 10 November 1858.

15. Tanner to Fitch, 10 November 1858.

16. Letter from Martha Tanner to A. M. Fitch, Indian agent, Mackinac Agency, 10 January 1860, BBC M-95-5.

17. Letter from Martha Tanner to Mrs. Baird, 8 July 1845, Henry and Elizabeth Baird Papers, 1798–1937, Wisconsin Historical Society, Wis. Mss. V, box 1, folder 9, https://content. wisconsinhistory.org/digital/collection/baird/id/1663/rec/6.

18. Letter from Martha Tanner to A. M. Fitch, Indian agent, Mackinac Agency, 10 January 1859, BBC M-95–5/c-1386.

19. Letter from Martha Tanner to A. M. Fitch, Indian agent, Mackinac Agency, February 1860, BBC M-95-5, 12.

20. Note from "Borough of Michilimackinac Records, 1817–1861," stamp dated 8 December 1997, vertical files, Petersen Library, Mackinac State Historic Parks (MSHP), Mackinaw City, MI. The note states "December 29, 1851—[The] Village voted to close [the] old Catholic cemetery to interments and to ban disinterments except in January, February or March."

21. Mackinac State Historic Parks, "1938 Survey of Ste. Anne's Cemetery," S. Alicia Poole Papers, Petersen Library (Mackinaw City, MI), Alice Poole Vertical File.

22. Letter from James Bennett to Martha A. Tanner, Mackinac County Courthouse, Register

of Deeds Office, St. Ignace, MI, M:221.

23. Martha died on 25 July 1887. Alice Poole noted that one of the island residents told her that Martha's father, John Tanner, was buried next to her in Ste. Anne's Cemetery in an unmarked grave, close to Lucy and his last wife, Therese Akwemikons.

24. Mackinac State Historic Parks, "1938 Survey of Ste. Anne's Cemetery."

24A, B & C. Hester Terrien, sister, and Peter

1. "Baptismal Register," *Mackinac Register, 1695–1888*, 24.
2. "Baptismal Register," *Mackinac Register, 1695–1888*, 42.
3. *Liber Matrimonium, Mackinac Register, 1695–1888*, 38.
4. "Baptismal Register," *Mackinac Register, 1695–1888*, 168.
5. "Baptismal Register," *Mackinac Register, 1695–1888*, 178.
6. "Baptismal Register," *Mackinac Register, 1695–1888*, 185.
7. "Baptismal Register," *Mackinac Register, 1695–1888*, 178. The name is speculation. Anna is clear, but the first name is not.
8. "Michigan Mortality Schedules, 1850–1880," *Family Search*, database, https://familysearch.org, under Oliver Therrin, 1859.
9. *Liber Defunctorum, Mackinac Register, 1695–1888*, 100.
10. St. Ignatius Loyola (St. Ignace, MI), "Marriages, 1838–1893," bk. 1, p. 26–27 (Noel Leveille and Elisabelle Lauzon marriage, 1865), parish rectory.
11. "Find a Grave Index," *Family Search*, database, https://familysearch.org, under Elizabeth Isabelle *Lozon* Leveille, 20 January 1833–29 July 1902, Burial: Gros Cap Cemetery, Gros Cap, Mackinac County, MI, record ID 24121327, *Find a Grave*, http://www.findagrave.com.

24A. Hester Terrien

1. "Baptismal Register," *Mackinac Register, 1695–1888*, 168.
2. "Michigan Marriages, 1822–1995," *Family Search*, database, https://familysearch.org, under William O. Hildreth and Esthere I. Thirien, 11 May 1874, Family History Library (FHL) microfilm 1,007,362.
3. Northeast Michigan Genealogical and Historical Society (NEMGS), *St. Bernard Church Records, Alpena, Michigan: Baptisms, 1864–1894; Marriages, 1870–1894; Funerals, 1870–1925* (Alpena, MI: NEMGS, 1995), p. 75, Gabriel Clarence Hildreth baptism.
4. "Michigan Marriages, 1822–1995," *Family Search*, database, https://familysearch.org, under Clarence G. Hildreth in entry for William F. Hildreth and Antoinette Vandusen, 9 June 1927, citing reference No. 6247, FHL microfilm 2,020,880.
5. "Find a Grave Index," *Family Search*, database, https://familysearch.org, under Clarence G. Hildreth, 26 March 1876–27 June 1933, Burial: Lone Oak Cemetery, Leesburg, Lake

County, FL, record ID 30545969, *Find a Grave*, http://www.findagrave.com.

6. "Find a Grave Index," *Family Search*, database, https://familysearch.org, under Isabelle Joan Hildreth, 16 July 1877–1 October 1878, Burial: Holy Cross Cemetery, Alpena, Alpena County, MI, record ID 37679185, *Find a Grave*, http://www.findagrave.com.

7. "Michigan Deaths and Burials, 1800–1995," *Family Search*, database, https://familysearch.org, under William Hildreth in entry for Isabella J. Hildreth, 1 October 1878, citing Alpena, reference 328, FHL microfilm 965,728.

8. NEMGS, *St. Bernard Church Records, Alpena, Michigan*, p. 36, Mary Agnes Hildreth baptism.

9. "Find a Grave Index," *Family Search*, database, https://familysearch.org, under Mae A. Hildrith Beu, 1933, Burial: Erie Cemetery, Erie, Erie County, PA, record ID 139137827, *Find a Grave*, http://www.findagrave.com.

10. "Michigan Births, 1867–1902," *Family Search*, database with images, https://familysearch.org, under Wm. Hildreth, 12 October 1881, citing item 1, p. 74, rn. 1731, Alpena, Alpena Conty, MI, Department of Vital Records, Lansing, FHL microfilm 2,320,574.

11. Lorraine LaCross, Rhea LaCross, and NEMGS, *St. Anne Church Records: Alpena, Michigan, 1822–1922*, vol. 1, *Baptismal Records, 1883–1896* (Alpena, MI: NEMGS, 1997), p. 41. Baptism of Ellen A. Hildreth.

12. "Find a Grave Index," *Family Search*, database, https://familysearch.org, under Esther Hildreth, 14 July 1906, Burial: Holy Cross Cemetery, Alpena, Alpena County, MI, record ID 132636933, *Find a Grave*, http://www.findagrave.com.

24B. Genevieve Terrien

1. "Michigan Marriages, 1822–1995," *Family Search*, database, https://familysearch.org, under Don A. Cheeseman and Jennie Therrien, 1 June 1903, Family History Library (FHL) microfilm 1,007,362.

2. "Michigan Deaths and Burials, 1800–1995," *Family Search*, database, https://familysearch.org, under Jane Cheeseman, 30 June 1921, citing Moran Township, Mackinac County, MI, reference yrs. 1899–1946, p. 102, FHL microfilm 1,007,364.

3. This information was shared with the author in 2013 by Gregory Robert "Bob" Cheeseman. He told the author that Alonzo was a polygamist, according to the Mormon faith, and that Amy Thorne was Alonzo's the third wife. The family has remained in the St. Ignace area.

24c. Peter Isaac Terrien

1. "Baptismal Register," *Mackinac Register, 1695–1888*, 178. His birth date was not recorded.

2. "Michigan Marriages, 1822–1995 *Family Search*, database, https://familysearch.org, under

Peter Ferriant and Angeline Belonga, 2 November 1886, citing Family History Library (FHL) microfilm 1,007,362. This item was found under the name "Ferriant." Some family members pronounce the family name as "Therrient," adding a "t" on the end.

3. "Michigan, County Births, 1867–1917," *Family Search*, database, https://familysearch.org, "Births, 1873–1898," vol. 1, image 129 of 291, Mackinac County, MI.

4. "United States World War I Draft Registration Cards, 1917–1918," *Family Search*, database with images, https://familysearch.org, under Scotty Oliver Therrien, 1917–1918, citing Mackinac County, MI, NARA microfilm publication M1509 (Washington, DC: National Archives and Records Administration, n.d.), Family History Library (FHL) microfilm 1,675,810.

5. "Indiana Marriages, 1811–2007," *Family Search*, database with images, https://familysearch.org, under Oliver Scott Terrient and Rose Lillie Gallagher, 1 May 1926, citing Lake, Indiana, FHL microfilm 2,414,790. These records are marked "unofficial."

6. "Michigan Marriages, 1868–1925," *Family Search*, database, https://familysearch.org, under Bernard Brake and Elizabeth Terriant, 1916.

7. "Find a Grave Index," *Family Search*, database, https://familysearch.org, under Roma Elizabeth *Therrien* Brake, 5 June 1892–7 September 1962, Burial: Northview Cemetery, Dearborn, Wayne County, MI, record ID 114120397, *Find a Grave*, http://www.findagrave.com.

8. "Michigan Marriages, 1868–1925," *Family Search*, database, https://familysearch.org, under Bert Squires and Florence Therrin, 1913.

9. "Michigan, County Births, 1867–1917," *Family Search*, database, https://familysearch.org, under Lawrence Terrient, 5 August 1896.

10. "Michigan Deaths and Burials, 1800–1995," *Family Search*, database, https://familysearch.org, under Lawrence Terrient, 26 August 1896, citing Holmes, Mackinac County, MI, reference yrs. 1873–1899, p. 91, FHL microfilm 1,007,364.

11. "Michigan Marriages, 1868–1925," *Family Search*, database, https://familysearch.org, under Herbert Therrian and Katherine Martin, 1916.

12. "Michigan Deaths and Burials, 1800–1995," *Family Search*, database, https://familysearch.org, under Peter Therien, 9 August 1900; citing Mackinac Island, Mackinac, MI, reference yrs. 1899–1946, p. 8; FHL microfilm 1,007,364.

13. "Michigan Deaths and Burials, 1800–1995," *Family Search*, database, https://familysearch.org, under Peter Therrien, 3 November 1911, citing Mackinac Island, Mackinac County, MI, reference yrs. 1899–1946, p. 56, FHL microfilm 1,007,364.

14. "Michigan Deaths and Burials, 1800–1995," *Family Search*, database, https://familysearch.org, under Angeline Terrien, 25 July 1929, citing Mackinac Island, Mackinac, MI, reference yrs. 1899–1946, p. 139, FHL microfilm 1,007,364.

61. Mrs. Margueritta Thompson (Margaret Pouillat)

1. *Holy Cross Church Records* (Cross Village, MI), microfilm publication, one roll, Bentley Historical Library (BHL), University of Michigan, roll 1, arranged mostly alphabetically; see family 135, "Antony Thompsen."

2. *Ste. Croix Parish Records* (Wikwemikong, Manitoulin Island, ON), 2 registers, May 8, 1838–September 25, 1854, register 1, p. 86 (Pierre Pouliot and Josette Larivière marriage, 1842), FHL microfilm 1,311,360.

3. *Liber Defunctorum, Mackinac Register, 1695–1888*, 99. See under Josette Larivierre. It says born on Drummond Island.

4. Emmet County, *Vital Records Search*, searchable database, http://apps.emmetcounty.org/clerk/deathrecords.aspx, under "Peter Pauet," liber 1, folio 98.

5. "Michigan Marriages, 1868–1925," *Family Search*, database, https://familysearch.org, under Anthony I. Thompson and Marguerite Pouott, 1870.

6. "Find a Grave Index," *Family Search*, database, https://familysearch.org, under Anthony J. Thompson, 1915, Burial: Veterans Home Cemetery, Grand Rapids, Kent County, MI, record ID 16818895, *Find a Grave*, http://www.findagrave.com. Birth date taken from death certificate.

7. *Register of Enlistments in the United States Army, 1798–1914*, National Archives at Washington, DC, Records of the Adjutant General's Office (1780–1917), record group 94, microfilm M233, 81 rolls, "Roster of 1868," no. 172, Anthony Thompson; *Ancestry*, (Provo, UT: Ancestry.com Operations, 2007).

8. *Holy Cross Church Records*, BHL, roll 1; see family 135, Antony Thompsen.

9. "Michigan Deaths and Burials, 1800–1995," *Family Search*, database, https://familysearch.org, under Anthony Thompson in entry for Edward Thompson, 19 June 1920, citing Escanaba, Delta County, MI, reference v. 2, p. 113, Family History Library (FHL) microfilm 1,310,149.

10. *Holy Cross Church Records*, BHL, roll 1; see family 135, Antony Thompsen.

11. "Michigan, County Marriages, 1820–1940," *Family Search*, database with images, https://familysearch.org, under John B. Levack and Louise Thompson, 7 December 1889, Emmet, MI, FHL microfilm 966,507.

12. *Michigan, Divorce Records, 1897–1952* [database online] (Provo, UT: Ancestry.com Operations, 2014), p. 277, no. 27, *John Levack v. Louisa Levack*, Leelanau County.

13. "Michigan Marriages, 1868–1925," *Family Search*, database with images, https://familysearch.org, under Anthony J. Thompson in entry for Emery Welch and Louise Thompson Leveck, 1921.

14. "Michigan Death Certificates, 1921–1952," *Family Search*, database with images, https://familysearch.org, under Louise Welch, 18 September 1931, citing Lansing, Ingham, MI,

Division for Vital Records and Health Statistics, Lansing, FHL microfilm 1,972,739.

15. *Holy Cross Church Records*, BHL, roll 1; see family 135, Antony Thompsen.
16. *Holy Cross Church Records*, BHL, roll 1; see family 135, Antony Thompsen.
17. *Holy Cross Church Records*, BHL, roll 1; see family 135, Antony Thompsen.
18. *Holy Cross Church Records*, BHL, roll 1; see family 135, Antony Thompsen.
19. *Holy Cross Church Records*, BHL, roll 1; see family 135, Antony Thompsen.
20. *Holy Cross Church Records*, BHL, roll 1; see family 135, Antony Thompsen.
21. *Holy Cross Church Records*, BHL, roll 1; see family 135, Antony Thompsen.
22. "Michigan Marriages, 1822–1995," *Family Search*, database, https://familysearch.org, under Anthony J. Thompson and Emily L. Hazen, 26 December 1887, FHL microfilm 2,342,482.
23. "Michigan Marriages, 1822–1995," *Family Search*, database, https://familysearch.org, under Anthony J. Thompson and Emma L. Drone, 14 December 1892, FHL microfilm 2,342,494.
24. "United States Census, 1910," *Family Search*, database with images, https://familysearch.org, under Anthony J. Thompson, Grand Rapids, Kent County, MI, citing enumeration district (ED) ED 126, sheet 9B, NARA microfilm publication T624 (Washington, DC: National Archives and Records Administration, 1982), roll 655, FHL microfilm 1,374,668.
25. Michigan Veterans Home Residents Resident Listing [formerly Michigan Old Soldiers' Home], Western Michigan Genealogical Society, under Anthony G. Thompson, registration no. M-4542, http://data.wmgs.org.

66. William Valier

1. St. Ignatius Loyola (St. Ignace, MI), "Marriages, 1838–1893," bk. 1, p. 28–29 (Guilelmus Valliere and Rosalia Paquin marriage, 1851), parish rectory.
2. *Programme de recherche en démographie historique (PRDH)* (Université de Montréal, Canada), 1621–1849, certificate 3008449, Rosalie Paquin, transcription, https://www.prdh-igd.com.
3. St. Ignatius Loyola (St. Ignace, MI), "Births, 1838–1893," bk. 3, p. 50 (Antoine Valliere, 1852), parish rectory.
4. "Michigan Marriages, 1868–1925," *Family Search*, database with images, https://familysearch.org, under Antwin Vallier and Lucey Martinow, 1872.
5. St. Ignatius Loyola (St. Ignace, MI), "Births, 1838–1893," bk. 3, p. 5 (Rosine Valliere, 1854), parish rectory. Father listed as Guillaume Valliere.
6. St. Ignatius Loyola (St. Ignace, MI), "Marriages, 1838–1893," bk. 1, p. 34–35 (Guilelmus Valliere and Juliana Martineau marriage, 1876), parish rectory.
7. St. Ignatius Loyola (St. Ignace, MI), "Births, 1838–1893," bk. 3, p. 69 (Josephine Valliere,

1857), parish rectory.

8. St. Ignatius Loyola (St. Ignace, MI), "Record of Interments: 1894–1988," p. 47 (Mrs. Josephine Johnson burial, 1940), parish rectory. Remarks column states, "Excellent Catholic daughter of Wm. Valliere."

9. St. Ignatius Loyola (St. Ignace, MI), "Births, 1838–1893," bk. 3, p. 77 (John Benjamin Valliere, 1859), parish rectory. Father listed as Guillaume Valliere.

10. St. Ignatius Loyola (St. Ignace, MI), "Births, 1838–1893," bk. 3, p. 86 (Thomas Leander Valliere, 1861), parish rectory.

11. "Michigan Deaths and Burials, 1800–1995," *Family Search*, database with images, https://familysearch.org, under Antony Vallier in entry for Thomas Vallier, 6 October 1922, citing Garfield Township, Mackinac County, MI, reference yr 1899–1946, p. 104, FHL microfilm 1,007,364.

12. St. Ignatius Loyola (St. Ignace, MI), "Births, 1838–1893," bk. 3, p. 93 (Joseph Valliere, 1863), parish rectory.

13. "Michigan Deaths, 1867–1897," *Family Search*, database with images, https://familysearch.org, under William Valin, 19 April 1895, citing p. 198, rn. 29, St. Ignace, Mackinac County, MI, Department of Vital Records, Lansing, FHL microfilm 2,363,834.

14. St. Ignatius Loyola (St. Ignace, MI), "Record of Interments: 1894–1988," p. 47 (Rose Vallier burial, 1910), parish rectory.

50. Mrs. Henry Vaillancourt (Catherine LaCroix)

1. "Baptismal Register," *Mackinac Register, 1695–1888*, 7. The baptism states Catherine is the daughter of Isidore LaCroix and "*Angelique de la nation des Osages*" (Angelique of the Osage nation).

2. On page 11 of the same register, a woman with unknown parents, who were both of the Osage Nation, took the name Catherine Angelique for her baptismal name. She was born "*vers l'annee mil huit* [sic] *cent quatre vingt trois*" [born near the year 1783] and baptized 15 October 1825. This woman was most likely Catherine LaCroix's mother.

3. Larry Wyckoff, trans., "Mixed-Blood Census Register, Ottawas and Chippewas of Michigan, Treaty of March 26, 1836," *Roots Web*, http://www.rootsweb.ancestry.com/~mimacki2/annuities/1836mb.pdf, n.d., no. 254 Catherine Vincencourt, and daughter Catherine, no. 255. Catherine, no. 254, was listed as the wife of Henry Vincencourt Jr. This is incorrect. Henry's father was Joseph Vaillancourt.

4. "Baptismal Register," *Mackinac Register, 1695–1888*, p. 44. See under Vayancour.

5. Inspection Return of Capt. Benjamin K. Pierce, 1817, under Henry Valencourt, line 91, image 16 of 69, Henry and Elizabeth Baird Papers, 1798–1937, Wis Mss V, box 5, folder 4, WIHV94-A1354, Wisconsin Historical Society, https://content.wisconsinhistory.org/

digital/collection/baird/id/3956/rec/4. Also, from *History of the Upper Peninsula of Michigan* (Chicago: Western Historical Company, 1883), comes this affidavit, page 361:

"I, Henry Vaillancourt born in Michilimackinac, Aged 9 years, 4 feet, 4 inches high, of Dark complexion, Black eyes, Dark hair, do hereby Acknowledge to have this day Voluntarily enlisted as a Soldier in the Army of the United States of America, for the period of five years unless sooner Discharged by proper authority do also Agree to accept such bounty, pay, rations and clothing as is, or may be established by law And I Henry Vaillencourt, do solemnly swear that I will bear true faith and Allegiance to the United State of America, and that I will served them honestly and faithfully against their enemies and opposers, wheresoever, and that I will observe and obey the orders of the President of the United States and the orders of the officers appointed over me according to the rules and articles of war."

Henry's X mark is used as signature, dated 1 March 1812. Punctuation and capital letters per document.

6. "Chicago's Early Postmasters," *Northern Tribune*, 19 February 1885, https://www.newspapers.com/image/171977395/?terms=Chicago%27s%2BFirst%2BPostmastes, para. 9.

7. Elizabeth Collins, "The Beats of Battle Images of Army Drummer Boys Endure," *U.S Army*, http://soldiers.dodlive.mil/2013/12/the-beats-of-battle-images-of-army-drummer-boys-endure, web page archived by the Department of Defense, no longer available online.

8. Collins, "The Beats of Battle Images of Army Drummer Boys Endure."

9. "Muster Roll of 1812," *History of the Upper Peninsula of Michigan* (Chicago: Western Historical Company, 1883), pp. 261–262. The Muster Roll lists the following member of the Vaillancourt family: Joseph Vaillancourt, father, and sons Francis, John P. (Jean Baptiste), and Henry.

10. *Register of Enlistments in the United States Army, 1798–1914*, National Archives at Washington, DC, Records of the Adjutant General's Office (1780–1917), record group 94, microfilm M233, 81 rolls, enlistment roster including Henry Valincourt, citing line 17.

11. *Register of Enlistments in the United States Army, 1798–1914*, enlistment roster, Henry Valincourt, line 17

12. *American Fur Company Records, 1803–1806*, and *1817–1843*, microfilm edition, Bentley Historical Library (BHL), University of Michigan, reel 3.

13. Records of the Superintendency of Michigan: Mackinac Agency Records; Letters Received, May 7, 1916–November 1, 1831; May 1, 1833–December 1834; January 3, 1835–June 29, 1936, microfilm publication no. 1, 3 microfilms (Washington, DC: National Archives and Records Service, 1942), roll 71, pp. 41–42.

14. Henry Rowe Schoolcraft, "Abstract of Licenses Granted by Henry R. Schoolcraft, Acting

Superintendent of Michigan [Indian Affairs] during the Year Ending 30th September 1839," *The Papers of Henry Rowe Schoolcraft, 1782–1878* (Washington, DC: Library of Congress Photoduplication Service), roll 8.

15. *Liber Matrimonium, Mackinac Register, 1695–1888*, 18.

16. "Baptismal Register," *Mackinac Register, 1695–1888*, 51.

17. *Liber Matrimonium, Mackinac Register, 1695–1888*, 37.

18. "Baptismal Register," *Mackinac Register, 1695–1888*, 89.

19. *U.S., Civil War Records and Profiles, 1861–1865, Ancestry* [database online] (Provo, UT: Ancestry.com Operations), Henry Vancourse.

20. George H. Turner, *Record of Service of Michigan Volunteers in the Civil War, 1861–1865*, vol. 37 (Kalamazoo, MI: Ihling Bros. & Everard, 1900), p. 134, https://catalog.hathitrust.org/Record/003931700. See under Henry Vancourse.

21. Turner, Record of Service of Michigan Volunteers in the Civil War, 1861–1865.

22. "Organization Index to Pension Files of Veterans Who Served Between 1861 and 1900," citing pension applications 1861–1942, T289 (Washington, DC: National Archives, n.d.), roll number 248, entry for Henry Viancouer (Company K, 7th MI Cavalry), *fold3*, https://www.fold3.com.

23. "Baptismal Register," *Mackinac Register, 1695–1888*, 97.

24. "Baptismal Register," *Mackinac Register, 1695–1888*, 105.

25. "Baptismal Register," *Mackinac Register, 1695–1888*, 111.

26. "Baptismal Register," *Mackinac Register, 1695–1888*, 126.

27. *Liber Matrimonium, Mackinac Register, 1695–1888*, 60/61.

28. "Michigan Marriages, 1822–1995," *Family Search*, database, https://familysearch.org, under Vincent Valiencourt and Grace Anna Bourisaw, 12 February 1911, FHL microfilm 1,007,362.

29. "Find a Grave Index," *Family Search*, database, https://familysearch.org, under Vincent Vallincourt, 1917, Burial: Ste. Anne's Cemetery, Mackinac Island, Mackinac County, MI, record ID 40035348, *Find a Grave*, http://www.findagrave.com.

30. "Baptismal Register," *Mackinac Register, 1695–1888*, 136.

31. "Baptismal Register," *Mackinac Register, 1695–1888*, 165.

28. Mrs. Thomas Valliere (Josette Thibault)

1. Gabriel Drouin, comp., *Drouin Collection* (Montreal, Quebec: Institut Généalogique Drouin); Basilique Notre-Dame de Québec (Quebec City, Canada), "*Registres*, 1797–1798," p. 63, Damase Leandre Valliere, *Quebec Canada, Vital and Church Records (Drouin Collection), 1621–1968, Ancestry*, https://www.ancestry.com.

2. Bernice Cook Edmunds, "Valliere Genealogy," *Ancestry* 4, no. 1 (April 1986): 9–13.

3. Edmunds, "Valliere Genealogy."

4. Gabriel Drouin, comp., *Drouin Collection* (Montreal, Quebec: Institut Généalogique Drouin); St.-Antoine-du-Padoue (Baie-du-Febvre, Quebec, Canada), "*Registres*, 1823," folio p. 12, Amiable Goudreau, *Quebec, Canada, Vital and Church Records (Drouin Collection), 1621–1968, Ancestry*, https://www.ancestry.com. St. Ignatius Loyola (St. Ignace, MI), "Marriages, 1838–1893," bk. 1, p. 7 (Amabilis Goudraux and Marie Brouillard marriage, 1847), parish rectory.

5. John T. Nevill, "Early Epoufette Days Were Happy Ones for Aunt Jane," *Evening News* (Sault Ste. Marie, MI), 26 March 1952. (This year was not archived.)

6. St. Ignatius Loyola (St. Ignace, MI), "Births, 1838–1893," bk. 3, p. 27 (Maria Goudro, 1844), parish rectory.

7. "Find a Grave Index," *Family Search*, database, https://familysearch.org, under Amable Goudreau, 1882, Burial: Saint Ignatius Catholic Cemetery, St. Ignace, Mackinac County, MI, record ID 35618087, *Find a Grave*, http://www.findagrave.com.

8. "Find a Grave Index," *Family Search*, database, https://familysearch.org, under Mary Goudreau, 1895, Burial: Saint Ignatius Catholic Cemetery, St. Ignace, Mackinac County, MI, record ID 70083222, *Find a Grave*, http://www.findagrave.com.

9. Michigan State Archives, "Death Records, 1897–1920," *Michiganology*, entry for Margaret Wagley, 1904, https://michiganology.org. Margaret's birth date is 25 December 1826.

10. The Traverse Region, Historical and Descriptive: With Illustrations of Scenery and Portraits and Biographical Sketches of Some of its Prominent Men and Pioneers (Chicago: H. R. Page, 1884), p. 142, https://quod.lib.umich.edu/m/micounty/ BAD0776.0001.001.

11. *Holy Cross Church Records* (Cross Village, MI), microfilm publication, one roll (Ann Arbor, MI: Bentley Historical Library, University of Michigan), roll 1, arranged mostly alphabetically; see family 142, "Joannes Wagley."

12. "Local and Personal," *Petoskey Record*, 9 November 1904, col. 1, p. 1.

13. Sally Ann Cummings, *Correspondence, Field Notes, and the Census Roll of All Members or Descendants of Members Who Were on the Roll of the Ottawa and the Chippewa Tribes of Michigan in 1870, and Living on March 4, 1907 (Durant Roll)* (Washington, DC: National Archives and Records Administration, 1996), p. 22. See Margaret Wagley, no. 103.

14. Michigan State Archives, "Death Records, 1897–1920," *Michiganology*, entry for Isabel Blanchard, 1903, https://michiganology.org. Her birth date was derived from seventy years, nine months, and seventeen days from date of death (17 May 1903).

15. "Michigan Deaths, 1867–1897," *Family Search*, database with images, https://familysearch.org, under Joseph Blanchard, 29 April 1880, citing p. 165, rn. 1, Moran, Mackinac County, MI, Department of Vital Records, Lansing, Family History Library (FHL) microfilm

2,363,668.

16. St. Ignatius Loyola (St. Ignace, MI), "Record of Interments, 1894–1988," p. 8 (Elizabeth Blanchard, 1903), parish rectory.

17. St. Ann Catholic Church (Penetanguishene, Ontario), *Registre des baptêmes, des mariages et des sépultures de l'année 1835 [à 1846]*, parish records, entry of 27 March [1836], baptism of Sophie Valière, 3 microfilm reels, not paginated, FHL 1305885.

18. Michigan State Archives, "Death Records, 1897–1920," *Michiganology*, entry for Sophia Sawyer, 1900, https://michiganology.org.

19. Kathleen M. Hendricks, comp., *St. Mary's Catholic Church Baptisms: Sault Sainte Marie, Michigan, 1811–1900* (Sault Ste. Marie, MI: Holy Name of Mary Proto-Cathedral, 2005), entry 281.

20. St. Ignatius Loyola (St. Ignace, MI), "Marriages, 1838–1893," bk. 1, p. 18–19 (Samuel Vallier and Marguerite Abbott marriage, 1851), parish rectory.

21. John L. Hagen and Georgia M. Rhoades, comp., *Moran Township: When the Moon Is High* (St. Ignace, MI: Moran Township Board of Trustees, 1997), 10–85.

22. Hagen and Rhoads, *When the Moon Is High*, 10–85.

23. St. Ignatius Loyola (St. Ignace, MI), "Baptisms, 1838–1893," bk. 3, p. 16 (Marie Anna Vaillet, 1841), parish rectory.

24. St. Ignatius Loyola (St. Ignace, MI), "Marriages, 1838–1893," bk. 1, p. 28–29 (Jean Baptiste Champagne and Marianne Valliere marriage, 1867), parish rectory.

25. St. Ignatius Loyola (St. Ignace, MI), "Marriages, 1838–1893," bk. 1, p. 28–29 (James Vallier and Frosine Lajoie marriage, 1868), parish rectory.

26. St. Ann Catholic Church (Penetanguishene, Ontario), *Registre des baptêmes, des mariages et des sépultures de l'année 1835 [à 1846]*, entry of 11 December 1846, baptism of David and Euphrosine Baril dit Lajoie, twins, FHL 1305885. Louis Baril dit Lajoie came to St. Ignace around 1849 from Penetanguishene area. He worked served several years as a voyageur with the Hudson's Bay Company at La Cloche, Ontario, called the Huron Company. His family originated in Berthier area of Quebec. His wife was Marie Leveque, daughter of Henry A. Levake (Levesque) and Therese Relle.

27. St. Ignatius Loyola (St. Ignace, MI), "Record of Interments, 1894–1988," p. 10 (Frezen Vallier, 1905), parish rectory.

28. "Michigan Deaths and Burials, 1800–1995," *Family Search*, database, https://familysearch.org, under James Vallier, 6 Oct 1915, citing St. Ignace, Mackinac County, MI, reference yrs. 1899–1946, p. 71, FHL microfilm 1,007,364.

29. "Michigan Marriages, 1868–1925," *Family Search*, database, https://familysearch.org, under Frederick Lavaque and Alice Valier, 1893.

30. "Michigan Deaths, 1867–1897," *Family Search*, database, https://familysearch.org, under

Alice Lavake, 13 March 1896, citing p. 173, rn. 2, Moran Township, Mackinac County, MI, Department of Vital Records, Lansing, FHL microfilm 2,363,835.

31. St. Ignatius Loyola (St. Ignace, MI), "Baptisms, 1838–1893," bk. 3, p. 35 (Celestina Vallier, 1847), parish rectory.

32. St. Ignatius Loyola (St. Ignace, MI), "Baptisms, 1838–1893," bk. 3, p. 40 (Thomas Leander Vallier, 1849), parish rectory.

33. St. Ignatius Loyola (St. Ignace, MI), "Marriages, 1838–1893," bk. 1, p. 32–33 (Thomas Vallier and Marianne Martin marriage, 1873), parish rectory.

34. St. Ignatius Loyola (St. Ignace, MI), "Baptisms, 1838–1893," bk. 3, p. 50 (Carolina Vallier, 1852), parish rectory.

35. "Record of Deaths, Made by Jas. Blanchard, Gros Cap, Mich.," n.d., Orr Greenlees folder, box 2, Emerson R. Smith Papers, Bentley Historical Library, University of Michigan. Citing page 5, Thomas Valier (1882), this booklet appears to be a typed copy of a handwritten original. The location of the original is unknown. This record of deaths contains information not found in state records or in church records and is an invaluable source to Mackinac-area researchers. It is not known if the dates are death dates or burial dates.

36. "Record of Deaths, Made by Jas. Blanchard, Gros Cap, Mich.," citing Mrs. Thomas Valier Sr. (1889).

Bibliography

Abbott, John, Graeme S. Mount, and Michael J. Mulloy. *The History of Fort St. Joseph*. Toronto: Dundurn Press, 2000.

Bak, Richard. *A Distant Thunder*. Ann Arbor, MI: Huron River Press, 2004.

Barry, James P. *Old Forts of the Great Lakes Sentinels in the Wilderness*. Lansing: Thunder Bay Press, 1994.

Borneman, Walter R. *1812: The War that Forged a Nation*. New York: Harper Perennial, 2004.

Brumwell, Jill Lowe. *Drummond Island History: Folklore and Early People*. Black Bear Press, 2003.

Cleland, Charles E. *Rites of Conquest: The History and Culture of Michigan's Native Americans*. Ann Arbor: University of Michigan Press, 1993.

———. *Faith in Paper: The Ethnohistory and Litigation of Upper Great Lakes Indian Treaties*. Ann Arbor: University of Michigan Press, 2012.

Cochrane, Timothy. *Early Accounts of the Anishnaabeg and the North Shore: Gichi Bitobig, Grand Marais*. Minneapolis: University of Minnesota Press, 2018.

Commission, Mackinac Island State Park. *Mackinac Island Its History in Pictures*. Mackinac Island State Park Commission, 1973.

Denissen, Christian. *Genealogy of the French Families of the Detroit River Region 1701–1936*, volumes 1 and 2. Detroit: Detroit Society for Genealogical Research, 1987.

Dorson, Richard M. *Bloodstoppers & Bearwalkers: Folk Traditions of the Upper Peninsula*.

Cambridge: Harvard University Press, 1952.

Dupuis, David. *St. Anne's of Penetanguishene Huronia's First Mission*. Penetanguishene, ON: St. Anne's Building Committee, 2001.

Danziger, Edmund Jefferson, Jr. *The Chippewas of Lake Superior*. Norman: University of Oklahoma Press, 1979.

Fischer, Marilyn, ed. *Seul Choix Point, Gulliver, Michigan*. Gulliver, MI: Gulliver Historical Society, 2001.

Hagen, John L., and Georgia M. Rhoades, compilers. *When The Moon Is High*. St. Ignace, MI: Moran Township Board of Trustees, 1997.

Hendricks, Kathleen M., compiler. *St. Mary's Catholic Church Baptisms: Sault Saint Marie, Michigan, 1811–1900*. Sault Ste. Marie, MI: Holy Name of Mary Proto-Cathedral Parish, 2005.

Herek, Raymond J. *These Men Have Seen Hard Service: The First Michigan Sharpshooters in the Civil War*. Detroit: Wayne State University Press, 1998.

Ilko, John A. *An Annotated Listing of Ojibwa Chiefs*. Troy, NY: Whitston, 1995.

Johnston, Patricia Condon. *Eastman Johnson's Lake Superior Indians*. Afton, MN: Johnston, 1983.

Lantz, Raymond C. *Ottawa and Chippewa Indians of Michigan, 1855–1868*. Bowie, MD: Heritage, 1993.

Lasley, Corey C. *The Lasley Family of Old Mackinac: Samuel C. Lasley, His Descendants, and Their Connections, 1775–2015*. Self-pub., 2016.

Mackinac State Historic Parks. *Mackinac: An Island Famous in These Regions*. Lansing, MI: Mackinac State Historic Parks, 1998.

May, George S. *War 1812: The United States and Great Britain at Mackinac, 1812–1815*. Mackinac Island, MI: Mackinac State Historic Parks, 2004.

McBride, Genevieve G., ed. *Women's Wisconsin: From Native Matriarchies to the New Millennium*. Madison: Wisconsin State Historical Society Press, 2005.

Peters, Bernard C. "Hypocrisy on the Great Lakes Frontier: The Use of Whiskey by the Michigan Department of Indian Affairs." *Michigan Historical Review* (1992): 1–13.

Porter, Phil. *A Desirable Station: Soldier Life at Fort Mackinac, 1867–1895*. Mackinac Island, MI: Mackinac Island State Park Commission, 2003.

Rentmeester, Les and Jean. *The Wisconsin Creoles*. Melbourne, FL: Les and Jean Rentmeester, 1987.

Russell, Donna Valley., ed. *Michigan Censuses 1710–1830*. Detroit: Detroit Society for Genealogical Research, 1982.

Schenck, Theresa M. *All Our Relations: Chippewa Mixed Bloods and the Treaty of 1837*. Madison, WI: Amik Press, 2009.

Sleeper-Smith, Susan. "'[A]n Unpleasant Transaction on This Frontier': Challenging Female Autonomy and Authority at Michilimackinac." *Journal of the Early Republic* (2005): 417–443.

Smith, Emerson R. *Before the Bridge.* St. Ignace, MI: Kiwanis Club of St. Ignace, 1957.

Stallard, Patricia Y. *Fanny Dunbar Corbusier: Recollections of her Army Live, 1869–1908.* Norman: University of Oklahoma Press, 2003.

Tanner, Helen Hornbeck, ed. *Atlas of Great Lakes Indian History.* Norman: University of Oklahoma Press, 1957.

Van Kirk, Sylvia. *Many Tender Ties: Women in Fur Trade Society, 1670–1870.* Norman: Oklahoma University Press, 1980.

Van Noord, Roger. *Assassination of a Michigan King: The Life of James Jessie Strang.* Ann Arbor: University of Michigan Press, 2011.

Widder, Keith R. *Battle for the Soul: Métis Children Encounter Evangelical Protestants at Mackinaw Mission, 1823–1837.* East Lansing: Michigan State University Press.

———. "Magdelaine LaFramboise: The First Lady of Mackinac Island." *Mackinac History* (2007): 1–12.

Wright, John C. *The Crooked Tree: Indian Legends of Northern Michigan.* Holt, MI: Thunder Bay Press, 1996.

Fort Mackinac, 1850. From an unknown artist's sketchbook.